Adobe®
After Effects® 5.0

Classroom in a Book®

Adobe

www.adobe.com/adobepress

Contents

Lesson 10

Building the Final Animation

Lesson 11

The Render Queue and Output Formats

Getting Started

Adobe® After Effects® 5.0 provides the core 2D and 3D tools for compositing, animation, and effects that motion-graphics professionals, Web designers, and video professionals need. After Effects is widely used for digital post-production of film, motion graphics, video multimedia, and the Web. You can composite layers in various ways, apply and combine sophisticated visual and audio effects, and animate both objects and effects.

About Classroom in a Book

Adobe After Effects 5.0 Classroom in a Book® is part of the official training series for Adobe graphics and publishing software. The lessons are designed so that you can learn at your own pace. If you're new to Adobe After Effects, you'll learn the fundamental concepts and features you'll need to use the program. Classroom in a Book also teaches many advanced features, including tips and techniques for using the latest version of this application.

The lessons in this edition include opportunities to use new features, such as compositing layers in 2D and 3D space, viewing 3D from different perspectives, creating and editing expressions, editing masks, defining parent-child relationships between layers, animating lights and cameras, using an enhanced interface with new conveniences, and more.

Prerequisites

Before beginning to use *Adobe After Effects 5.0 Classroom in a Book*, make sure that your system is set up correctly and that you've installed the required software and hardware. You should have a working knowledge of your computer and operating system. You know how to use the mouse and standard menus and commands and also how to open, save, and close files. If you need to review these techniques, see the printed or online documentation included with your Microsoft® Windows® or Apple® Mac® OS documentation.

Installing Adobe After Effects

You must purchase the Adobe After Effects 5.0 software separately. For system requirements and complete instructions on installing the software, see the *Install Readme.wri* (Windows) or *Install Readme.txt* (Mac OS) file on the application CD. You must install QuickTime 4.0 or later, which is also included on your After Effects application CD.

Install the After Effects and QuickTime applications from the Adobe After Effects 5.0 application CD onto your hard disk; you cannot run the program from the CD. Follow the on-screen instructions.

Make sure your serial number is accessible before installing the application; you can find the serial number on the registration card or on the back of the CD case.

Allocating RAM to After Effects

Creating movies is memory-intensive work for a desktop computer. The more random access memory (RAM) available to After Effects, the faster the application will work for you. It's a good idea to allocate as much RAM to After Effects as possible. For these lessons, a minimum allocation of 128 MB is strongly recommended.

Windows Exit as many other programs as possible while you work in After Effects. Windows automatically allocates RAM to the application.

Mac OS The default RAM allocation is 30 MB. You must manually change that allocation. To do this, quit After Effects if it is running, and then select the After Effects program icon (not an alias) in the Finder. Then follow the standard Mac OS procedure for changing the Preferred Size setting in the After Effects Info window. For details about adjusting memory usage for your Mac OS, see your Mac OS online Help.

For more information about optimizing performance, go to the Adobe Web site and search the After Effects Support Knowledgebase "Top Issues" page.

Installing the Classroom in a Book fonts

To ensure that the lessons appear on your system with the correct fonts, you may need to install the Classroom in a Book font files. The fonts for the lessons are located in the Fonts folder on the *Adobe After Effects Classroom in a Book* CD, which is attached to the inside back cover of this book. If you already have these on your system, you do not need to install them. If you have Adobe Type Manager (ATM), see its documentation on how to install fonts. If you do not have ATM, installing it from the Classroom in a Book (CIB) CD will automatically install the necessary fonts.

💡 *You can also install the Classroom in a Book fonts by copying all of the files in the Fonts folder on the* Adobe After Effects Classroom in a Book *CD to the Program Files/Common Files/Adobe/Fonts (Windows) or System Folder/Application Support/Adobe/Fonts (Mac OS). If you install a Type 1, TrueType, OpenType, or CID font into these local Fonts folders, the font appears only in Adobe applications.*

Restoring default preferences

The preferences file controls the way the After Effects user interface appears on your screen. The instructions in this book assume that you see the default interface when they describe the appearance of tools, options, windows, palettes, and so forth. Because of this, it's a good idea to restore the default preferences, especially if After Effects is new to you.

Each time you exit After Effects, the palette positions and certain command settings are recorded in the preferences file. If you want to restore the palettes to their original default settings, you can delete the current After Effects preferences file. (After Effects creates a new preferences file if one doesn't already exist the next time you start the program.)

Restoring the default preferences can be especially helpful if someone has already customized After Effects on your computer. If your copy of After Effects hasn't been used yet, this file won't exist, so this procedure is unnecessary.

Important: *If you want to save the current settings, you can rename the preferences file instead of deleting it. When you are ready to restore those settings, change the name back and make sure that the file is located in the correct preferences folder.*

1 Locate the After Effects preferences folder on your computer:

• For Windows 2000: .../Documents and Settings/<*user name*>/Application Data/Adobe/After Effects/Prefs.

• For Windows 98 and Windows ME: .../Windows/Application Data/Adobe/After Effects/Prefs.

• For Windows NT: .../Winnt/Profiles/<*user name*>/Application Data/Adobe/After Effects/Prefs.

• For Mac OS: .../System/Preferences.

2 Delete or rename the Adobe After Effects 5 Prefs.txt file (Windows) or the Adobe After Effects 5 Prefs file (Mac OS).

3 Start Adobe After Effects.

Note: (Windows only) If you do not see the Prefs file, be sure that the Show all files option is selected for Hidden files on the View tab of the Folder Options dialog box.

Copying the lesson files

The lessons in *Adobe After Effects 5.0 Classroom in a Book* use specific source files, such as image files created in Adobe Photoshop and Adobe Illustrator, audio files, and prepared QuickTime movies. To complete the lessons, you must copy these files from the *After Effects Classroom in a Book* CD (inside the back cover of this book) to your hard drive.

Setting up a folder structure

Before you copy the source files to your hard drive, create the folder structure that you will use throughout these lessons. Because the project builds from lesson to lesson, this structure is very important as you progress, so be sure to take the time to set it up now.

On your hard drive, create a new folder in a convenient location and name it **AE_CIB job**, following the standard procedure for your operating system:

Windows In the Explorer, select the folder or drive in which you want to create the new folder, and choose File > New > Folder. Then type the new name.

Mac OS In the Finder or desktop, choose File > New > New Folder. Type the new name and drag the folder into the location you want to use.

Inside your new AE_CIB job folder, create eight more folders and name them as follows:

- _aep
- _ai
- _audio
- _mov
- _psd
- _txt
- Sample_Movies
- Finished_Projects

You'll use these folders to store files by type, with Adobe Illustrator files in your _ai folder, your After Effects project files in the _aep folder, and so forth.

Copying the source files

The source files for the lessons are relatively small files. You can install all the files for those folders now. The Sample_Movie files are large, so unless you have many gigabytes of free storage space on your computer, it's best to copy the sample movies as needed for each lesson and then remove them from your hard disk after you finish viewing them.

If you use After Effects on a Windows computer, you'll also need to unlock the files before you use them. This is not necessary if you are using a Macintosh computer.

1 Insert the *Adobe After Effects Classroom in a Book* CD into your CD-ROM drive.

2 Copy the source files from the following five folders on the CD to the folders of the same name on your hard drive: _ai, _audio, _mov, _psd, and _txt. There is no _aep folder to copy because you'll use this folder for the project folders you create in each lesson.

3 Unlock the files you copied (Windows only) by doing one of the following:

• If you copied all of the lessons, double-click the unlock.bat file in the AE_CIB/Lessons folder.

• If you copied a single lesson, drag the unlock.bat file from the Lessons folder on the CD into the AE_CIB job folder, and then double-click the unlock.bat file inside that folder.

• If you want to unlock the files individually, right-click the file, and select Properties from the contextual menu. In the file Properties dialog box, under Attributes, deselect the Read-only option.

About copying the sample movies and projects

You will create and render one or more QuickTime movies in most lessons in this book. The files in the Sample_Movies folder are low-resolution examples that you can use to see the end products of each lesson and to compare them with your own results. These files tend to be large, so you many not want to devote the storage space or time to copying all the sample movies before you begin. Instead, find the appropriate Lesson folder in the Sample_Movies folder on the CD and copy the files it contains into your Sample_Movies folder as you begin work on a lesson. (You cannot play movies from the CD.) After you finish viewing the movie, you can delete it from your hard drive.

The Finished_Projects files are samples of the completed projects for each lesson. Use these files for reference if you want to compare your work in progress with the files used to generate the sample movies. These files vary in size from relatively small to a couple of megabytes, so you can either copy them all now if you have available storage space or copy just the finished sample for each lesson as needed, and then delete the sample when you finish that lesson.

How to use these lessons

This entire book represents a single project, based on a hypothetical scenario in which Adobe Systems hires your company to create an 18-second movie that they will use for NTSC broadcast and on the Web. The designer for this project has separated the project into more than a dozen independent elements that you create and render separately. In the later lessons of the book, you'll bring all the elements together in stages to create the final composite and render it to the various formats your client requires.

Each lesson provides step-by-step instructions for creating one or more specific elements of that project. These lessons build on each other—in terms of concepts, skills, and the job files themselves—so the best way to learn from this book is to go through the lessons in sequential order. In this book, some techniques and processes are explained and described in detail only the first few times you perform them.

Note: Many aspects of the After Effects application can be controlled by multiple techniques, such as a menu command, a button, dragging, and a keyboard shortcut. Only one or two of the methods are described in any given procedure, so that you can learn different ways of working even when the task is one you've done before.

The organization of the lessons is also design-oriented rather than feature-oriented. That means, for example, that you'll work with three-dimensional effects and layers in different ways over several chapters rather than in just one chapter entirely devoted to 3D, as you'd find in the *After Effects 5.0 User Guide*.

Additional resources

Adobe After Effects Classroom in a Book is not meant to replace documentation that comes with the program. This book explains only the commands and options actually used in the lessons, so there's much more to learn about After Effects. The *Classroom in a Book* aims to give you confidence and skills so that you can start creating your own projects. For more comprehensive information about program features, see:

• The *Adobe After Effects 5.0 User Guide*, which is included with the Adobe After Effects 5.0 software and contains descriptions of all features.

• Online Help, an online version of the user guide, which you can view by starting After Effects and choosing Help > Contents (Windows) or Help > Help Contents (Mac OS).

• The Adobe Web site (www.adobe.com), which you can explore by choosing Help > Adobe Online if you have a connection to the World Wide Web.

Adobe Certification

The Adobe Training and Certification Programs are designed to help Adobe customers improve and promote their product proficiency skills. The Adobe Certified Expert (ACE) program is designed to recognize the high-level skills of expert users. Adobe Certified Training Providers (ACTP) use only Adobe Certified Experts to teach Adobe software classes. Available in either ACTP classrooms or on-site, the ACE program is the best way to master Adobe products. For Adobe Certified Training Programs information, visit the Partnering with Adobe Web site at http://partners.adobe.com.

A Message from Belief

When Adobe approached Belief, a broadcast design studio in Santa Monica, California, to do the After Effects 5.0 Classroom in a Book, I was truly honored. Belief has long been a champion for doing motion graphics on desktop computers and has been using After Effects way back when it was called CoSA. In fact, when my partner Steve Kazanjian and I started Belief, we set out to do the impossible at the time, which was to build the entire studio around desktop machines. Today this practice is becoming more common, which is great for artists for there are more opportunities for their visions to be experienced.

Belief has continually tried to share with the design community, and creating this book was a great opportunity to continue this tradition. We have inspired the exploration of experimental motion graphics with the artists from our studio and around the world with the "Untitled" series. Steve and I have taught classes and given lectures encouraging artists to get into this rewarding industry. I believe strongly in the potential of After Effects and have been impressed how the Adobe team has continued to evolve the product, adding many new features without alienating their core users. I hope this book will not only inspire but will teach users a new way of approaching projects. Inexpensive tools like After Effects empower artist visions to dance across movie screens, television sets, and—with the Internet—our home computer screens.

The key to the Belief approach is to break projects into elements. Making a project modular is a way to simplify projects and thus make it easier to handle client changes. Creating motion graphics for money is a commercial art form and clients have final say, but that doesn't mean the work you produce can't be amazing. I have noticed many students creating animations using only one composition with hundreds of layers. Those who have been taught to approach projects this way should try to erase that memory and begin fresh with a new outlook. You will soon find as you continue through the book, that a modular element based approach is a much more efficient way of working.

This Classroom in a Book is unique because the lessons are designed in sequential order to create the elements needed to produce one fully realized, complicated animation. When you complete the book, you will know many new principles that you can apply to any project you undertake. Get ready to open your mind while I leave you these departing thoughts. Technique is the key: Don't learn how to drive from A to Z, learn how to navigate. Keep working until you not only complete the lesson but understand what you did and why. You may get confused but try not to get frustrated; you're not an old dog and you will be able to learn new tricks! And finally, remember that great animations ALWAYS begin with great design!

Mike Goedecke, Partner
Belief
www.belief.com

Lesson 1

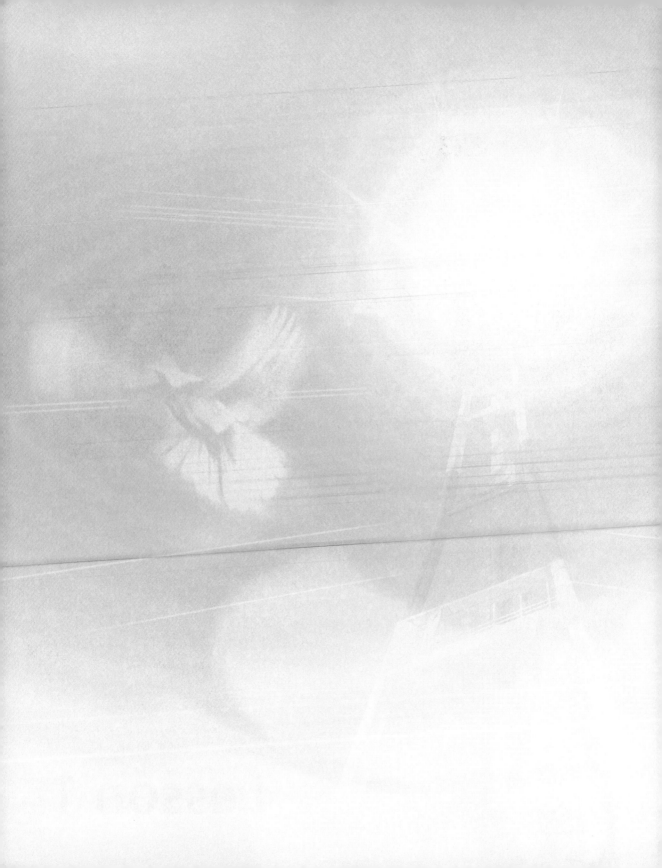

1   Creating 2D Elements from Hexagons

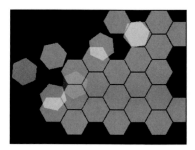 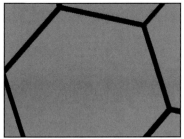 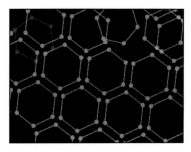

In this lesson, you'll dive right into your job to create an entire element, from importing a simple geometric image to rendering the QuickTime movie. The art is abstract, but you'll make it interesting by rolling hexagons into patterns and making them turn, fade, and zoom in a complex series of movements. You'll get lots of experience using After Effects basic transform properties in ways that go far beyond the basics.

In this lesson, you'll learn to do the following:

- Create After Effect project files
- Import Adobe Photoshop files
- Interpret imported alpha channels
- Create compositions and add layers to them
- Change the background color of a composition
- Work with transform properties
- Create and adjust keyframes to create animations
- Duplicate layers
- Change layer In points
- Replace footage layers
- Create RAM previews
- Rename layers
- Precompose multiple layers
- Adjust velocity graphs
- Render elements

You're about to begin work on two of the elements to be used in the final piece. Both elements animate to form a precise honeycomb of hexagons that fly in from off-screen at different times and from different directions. You'll use just two still files to do the job.

After an optional break, you'll continue this project, adding more levels of complexity to the honeycomb shape you'll create now. Finally, you'll replace the artwork to create a second standalone element for your final animation.

This lesson takes a total of at least two hours, but it is divided so that you can do the work in three sessions of about 30-45 minutes each.

Getting started

In the previous chapter, you created a folder structure on your hard drive and copied all the source files for all lessons into an AE_CIB job folder. If you have not created the folder structure described in "Setting up a folder structure" on page 4, take the time to do that now.

You probably did not copy all the sample movies and finished project files, so you need to copy the Lesson 1 sample files now.

1 Reinsert the *After Effects 5.0 Classroom in a Book* CD into your CD-ROM drive.

2 In your Windows Explorer (Windows) or on your desktop Finder (Mac OS), open to the AE_CIB job folder on your hard drive.

3 In your desktop Windows Explorer (Windows) or desktop (Mac OS), double-click the CD icon to open it. Open the AE_CIB folder on the CD, and then the Sample_Movies folder so that you can see the Lesson01 folder.

4 Select the Lesson01 folder on the CD and drag it into the Sample_Movies folder on your hard drive.

5 On the CD, open the Finished_Projects folder and drag the Hexagons01_finished.aep file into the Finished_Projects folder on your hard drive.

In this lesson, you'll use two source files:

• Hexagon01.psd

• Hexagon02.psd

Make sure that these files are already in the _psd folder inside the AE_CIB job folder on your hard drive, or copy them now. The file structure on your hard drive is very important, so don't overlook or postpone that task.

Close the CD windows and eject the CD. Return it to the pocket on the back cover of this book or another safe storage place. You will copy more sample movies and finished project files from the CD at the beginning of each lesson.

Viewing the sample movie

The Sample_Movies folder now contains finished versions of the animations you'll create in this lesson. To see the results you're aiming for, play the movies now.

1 In your Windows Explorer (Windows) or Finder (Mac OS), open the Sample_Movies folder and the Lesson01 folder inside it, and then double-click Hexagons_final.mov to open it in the QuickTime Player.

2 Click the Play button to view the movie.

3 Again on the desktop, double-click the HexOutlines_final.mov to open and play that movie in the QuickTime Player.

4 When you're finished, close the windows and quit the QuickTime player.

💡 *Your processor attempts to play back movies at as close to real time as possible. To see these movies play back faster, try shrinking the QuickTime window to half size.*

If necessary to save storage space on your hard disk, you can delete the Hexagons_final.mov and HexOutlines_final.mov from the Sample_Movies folder now.

Creating a project

After Effects files are called *projects* and can be recognized by the .aep extension to the filename. Your first task is to create a new project. After Effects can have just one open project at a time.

1 Start After Effects 5.0, if it is not already open. Or, if another After Effects Project is open, save and close that project now by choosing File > Save and then File > Close.

2 Choose File > New > New Project. The Project window title bar now reads Untitled Project.aep.

3 Choose File > Save As.

4 In the Save Project As dialog box, find and open the _aep folder in the AE_CIB job folder you created earlier.

5 In File Name, type **Hexagons01_work.aep**.

Note: *Naming this project with _work in the filename helps you tell it apart from the Hexagons01_finished.aep (finished sample) that you copied from the CD to your Finished_Projects folder.*

6 Click Save.

When the dialog box closes, the Project window title bar displays the new project name.

Make sure that the Info and Time Controls palettes are open. If you're not sure, look on the After Effects Window menu and make sure that both Info and Time Controls are selected (indicated by a checkmark). If not, choose those commands now to open them.

Building the first hexagon composition

In this section, you'll work extensively with the transform properties to create a complex, animated composition. By duplicating simple images, your composition uses minimal storage and yet remains flexible.

Importing footage for the first composition

You need to import the source file. The image you'll use was created for you in Photoshop and uses an *alpha channel* to define a simple hexagonal shape. Alpha channels are areas of transparency that can be defined in the application used to create a file. When you import a file containing an unlabeled alpha channel, you must specify how After Effects interprets that alpha channel.

1 Choose File > Import > File.

2 In the Import File dialog box, open the _psd folder inside your AE_CIB job folder and select Hexagon01.psd.

3 Click Open (Windows) or Import (Mac OS).

4 In the Interpret Footage dialog box, select the Straight – Unmatted option, and then click OK.

The Hexagon01.psd file now appears in the Project window list. If it is not already selected, click the filename to see a thumbnail of the image and some information about it in the top of the Project window. This information includes the image size (400 x 400 pixels), the color depth (Millions of Colors+), and the interpretation of the alpha channel (Straight).

Interpreting alpha channels

Alpha channels play a key role in your using After Effects to create interesting, professional-quality motion graphics. Although you can do all the lessons in this book without understanding much about alpha channels, you'll need to have a comfortable mastery of this subject when you start doing projects on your own. Whether you delve into alpha channels now or decide to come back to this topic later is up to you.

When you import a file with an unlabeled alpha channel into a project, a message appears, asking how to treat the alpha channel. The alpha-channel interpretation method affects the layer's appearance in the composition and in the finished piece. Your best choice depends on how the alpha channel was originally created, because that determines which method for interpreting the alpha channel is correct.

The main choices available in the Interpret Footage dialog box are:

• Ignore

• Straight – Unmatted

• Premultiplied – Matted with Color

Straight – Unmatted: In the case of the Hexagon01.psd file used in Lesson 1, the transparency is defined only in the alpha channel. The RGB channels act as a solid white "fill" for the alpha or matte channel. This is similar to the way a sheet of rolled-out dough acts beneath a cookie-cutter. This type of alpha channel is called straight alpha. Therefore, when this file is imported into After Effects, the alpha channel should be interpreted as Straight - Unmatted.

Ignore: This interpretation method disregards any alpha-channel (transparency) information defined within the original file, giving the layer a solid (100% opaque) background. You'll have a chance to use Ignore in an optional exercise in Lesson 8.

Premultiplied – Matted With Color: This choice removes the original background color from the semi-transparent edges of the artwork. This prevents the appearance of a halo around the image.

Note: Some files can be properly interpreted using either Premultiplied or Straight.

If you don't know how the alpha channel was created for a file you are using, click the Guess button. After Effects attempts to analyze which type of alpha channel the file uses and apply the appropriate interpretation method. If it cannot determine this, After Effects warns you with an alert sound.

The Interpret Footage dialog box also includes an Invert Alpha option. Selecting (checking) this option reverses the existing alpha channel.

You can read more about alpha channels in After Effects 5.0 online Help and in documentation for Adobe Photoshop, Adobe Illustrator, Adobe Premiere, and other applications capable of creating images with alpha channels. Also see the Adobe Web site for technical articles about alpha channels.

Organizing the project

It is just as important to organize files within an After Effects Project as it is that you organize the files for a job on your hard drive. Just as you created the organizational folders on your drive at the beginning of this job (in "Setting up a folder structure" on page 4), you'll now create folders that give order to this After Effects Project.

1 Choose File > New > New Folder. Or, click the folder icon (▭) on the lower edge of the Project window. An untitled folder appears in the Project window.

2 Type **psd files** and then press Enter (Windows) or Return (Mac OS) to name the folder.

3 Drag the Hexagon01.psd file into the psd files folder.

4 Use the arrow to expand the psd files folder so that you see the Hexagon01.psd nested in it.

In this lesson you'll import only .psd files, so you don't need any other folders. Later, in more complex projects with many kinds of files, you'll create a Project-window folder for each file type that you import.

Creating the first composition

You start building your animation by creating a new composition. Compositions are the basic units of an After Effects project in which you place and manipulate images, movies, audio, and even other compositions.

·

Delivery formats

At this point in the project, it's important to consider what format you'll use for the final delivery of your project (such as film, Web, or television), because this determines the size at which you build your elements. You specify these settings at the composition level.

You know from the job scenario described in the introductory chapter that this animation is intended primarily for NTSC broadcast. This means that your final animation should be rendered at D1 resolution (720 x 486). Therefore, as you build your elements you need to construct them in compositions that are large enough for their required size in the final animation.

This D1 resolution is a non-square pixel format. However, in these lessons you build elements using square pixel aspect ratio and place your final composition into a 720 x 486 D1 NTSC composition before you render the final animation for delivery.

1 Choose Composition > New Composition.

2 In the Composition Settings dialog box, type **Hexagon Final Comp** in Composition Name.

Note: Final *indicates that this is the composition that you will render at the end of the lesson. This name distinguishes it from other intermediate compositions that you'll create in this lesson.*

3 Using the Preset pop-up menu, select the NTSC D1 Square Pix, 720 x 540 option.

4 Make sure that the following settings are shown:

- Width: 720

- Height: 540

- Lock Aspect Ratio: unselected (no checkmark)

- Pixel Aspect Ratio: Square Pixels

- Frame Rate: 29.97

- Resolution: Full. (You can select a lower resolution. Use Half or lower if your system has only the minimum amount of RAM, a standard monitor size, or a slow processor.)

- Start Timecode: 0;00;00;00

5 In Duration, type **400** for four seconds.

6 When all these options are set, click OK.

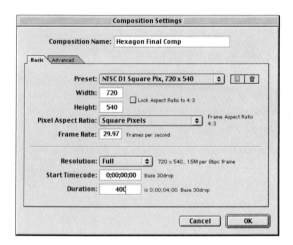

The Hexagon Final Comp now appears in the Project window and in the title bar of two new windows: the Composition window and the Timeline window. If necessary, resize these windows so that they all fit on your screen. The Composition window, which usually shows you how your composition looks, is empty (solid black, or whichever background color is currently selected) because you haven't added any images to your new composition.

The Timeline window is also empty, but you can see the numerous controls in it that you'll use to manipulate items in compositions. Notice that the right side of the Timeline window shows the duration you specified: four seconds.

You can make your Timeline window more efficient for the work you'll do in this lesson by closing the Parent panel. To do this, right-click (Windows) or Control + click (Mac OS) the word Parent in the panel heading to open the contextual menu and choose Hide This.

Placing footage in a composition

When you add footage to a composition, you position it in terms of both space and time. You can change these positions later, but it's efficient to put it where you want it now.

The *In point* is the point in time at which the footage first appears or begins playing in a composition. The layer In point is automatically set at the position of the *current-time marker* (🖤) when you bring the layer into the composition. You want this image to start appearing at the very first frame (00;00;00;00), so that's the number you want to see in the underlined *current-time display*, in upper left corner of the Timeline window. There are several methods you can use to change the position of the current-time marker.

1 If the current-time marker is not at 0:00, do any one of the following:

• Click the current-time display to open the Go To Time dialog box, type **0** (the number zero), and click OK.

• Drag the current-time marker as far to the left as possible.

• Press the Home key.

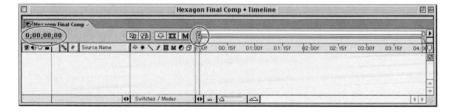

2 In the Project window, select the Hexagon01.psd file and drag it into the Composition window.

3 Continue dragging until the bounding box (outline indicating the dimensions of the image) is positioned slightly above center on the right side of the composition.

When you release the mouse, the hexagon appears in the Composition window. The file also appears as Layer 1 in the Timeline window, where it is listed as Hexagon01.psd—the name of the source file.

Note: *If the background in the Composition window is white, you won't be able to see the hexagon (because it is also white). To fix this, choose Composition > Background Color to open the Background Color dialog box. Click the color swatch to open the color picker, and select the black color sample. Then click OK to close both dialog boxes.*

Transform Properties

The transform properties are the core of After Effects. After you master the techniques for manipulating these settings and adding keyframes for these five properties, the possibilities are virtually endless. In this book, almost every adjustment that you make to a layer within After Effects is based on the principles that you learn for working with the transform properties.

To access the transform properties for a layer, you have two options. You can click the arrow to the left of a layer name to reveal Masks, Effects, and Transform categories. Then, click the arrow next to Transform to reveal the five transform properties for that layer: Anchor Point, Position, Scale, Rotation, and Opacity. You can make changes to the values shown here to affect your layer.

Frequently, you need to see only some of the transform properties—not all of them—and you aren't interested in the Masks or Effects categories. Opening all these categories can be distracting and inconvenient because the list becomes so long you may need to scroll to find the property you want to see. The solution is to use a simple, single-key shortcuts to open a transform property, without opening the category levels or other properties. This keeps your Timeline window easier to use. These shortcuts are:

A = Anchor Point

P = Position

S = Scale

R = Rotation

T = Opacity

When you use a second shortcut, that transform property replaces the first one you opened, keeping the Timeline window trim and efficient. To reveal multiple transform properties for a layer, press Shift as you press the additional property shortcuts.

You don't need to memorize these properties now, because the procedures in this book remind you which shortcut to use for transform-property displays. For more information, see "Viewing layer properties in the Timeline window" in After Effects online Help.

Transforming the image

After Effects reserves the term *transform* to specific layer properties, including the layer position, scale, rotation, opacity, and the placement of the anchor point. By the time you finish your work with the hexagons element, you will apply each of these transform properties at least once and some many times, in a variety of situations and combinations.

Moving the image to an exact position

Because you'll be creating a precise pattern using the Hexagon01.psd, your next step is to fine-tune its position within the composition.

1 If the layer is not selected, click the image in the Composition window or click the layer name in the Timeline window.

💡 *To avoid scrolling to see an image in the Composition window, use the magnification pop-up menu in the lower left corner of the window or press the comma key (,) to zoom out. To increase redraw and processing speed while you work, you can reduce resolution of the Composition window from Full to a lower value (such as Half or Third), using that pop-up menu. These settings affect only your working views, not the size or the quality of your final output.*

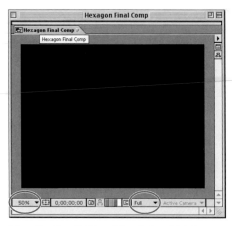

Magnification (left) and Resolution (right)

2 Press P on your keyboard. The Position property appears below the layer in the Timeline window.

3 Move the layer to (or close to) the X, Y coordinates 468, 242 by doing any of the following:

• Drag the layer within the Composition window, using the coordinate display in the Info palette or the Position property in the Timeline window to guide you.

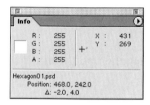

If you can get close to 468 and 242 but have trouble getting them exactly, try using the arrow keys on your keyboard to nudge the image a few pixels at a time.

• Drag the underlined Position property coordinates in the Timeline window to *scrub*. Drag right to increase the value or left to lower it.

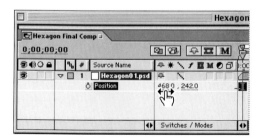

• Click the position coordinates in the Timeline window and type **468** for X and **242** for Y.

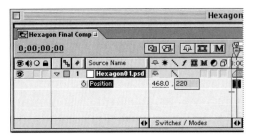

Note: *These X, Y coordinates mark the position of the* anchor point *of the layer within the Composition window. By default, After Effects sets the anchor point at the center of the layer.*

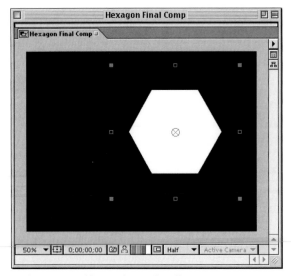

Anchor point and layer selection handles

Adjusting the image size

In real life, you often have to work with images that are not the ideal size for your composition. In this task, you'll decrease the size of the hexagon image so that the final bar of hexagons that you build fits in the composition frame the way you want.

1 In either the Composition window or the Timeline window, select the Hexagon01.psd layer.

2 Press S on your keyboard. The Scale property appears below the layer in the Timeline window, replacing the Position property.

3 Change the Scale value to 57%, either by scrubbing the value or by selecting it, typing the new value, and pressing Enter (Windows) or Return (Mac OS).

The hexagon appears in the Composition window at the reduced size.

Setting keyframes to rotate the image

Next, you want the hexagon to rotate as it falls into place. In the following task, you'll animate the hexagon so that it rotates 180° over the first 15 frames of the four-second composition.

You use two or more *keyframes* to specify how things change over time within the composition. A keyframe is a reference point that links a layer property value to a place in time. To make the image rotate, you set one keyframe for its beginning Rotation value and another keyframe for its final Rotation value. After Effects calculates the intermediate rotation values so you don't have to create keyframes for each individual frame between the two reference points.

1 Move the current-time marker to 0:00, if necessary (by pressing the Home key, dragging the current-time marker, or clicking the current-time display to open the Go To Time dialog box and typing **0**).

2 Select the Hexagon01.psd layer in the Timeline window.

3 Press R to open the Rotation property for the layer. There are two underlined numbers for rotation. The first is the number of revolutions. The second is the number of additional degrees.

4 Leaving the first number (revolutions) at zero, change the second number (degrees): Scrub or type **-180°**, being careful to make the number negative.

5 Click the stopwatch icon to the left of the Rotation property. The stopwatch icon now includes hands (⚬), and a small diamond shaped icon(♦), representing a keyframe, appears in the timeline at the position of the current-time marker (0:00).

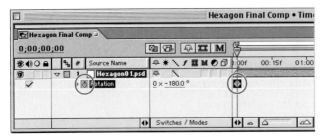

Rotation stopwatch (left) and keyframe (right)

6 Drag the current-time marker to 0:15, or click the current-time display and type **15** in the Go To Time dialog box.

7 Scrub or type to change the second rotation value to **0°** (zero). A new keyframe automatically appears at the position of the current-time marker (0:15).

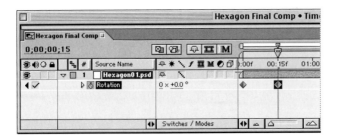

Important: *When setting keyframes for any property within After Effects, be careful to click the stopwatch only once. The clock hands inside the stopwatch icon indicate that the property can change over time, so After Effects automatically adds keyframes when you move the current-time marker and change a value for that property. If you click the stopwatch a second time, this indicates that the property remains the same throughout the composition, so After Effects removes all the keyframes for that property (and the hands disappear in the icon). However, if you accidentally clear a selected stopwatch, choose Edit > Undo, or press Ctrl + Z (Windows) or Command + Z (Mac OS) to undo that action and avoid having to redo the work of creating the deleted keyframes. If you want to remove a specific keyframe, simply select that keyframe and press Delete.*

Previewing the first animation

You can preview your composition to see results of setting the keyframes.

1 Press the Home key to move the current-time marker to 0:00.

2 Press the spacebar or click the Play button (▸) in the Time Controls palette to play the animation.

Note: *While the preview plays, the current-time marker moves across the timeline, and a green line appears above it. After the marker passes 0:15, the hexagon does not move again until the preview loops back to the starting point.*

3 When you finish watching, click the Play button again to pause the preview or press the spacebar again to stop it.

You're finished working with the Rotation property for now, so press the (`) accent grave key to hide it again. Or, you can just press R.

💡 *Many After Effects controls, including the buttons on the Time Controls palette, have tool tips: small windows that appear after a few seconds when the pointer hovers over the button, tool, or option. If you do not see these, choose Edit > Preferences > General and make sure Show Tool Tips is selected (checked).*

Creating an animated pattern from a simple image

You need many more hexagon layers to build your hexagon element. Instead of repeating all the changes you've made to the first layer on each additional hexagon, you'll duplicate the first layer many times. This not only reproduces the layer itself, but also duplicates any changes made or keyframes set for Scale, Position, and Rotation for each new layer, saving you a lot of time. Your first task is to create the duplicates.

1 Drag the current-time marker to 0:0, or press Home.

2 In the Timeline window or the Composition window, select the Hexagon01.psd layer, and then choose Edit > Duplicate. A new layer appears above the original layer in the Timeline window.

3 Duplicate the original layer eight more times, either by choosing Edit > Duplicate or by pressing Ctrl + D (Windows) or Command + D (Mac OS).

Notice how duplicating the first layer affects the windows:

• The appearance of the Composition window does not change. That's because the ten images are stacked directly above each other at exactly the same position coordinates.

• The Timeline window lists all ten layers as *Hexagon01.psd* because all ten layers use the same source file. The number to the left of the name identifies each layer according to its position in the *layer stack* (from top to bottom or front to back).

• All layers have Rotation, Scale, and Position settings that are identical to the first layer. To verify this, select one or more layers and then press R, S, or P.

Moving layers into a pattern

The next step is to arrange the ten hexagons so that they form a precise honeycomb formation. You'll place the layers in the order shown in the illustration below.

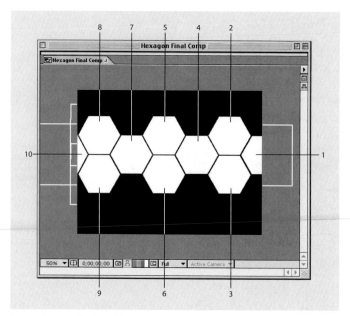

Layers 1–10 in final positions

You do not have to use the exact coordinates listed in the following procedure. If you do use them, make sure that the current layer coordinates are 468, 242. Otherwise, you can just arrange the hexagons visually so that they form a tile-like pattern with evenly wide spacing between the hexagons.

1 In the Timeline window, select the top layer (Layer 1). Notice the layer handles (small squares at the corners of the layer bounding box) that appear in the Composition window. Press P to open Position properties for the layer.

Note: If you don't see the layer handles, click the right-facing arrow button just above the vertical scroll bar in the Composition window to open the Composition window menu, and choose Layer Handles if it is not already checked.

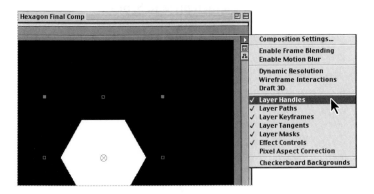

2 Drag Layer 1 to the far right of the composition. Most of the hexagon should be outside of the composition frame, with only a portion visible.

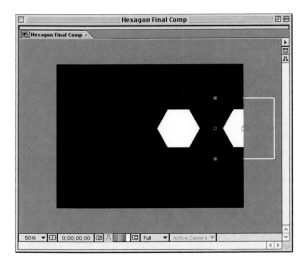

3 In the Timeline window, examine the Position coordinates shown for Layer 1.

4 If you want to use the same Position coordinates as the sample, drag the image in the Composition window until the coordinates are 723, 242. Or, scrub or type these Position coordinates in the Timeline window. To move a layer precisely, try these techniques:

• After you start to drag a layer, press Shift to constrain the movement either vertically or horizontally. Be careful not to press Shift before you drag or you'll resize the image instead of moving it.

• Press the arrow keys to nudge the image by small increments.

• For typing, use the Tab key to jump from one coordinate value to the next, all the way down the layer stack.

5 Select each layer in turn and move it to the position shown in the diagram at the beginning of this procedure. If you want to use the same coordinates as the sample, refer to the following list:

Layer 1   723, 242

Layer 2   595, 169

Layer 3   595, 316

Layer 4   Leave in its original position (468, 242)

Layer 5   341, 169

Layer 6   341, 316

Layer 7   214, 242

Layer 8   87, 169

Layer 9   87, 316

Layer 10   -40, 242

6 Choose File > Save.

Starting a new animation by creating keyframes

You now have the ten hexagons in a tight honeycomb formation. Next, you'll set a position keyframe for each layer.

1 Move the current-time marker to 0:15, either by dragging or typing.

2 Choose Edit > Select All to select all layers. Or, press Ctrl + A (Windows) or Command + A (Mac OS). Then, if the Position property is not already open, press P to open it for all layers.

3 Press Alt + P (Windows) or Option + P (Mac OS) to set a Position keyframe for all of the layers at once. Notice that the stopwatch icons (to the left of Position) now have hands, and diamond-shaped keyframe icons appear at 0:15 on the timeline for each layer.

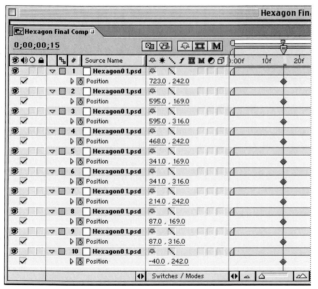

4 Choose Edit > Deselect All or press Ctrl + Shift + A (Windows) or Command + Shift + A (Mac OS) to deselect all layers. Leave the Position properties open.

This arrangement of the hexagons represents the final position in the hexagon pattern animation.

Continuing to animate the hexagons

You're now ready to create the starting position for each hexagon. You want the individual hexagons to fly into the composition, spinning and coming to rest in the precise honeycomb pattern. To do that, you'll assign each layer a starting point that is outside of the composition frame. Because it's helpful to see more of the pasteboard (the gray area outside the composition itself), your first step is to zoom out. This changes your working view only; it does not reduce or enlarge the objects in the rendered movie.

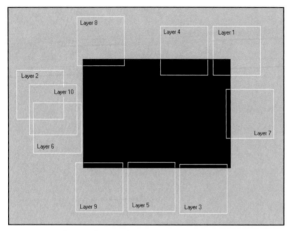

Layers 1–10 in starting positions

If you don't want to take the time to arrange the start position to match the ones shown below, simply drag the files to the approximate positions, as indicated by the illustration above. The alignment of the start positions is not as critical to the results as the precision of the final honeycomb pattern that you arranged earlier.

1 In the Composition window, choose 50% (or lower) from the magnification pop-up menu in the lower left corner. Or, press the comma key (,) to zoom out by one step.

2 Move the current-time marker to 0:00.

3 Move each hexagon to the approximate position shown in the illustration above this procedure, using whichever technique you prefer. If you want to use the exact coordinates shown in the sample, they are:

Layer 1   723, -51

Layer 2   -192, 169

Layer 3   595, 607

Layer 4   468, -49

Layer 5   341, 594

Layer 6   -125, 316

Layer 7   825, 242

Layer 8   87, -94

Layer 9   87, 595

Layer 10   -140, 242

Keyframes automatically appear for each layer (at 0:00) as you specify the new positions.

4 Preview your animation by pressing the spacebar, or press 0 (zero) on the numeric keypad to create a RAM preview. When you are finished watching the preview, press the spacebar to stop.

5 With the Timeline window active, press Ctrl + A (Windows) or Command + A (Mac OS) to select all layers, and then press the accent grave key (`) to hide the Position properties. Choose Edit > Deselect All to deselect the layers.

6 Choose File > Save to save your work.

♀ *After you create a RAM preview, you can drag the current-time marker to scrub through the composition. If you drag the current-time marker without building a RAM preview, After Effects updates the Composition window as quickly as it can (depending on the speed of the processor, the amount of RAM available, and the speed of the display card). For more information, see "Allocating RAM to After Effects" on page 2. See also "Saving a RAM preview as a rendered movie" and "Techniques for working efficiently" in After Effects online Help.*

.

RAM previews

What is a RAM preview? When you preview an animation by pressing the spacebar or clicking the Play button in the Time Controls, the playback speed shown is not real time. The composition plays back as close to real time as possible; actual speed varies based on the speed of your processor. Depending on the amount of RAM available on your system and the speed of your display card, you can run the composition at real time by creating a RAM preview.

To create a RAM preview, After Effects first loads the frames into RAM and then plays them back. The first cycle through the preview appears to be much slower. As After Effects builds the preview, a green line moves across the timeline, indicating the progress of the RAM preview build. After the preview is loaded into RAM, the animation plays back at real time or as close to real time as your system can handle.

The number of frames that appear in a RAM preview depends on how much information can be loaded into the RAM on your system. If the composition exceeds your RAM, After Effects builds a RAM preview of as many frames as possible and then plays those in real time. If the composition is very large and complex, you may see just a short segment of the timeline.

The time required to build a RAM preview depends on the speed of your CPU. The frame rate of the playback depends on the amount of RAM available and the speed of the display card installed in your system.

There are several ways to create a RAM preview:

• Choose Composition > Preview > RAM Preview.

• Click the RAM Preview button in the Time Controls palette.

• Press 0 (zero) on the numeric keypad.

Maximizing RAM previews When the composition is simple, creating a RAM preview is almost as fast as a simple preview. However, when compositions are more complex, the process of generating the RAM preview can become time-consuming, and the number of frames that you see may be limited by the amount of RAM available to After Effects. To get the most from your RAM previews, you can:

• Exit other applications (Windows) or increase the amount of memory allocated to After Effects (Mac OS).

• Lower the Resolution (in either the Composition window or Time Controls palette) to Half or Third. This affects only previews; when you render the composition, the image is rendered with full anti-aliasing.

• Reduce the magnification of the Composition window to 50% or lower.

• Set the Quality for your layers to Draft rather than Best.

• Turn off the Video switch for any layers you don't need to see in the preview.

• Limit the work area to preview smaller sections of the timeline.

RAM preview Options You can select options associated with RAM preview, including Frame Rate, Skip Frames, Resolution, and others. These options appear in the lower portion of the Time Controls palette, under RAM Preview Options. If you don't see options, click the arrow at the upper right corner of the Time Controls palette to open the Time Controls palette menu and select Show RAM Preview Options.

For more information about preview settings, see "Setting preview options" in After Effects online Help.

Adding complexity to the animation

You've created a fairly sophisticated animation for your hexagon element, but now you can add interest and complexity by changing a few more properties. First, you'll stagger the starting points for the layers, so that each hexagon begins to appear at a different point in time in the composition. Then, you'll adjust the opacity of the hexagons so that they fade in and then remain partially transparent.

Staggering the In points

The *In point* of a layer is the time at which the layer starts to appear in the composition. Right now, all your layers begin at 0:00, as shown by the position of the colored duration bar for each layer in the timeline. To create a more fluid animation, you'll offset the In points of the layers on the timeline.

1 At the bottom of the Timeline window near the center, click the double-headed arrow (◆) to open the In/Out panel.

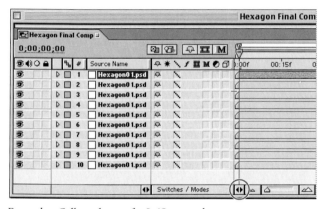

Expand or Collapse button for In/Out panels

2 Click the underlined In value for each layer, type a new value in the Layer In Time dialog box, and click OK to set In points that are staggered by exactly three frames per layer, as shown in the illustration below:

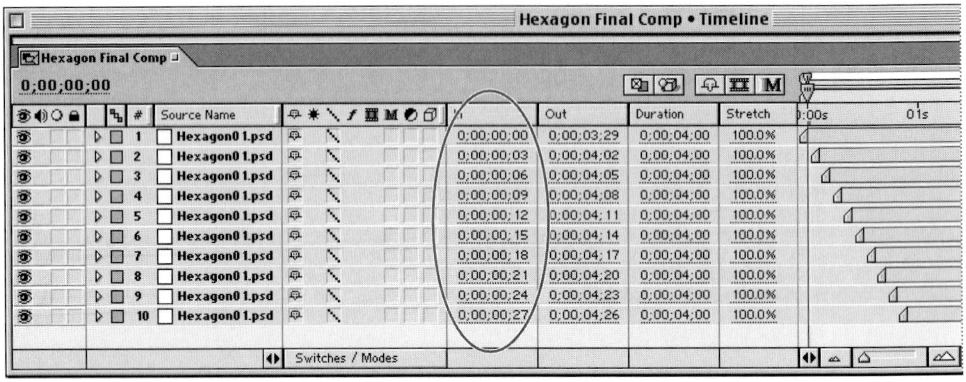

In point values

3 Press Home to move the current-time marker to 0:00, and then press the spacebar or 0 (zero) on the numeric keypad to preview your animation.

4 When you finish viewing the preview, click the double-headed arrow button again to close the In/Out panel in the Timeline window, and then choose File > Save to save your work.

The hexagons now fall into place, sequentially taking their positions from right to left.

Adjusting opacity for one layer

By making the hexagons semi-transparent, you create a more interesting interaction as they spin over each other to form the honeycomb. First, you'll set the opacity for one layer so that it dissolves in over nine frames.

1 Press Home to move the current-time marker to 0:00.

2 In the Timeline window, select Layer 1 and press T to reveal the Opacity property. The current value is 100%.

3 Set the Opacity value to 0 (zero), either by scrubbing the value or by clicking the value and typing.

4 Click the stopwatch to animate the opacity and set the first opacity keyframe at 0:00.

5 Move the current-time marker to 0:09.

6 In the Opacity value, scrub or type **50%**. A second keyframe appears (at 0:09).

7 Press Home to return the current-time marker to 0:00, and then press the spacebar or 0 (zero) on the numeric keypad to preview the composition.

The Layer 1 hexagon fades up and then remains at 50% opacity.

💡 *To remember the keyboard shortcut for opening the Opacity property, think T for transparency. The O key shortcut is reserved for another use.*

Pasting Opacity keyframes to other layers

Now you're ready to create the same dissolve on the other hexagons. For this, you'll use a time-saving cut-and-paste technique to add Opacity keyframes to the nine remaining layers.

1 Select the Opacity keyframes on the first layer by carefully dragging a small marquee around the two keyframes, as shown below. Or, you can click the word Opacity to select both keyframes.

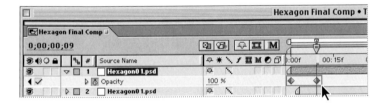

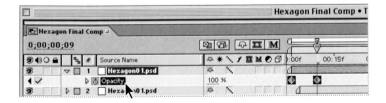

2 Choose Edit > Copy, or press Ctrl + C (Windows) or Command + C (Mac OS) to copy the keyframes.

3 Select the Layer 2, and press I (the letter *i*) to move the current-time marker to the In point for that layer (at 0:03).

4 Choose Edit > Paste, or press Ctrl + V (Windows) or Command + V (Mac OS) to paste the Opacity keyframes into Layer 2.

5 With Layer 2 selected, press T to see the new Opacity keyframes. The keyframes appear at time positions that maintain the same relationship to the current-time marker, so that the first appears at 0:03 and the second at 0:12. Then press T again to hide them.

6 Repeat steps 3 and 4 for each of the remaining eight layers.

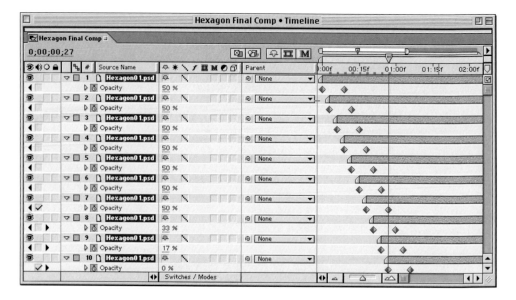

7 Preview the animation and save the project.

Precomposing multiple layers

Your next task is to unite your ten layers into a single layer by precomposing. This non-destructive process makes your project more manageable and also makes it possible for you to add transformations to the group as a whole.

1 With the Timeline or Composition window active, choose Edit > Select All to select all ten layers.

2 Choose Layer > Pre-compose.

3 In the Pre-compose dialog box, type **Hexagons Build Pre-comp** to name the precomposition so that it describes what happens inside the precomposition.

4 Make sure that the Move All Attributes into the New Composition option is selected and that Open New Composition is not selected, and then click OK.

Note: *The first option (Leave All Attributes in "Hexagon Final Comp") should be dimmed. It is not available when multiple layers are selected.*

In the Timeline window for Hexagon Final Comp, the Hexagons Build Pre-comp layer replaces the ten individual hexagon layers.

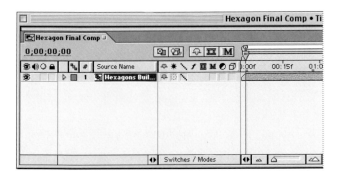

5 Choose File > Save to save the project.

Note: *You can still access and make changes to the original ten layers by double-clicking the Hexagons Build Pre-comp item in the Project window. Any changes you make within the Hexagons Build Pre-comp are immediately reflected in the Hexagon Final Comp.*

Nice work. You have completed the first phase of construction for the hexagon element, so you are almost half finished with Lesson 1. If you need to take a break, this is a good time to do that. If appropriate, close the project and quit After Effects.

Transforming a precomposition layer

So far, you have created an animated set of hexagons that fly onto the screen and settle into a honeycomb formation. Now, you're going to leverage that work to fill the frame with the hexagon pattern and add some of the subtle refinements that make your good work look even better.

You'll continue to transform the group of hexagons that you have created. The overall effect you'll create is one of complex motion in which the object appears to be moving in several ways: rotating, moving laterally, and coming closer —as if the viewer is traveling through the center of one of the hexagons.

Now you can transform all the hexagons as a unit without losing the transformations you applied earlier to the ten original layers. The new transformations add to the existing motions to create complex combinations of change upon change.

Reopening your project after a break

If you quit After Effects when you finished the previous section, you need to restart the application and open the file you've been working on.

1 Start After Effects and choose File > Open Project.

2 Find the _aep folder inside of the AE_CIB job folder that you created at the beginning of this lesson.

3 Select the Hexagons01_work.aep file, and click Open.

You can probably open the Hexagons01_work.aep file by choosing File > Open Recent Projects > and selecting the path and filename for this project file. After Effects typically lists the ten most recently opened projects in the Open Recent Projects submenu.

4 In the Project window, double-click Hexagon Final Comp to open it in the Composition and Timeline windows.

If the names in the Project window are truncated and difficult to read, you can drag the embossed bar at the right edge of the column heading to expand the column width.

Scaling and collapsing the precomposed layer

First, you'll adjust the size of the hexagons and collapse transformations for the precom-position layer to preserve image quality. In this case, you don't set keyframes for scale because you want the Scale property to remain unchanged over time.

1 If necessary, click the Hexagon Final Comp tab in the Timeline window to bring it forward.

2 Move the current-time marker to about 1:00 so that you can see the results of the scale change as you apply it.

3 In the Timeline window, select the Hexagons Build Pre-comp layer and press the S to open the Scale property.

4 In Scale, scrub or type **68%**. In the Composition window, layer handles indicate the layer's bounding box. The edges of some of the hexagons are currently out of view.

5 With the Hexagons Build Pre-comp layer still selected, choose Layer > Switches > Collapse. Or, you can click the Collapse Transformations switch in the Timeline window Switches panel (to the right of the layer names, by default) from Off ( ) to On (✳). This enables you to see the artwork beyond the edges of the bounding box and improves the quality of the layer.

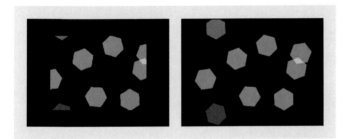

Before (left) and after (right) turning on Collapse Transformations switch

Note: Collapsing *(activating the Collapse switch) refers to the way After Effects calculates information for layers. When you collapse transformations for a nested precomposition layer, the image quality improves and the amount of time required to render the final movie is reduced. For more information, see "Maintaining image quality in nested compositions" and "Collapsing transformation properties" in After Effects online Help.*

Duplicating and renaming precomposed layers

The easiest way to fill the composition frame with hexagons is to create copies of the precomposed layer.

1 Select the Hexagons Build Pre-comp layer, then press S to hide the Scale property.

2 With the layer still selected, choose Edit > Duplicate. Or, press Ctrl + D (Windows) or Command + D (Mac OS).

3 Choose Edit > Duplicate again. The Timeline window now lists three layers.

4 Select Layer 1 and press Enter (Windows) or Return (Mac OS). The layer name becomes active and a cursor appears.

5 Type **Top** and press Enter (Windows) or Return (Mac OS) to enter the new name.

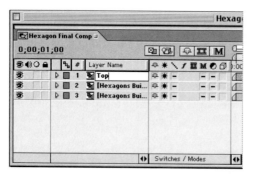

6 Select Layer 2 and repeat steps 3 and 4, typing **Middle** for the layer name.

7 Using the same steps, type **Bottom** to rename Layer 3.

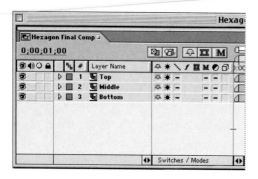

Moving precomposed layers

The three layers are stacked directly on top of each other, so that only the top layer is visible in the Composition window. You'll now move the layers into precise positions so that they line up in a complete pattern, filling the composition frame.

1 Move the current-time marker to about 2:00 so that you can see the results as you work.

2 Choose Edit > Select All to select all the layers, and press P to open the Position properties.

3 Choose Edit > Deselect All or press Ctrl + A (Windows) or Command + Shift + A (Mac OS) to deselect all three layers.

4 Move each layer so that the three fit snugly together, either by dragging (refer to the illustration below) or by changing the Position coordinates to the following values:

- Top: 449, 113
- Middle: 363, 263
- Bottom: 449, 413

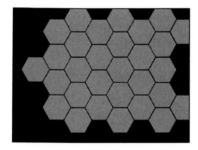

5 Choose Edit > Select All and press P again to hide the Position properties for all layers. Then choose Edit > Deselect All.

6 Press Home to move the current-time marker to the start of the composition, and press the spacebar or 0 (zero) on the numeric keypad to preview your work.

7 Save your project.

Changing the In points

Your next task is to create a more progressive entry for the hexagons by staggering the In points for each of the three layers, just as you did with the ten original layers.

1 In the Timeline window, click the double-arrow in the lower bar of the window to open the In/Out panel.

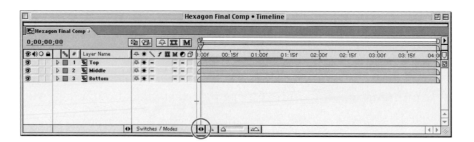

2 Type the following values for the layer In points:

- Top: **0:20**

- Middle: **0:12**

- Bottom: **0:04**

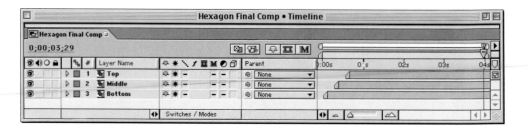

3 Click the button again to close the In/Out panel.

Again, save the project and then preview your work by pressing the spacebar or pressing 0 (zero) on the numeric keypad to create a RAM preview. The pattern now builds up not only from right to left but also from bottom to top.

Precomposing the three layers

Now you'll consolidate these three layers into a single precomposed layer before you apply the finishing touches.

1 With the Timeline window active, choose Edit > Select All to select all three layers.

2 Choose Layer > Pre-compose. The Pre-compose dialog box appears, with the Move All Attributes into the New Composition option already selected.

3 In New Composition Name, type **Hexagon 3 Bars Pre-comp** and click OK.

Note: It is a good practice to name a precomposition using a description of what takes place inside it. This helps to keep complex projects from becoming cluttered with unlabeled compositions and precompositions.

In the Timeline window, the Hexagon 3 Bars Pre-comp layer replaces the Top, Middle, and Bottom layers. Again, the individual layers are still accessible by clicking the Hexagon 3 Bars Pre-comp in the Project window to open it. If you open the precomposition make sure to close it again before you continue.

Applying a third level of motion and other refinements

So far, you've created two levels of motion: the movement of the individual hexagons rolling into formation and the movement of three precomposed bars of hexagons, entering the composition at different times and positions, Now, you transform the new precomposition layer that includes all those pieces. The transformations you applied to the layers nested within this precomposition are not lost or overwritten but remain as motions within motions.

Then you'll give this layer just three more "tweaks": shifting the Anchor Point, creating a drift-like movement, and accelerating the zoom.

Creating a zoom

You'll create the feeling of a camera zooming into the image by dramatically increasing scale over time.

1 Press Home to move the current-time marker to 0:00, and select the Hexagon 3 Bars Pre-comp layer in the Timeline window.

2 Press S to open the Scale properties, and then scrub or type to set the Scale value at 92%.

3 Click the stopwatch to create a keyframe.

4 Move the current-time marker to 3:29, by one of the following methods:

• Drag the current-time marker all the way to the right.

• Click the time display and type **329** in the Go To Time dialog box.

• Press the End key (since 3:29 is the last frame in the composition).

• Click the right end of the time ruler (the numbers above the duration bar in the timeline), at 3:29.

5 For the Scale value, scrub or type **1156%**. A new keyframe appears in the timeline, aligned with the current-time marker. Leave the Scale properties visible. The Composition window is almost entirely gray because you are seeing a close up view of one of the hexagons.

6 Move the current-time marker to 1:15. The edges of the hexagon look jagged now because of the extreme scale change.

7 In the Switches panel, click the Collapse switch (✱) to collapse the transformations so that image quality is preserved. The edges of the hexagon become smooth once the layer is collapsed.

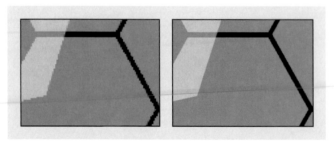

Before (left) and after (right) turning on Collapse Transformations switch

Note: *If the resolution of the Composition window is Half or lower, you may still see some jagged edges. To confirm that the edges are actually smoothed, temporarily change the resolution to Full.*

8 Move the current-time marker to 0:00 and then press the spacebar or 0 (zero) on the numeric keypad to preview or create a RAM preview of your work.

Now the hexagons quickly become very large as they enter the composition frame. You will continue to make adjustments to affect the appearance of their entry in the following procedures.

Note: The hexagons may appear larger than you expect at this stage. You'll correct this a little later in another procedure so that they look more like the sample movie.

When collapsing the transformations in this case, After Effects uses the scale of the source file to display this image rather than calculating the scale based on the reduced size of the hexagon layers in the previous composition (Hexagon Build Pre-comp). The Hexagon01.psd source file is plenty large enough to display the image at this size without sacrificing the image quality.

Rotating the entire honeycomb

The next step is to add a rotation that extends from the beginning (0:00) to the end (3:29) of the composition. You need the rotation keyframes at the same points in time as the scale keyframes you just added. You'll use some new techniques to simplify your task.

1 With the Hexagon 3 Bars Pre-comp layer selected and the Scale property still open, press Shift + R. The Rotation property opens but without replacing the Scale property display.

2 Move the current-time marker to 0:00 if it is not already there, but this time try one of the following techniques:

• Click the left *keyframe navigation arrow* for the Scale property to move the current-time marker to the first Scale keyframe at 0:00. Be careful not to click the check box.

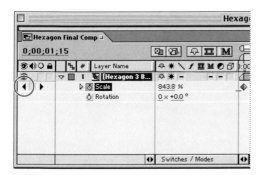

Keyframe navigation arrow

• Press J.

3 Click the Rotation property stopwatch to set a keyframe with values of 0 x 0° (at 0:00).

4 On the Scale property, click the right keyframe navigation arrow to move the current-time marker to the next Scale keyframe at 3:29. Or, press either K or End.

5 Change the Rotation value to 90°. A second keyframe appears in the Rotation properties.

6 Press J or Home to move the current-time marker back to 0:00.

7 Save your project and then preview the animation. If necessary, lower the resolution of the Composition window to see more frames in the RAM preview.

Moving the anchor point

Your composition now scales up until the center of the composition fills the frame. The *anchor point* is the focal point of the zoom and the center of the rotation as it spins. You can shift the target off center by moving the anchor point to add visual interest. (This also creates a nice opportunity for a transition into another scene later in the job.) You won't set a keyframe for the anchor-point position because you want it to remain at the same coordinates throughout the composition.

1 Move the current-time marker to 3:00.

2 In either the Timeline or Composition window, double-click the Hexagon 3 Bars Pre-comp to open the Layer window.

3 On the Layer window menu, choose Anchor Point Path, if it is not already selected.

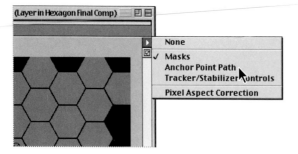

Crosshairs superimposed on the center of the layer indicate the current position of the anchor point (⊗).

4 With the layer still selected, press Shift + A to open the layer Anchor Point property in the Timeline window.

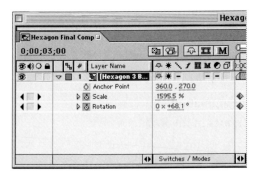

5 In the Layer window, drag the anchor point down and to the right to the coordinates 550, 295. Use the display in the Info palette as a guide, or you can scrub or type the Anchor Point values in the Timeline window.

Anchor point

6 Close the Layer window, save your work, and preview the animation.

The layer now rotates around the new anchor point and zooms into the center of the specified hexagon.

Changing position once more

As the layer zooms and rotates, it can also move sideways or up and down. By adding a small change in position, you'll give the overall movement of the layer a more natural flow, keeping it from looking too mechanical.

Before you start, press the comma key (,) or use the magnification pop-up menu in the lower left corner of the Composition window to reduce the zoom to the next lower value. Or, you can choose View > Zoom Out. At 0:00, you can then see the entire bounding box of the layer, which extends outside the composition frame and onto the pasteboard.

1 In the Timeline window, press Home to set the current-time marker at 0:00.

2 Select the Hexagon 3 Bars Pre-comp layer and press Shift + P to open the Position property without closing the Scale, Rotation, and Anchor Point properties.

3 Move the layer to the position coordinates 645, 390 by dragging, scrubbing the values, or typing in the Position property values, as shown here:

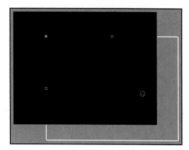

4 Click the Position stopwatch to set a keyframe.

5 Press K to move the current-time marker to the next keyframe at 3:29.

6 Change the position coordinates to 314, 539, so that the center of the hexagon completely fills the composition frame. A second keyframe appears automatically.

7 Save the project and preview the animation.

For an interesting view of the animation, drastically reduce the magnification to about 3% and then press the spacebar to create another preview. You'll see the movement of the whole layer, including the outline of what's outside the frame, on the pasteboard. Return the magnification to 50% or the appropriate size for your monitor when you are finished.

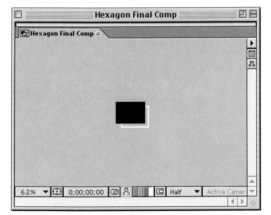 

Layer at 0:00 (left) and 3:29 (right)

Adding acceleration to the scale change

In real life, the appearance of an object doesn't increase very quickly when you approach it at steady speed from far away. As you get closer to the object, the rate at which the object fills your field of vision increases rapidly. You want to add this type of acceleration to the scaling of the layer. This is a subtle effect but the visual payoff is well worth the effort, so it's a good skill to learn.

1 With the Scale property visible in the Timeline window, click the arrow to expand the Scale property. Two graphs appear, the Value: Scale and the Velocity: Scale. Currently, the rate of change in Velocity: Scale graph is constant (linear) between the two keyframes.

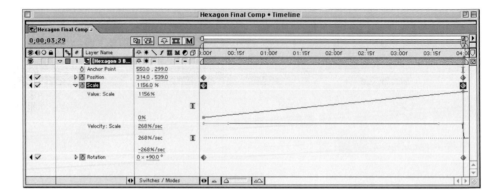

2 Click the word Scale to select both Scale keyframes.

3 On the Velocity Scale graph (below the Value: Scale graph), click the small handle just inside the 0:00 end of the graph and drag it slightly downward and then to the right until it reaches about the 2:00 position. When you release the handle, the Velocity: Scale percentage number updates.

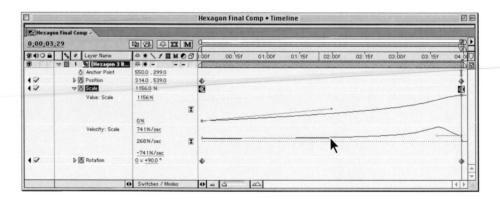

4 Select the similar handle near the 3:29 end of the graph and drag it upward, trying not to move it left or right. When you release the handle, the Velocity: Scale percentage value updates. Continue dragging the right handle upward until the line of the graph matches the illustration below.

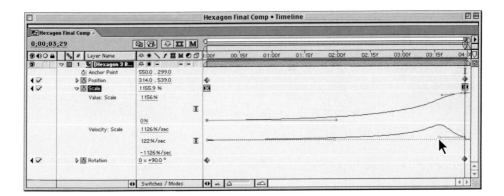

5 Press the accent grave key (`) to hide all the transform properties.

6 Save your project and preview the animation. You can now see many more of the hexagons at the beginning, similar to the way they appear in the sample movie.

Notice that the Scale keyframes change shape after you adjust the velocity. This indicates a difference in *keyframe interpolation*, caused by changing the rate of the scale change. For more information, see "Controlling change through interpolation" in After Effects online Help.

If you need to take another break, this is a good time to do that. The final section of the lesson takes about 20-30 minutes.

Reusing your work to create a second element

Your honeycomb animation is now complete, so you're ready to start working on a second hexagon element. This new composition is much easier to create than the first one because you're going to leverage that work by simply duplicating the original composition and plugging in different artwork.

Your ability to substitute new footage files within compositions instead of starting over from the beginning is a time-saver and a potential "life-saver." It makes it relatively quick and painless to do last-minute changes or to create multiple versions, such as different language versions for international distribution or multiple output formats.

Importing artwork for a second element

First, you need to import the new artwork into your project. If necessary, restart After Effects and open the Hexagons01_work.aep.

1 Choose File > Import > File. Or, press Ctrl + I (the letter *i*) (Windows) or Command + I (Mac OS).

2 Browse to the _psd folder you created, and select the Hexagon02.psd file that was copied from the CD.

3 Click Open (Windows) or Import (Mac OS).

4 In the Interpret Footage dialog box, click Straight – Unmatted, and click OK.

5 In the Project window, drag the Hexagon02.psd file into the psd files folder.

In the thumbnail image, you can see that this hexagon is only an outline with small circles at each of its points.

Replacing footage

Now, you'll replace the footage in the composition.

1 In the Project window, select the Hexagon Build Pre-comp and choose Edit > Duplicate. A duplicate item appears in the Project window with an asterisk (*) after the name.

2 With the duplicate composition selected, choose Composition > Composition Settings to open the Composition Settings dialog box.

3 Type **HexOutlines Build Pre-comp** for the name, and leave all other settings unchanged. Click OK to close the Composition Settings.

4 In the Project window, double-click the HexOutlines Build Pre-comp to open it in the Composition and Timeline windows.

5 With the Timeline window active, choose Edit > Select All to select all ten Hexagon01.psd layers.

6 In the Project window, select theHexagon02.psd file. Then, hold down Alt (Windows) or Option (Mac OS) as you drag the file into the Timeline window and then release the mouse button.

The source name for all of the layers changes to Hexagon02.psd and the new artwork appears in the Composition window. To see the differences, preview the composition.

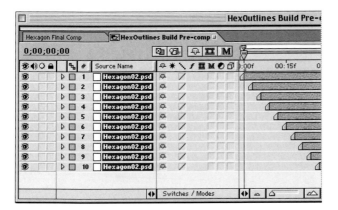

When you replace one source file with another one used in a composition, you don't have to redo the transformation changes and keyframes. The layer retains all the transform property changes and keyframes, and applies them to the replacement footage.

Duplicating and reusing a precomposition

You'll repeat the process for the remaining two compositions in this element.

1 In the Project window, select the Hexagon 3 Bars Pre-comp and choose Edit > Duplicate, or press Ctrl + D (Windows) or Command + D (Mac OS). A duplicate composition appears, again with the asterisk after its name.

2 With the duplicate composition selected in the Project window, choose Composition > Composition Settings to open the Composition Settings dialog box.

3 Type **HexOutlines 3 Bars Pre-comp** for the name, and leave all other settings unchanged. Click OK to close the Composition Settings.

4 In the Project window, double-click the HexOutlines 3 Bars Pre-comp to open it in the Composition and Timeline windows.

5 In the Timeline window, select all three layers.

6 In the Project window, select the HexOutlines Build Pre-comp. Then, hold down Alt (Windows) or Option (Mac OS) as you drag the file into the Timeline window and then release the mouse button.

7 Click the panel heading, Layer Name, to toggle to the Source Name panel, and notice that the source names have changed from Hexagon Build Pre-comp to HexOutlines Build Pre-comp. Preview the composition and save your work.

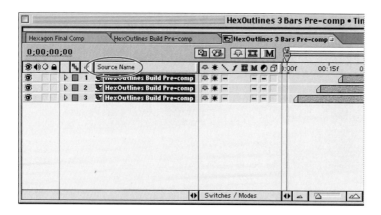

Duplicating another precomposition

Lastly, you'll repeat the same steps with the final composition for this new element.

1 In the Project window, select the Hexagon Final Comp and choose Edit > Duplicate.

2 Select the Duplicate item and press Ctrl + K (Windows) or Command + K (Mac OS) to open the Composition Settings.

3 Type **HexOutlines Final Comp** for the name, and leave all other settings unchanged. Click OK.

4 In the Project window, double-click the HexOutlines Final composition to open it in the Composition and Timeline windows.

5 In the Timeline window, select the Hexagon 3 Bars Pre-comp layer.

6 In the Project window, select the HexOutlines 3 Bars Pre-comp, press Alt (Windows) or Option (Mac OS) as you drag the file into the Timeline window, and release the mouse. The layer is replaced.

7 Save your work, and then press 0 (zero) on the numeric keypad to create and run a RAM preview.

As the composition plays, notice that the new hexagon outlines behave exactly like the ones they replaced, with the same characteristics for scale, position, rotation, and opacity. Your entire animation now plays back using the new artwork.

Rendering compositions

Rendering generates a movie of a composition in a destination format. When you work on large jobs with many components, it can be helpful to pre-render some of the elements: You build the element in its own project or composition, render it, and then import it into the final job composition or project.

There are many advantages to pre-rendering:

• It helps to organize large numbers of elements and reduces the number of compositions within the final project. This keeps the final project more streamlined.

• Pre-rendered elements don't require as many CPU cycles to process while you work as unrendered compositions do. Consequently, things like redraw and RAM previews are much more efficient.

• It speeds up the final job render because the element is processed as one layer, not many.

Both your hexagon elements are just the way you want them, so you can now render these compositions. The process is comparable to creating a RAM preview, but rendering takes more time and produces an independent file that is stored on your hard drive.

The time required for rendering depends on the size and complexity of the project and on the processing speed of your equipment. This project is still relatively small, so it shouldn't take too long—about a couple of minutes.

Rendering the Hexagons element

Your first task is to render the first composition, which is composed of solid hexagons from the Hexagon01.psd.

1 Close the Timeline and Composition windows.

2 Select the Hexagon Final Comp in the Project window.

3 Choose Composition > Make Movie.

4 In the Output Movie To dialog box, type **Hexagons.mov** in File Name, and save the file in the _mov folder you created in the AE_CIB job folder.

5 Click Save. The Render Queue window appears.

6 Click the underlined words *Current Settings* next to Render Settings.

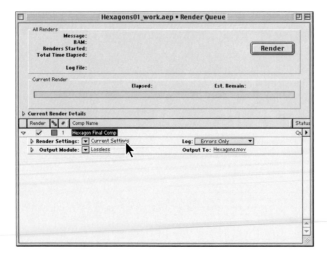

7 In the Render Settings dialog box, specify the following options:

• For Quality, select Best.

• For Resolution, select Full.

• Under Time Sampling, for Time Span, select Length of Comp from the pop-up menu. (These settings override any settings you used in the Composition or Timeline windows for the purposes of the render.)

8 Click OK to close the Render Settings dialog box.

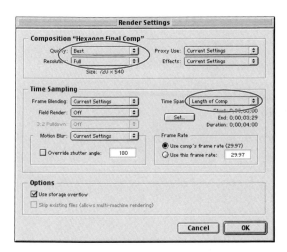

9 In the Render Queue window, click the arrow to open the pop-up menu for Output Module, and select Custom.

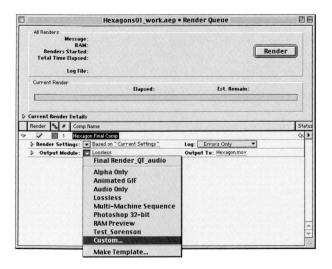

10 In the Output Module Settings dialog box, under Output Module, set the following options:

• In the Format pop-up menu, choose QuickTime Movie.

• Select the Import into Project When Done option.

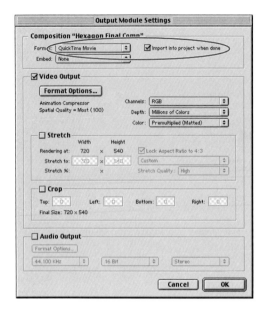

11 Under Video Output, click the Format Options button to open the Compression Settings dialog box, and make sure that the following options are selected:

• Under Compressor, choose Animation and Millions of Colors+ from the menus.

• The Quality slider is at Best.

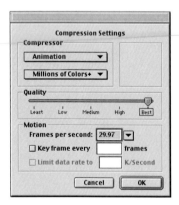

Note: The Frames per Second value is set in the Render Settings dialog box—not here.

12 Click OK to close the Compression Settings dialog box.

13 Click OK to close the Output Module Settings dialog box, returning you to the Render Queue window.

14 Choose File > Save to save the project before you render and then click Render.

Note: Although you could wait until you specify options for rendering the HexOutlines Final Comp before you render the Hexagons Final Comp, rendering now will give you a sense of how long it takes to render elements on your machine.

Rendering the HexOutlines element

Next, you render the HexOutlines element.

1 In the Project window, select the HexOutlines Final Comp and choose Composition > Make Movie.

2 In the Output Movie To dialog box, type **HexOutlines.mov** in File Name, and save the file in the _mov folder you created in the AE_CIB job folder. When you click OK, the HexOutlines Final Comp appears as the second item in the Render Queue.

3 Repeat steps 5 – 14, as described in the previous procedure, "Rendering the Hexagons element" on page 58.

4 When the render is complete, close the Render Queue.

5 The Hexagons.mov and HexOutlines.mov both appear in the Project window because you selected the Import into Project When Done option in step 10.

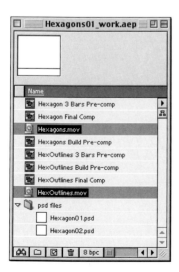

Viewing the rendered movies

You're almost finished with this lesson. All that remains is to check your results.

1 In the Project window, double-click the Hexagons.mov to open it.

2 Click the Play button (▶) to start the movie.

3 Repeat steps 1 and 2 for the HexOutlines.mov.

4 Close the player windows.

After you render a movie, you may discover elements you want to change. If so, you can make these changes in the appropriate composition(s) and save your work, but these do not affect the already-rendered movie. Instead, you must render the movie again to create a new movie that incorporates your changes. For more information, see "Saving time by pre-rendering nested compositions" in After Effects online Help.

*If you have trouble viewing your full-resolution rendered movie, try rendering a version of this movie at half-resolution just for your own viewing convenience. To do this, follow the rendering procedure above, but name it **Hexagon_lr.mov** in step 4, and select Half instead of Full for Resolution in step 7. However, if you do render a low-resolution movie, do not delete your full-resolution version of the rendered movie because you cannot use the half-resolution version in the final project—it won't have the dimensions you need. You must use full-resolution renderings when you combine elements in later lessons.*

Congratulations! You've now finished all of your work on both the Hexagons.mov and HexOutlines.mov elements. Later in the book, you'll combine these QuickTime elements with many others in one final composition to finish the job.

Lesson 2

2 | Building Elements from Squares

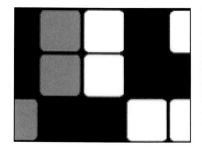  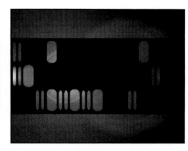

You don't need a lot of source files to get sophisticated results. You can create many complex animations using just the numerous controls, tools, and effects that are built into After Effects 5.0. But you can also take full advantage of files created in other Adobe products, such as Adobe Premiere, Adobe Photoshop, and Adobe Illustrator, when you incorporate them into your After Effects projects.

In this lesson, you'll learn to do the following:

- Import layered Photoshop files as compositions
- Use individual Photoshop layers as After Effects layers
- Create and use guide lines in your composition
- Use keyframe interpolation to control movements
- Set a work area
- Change Position keyframes by dragging
- Apply transfer modes
- Create a solid layer and apply the Lens Flare effect
- Combine rendered elements into a single composition

This lesson is organized in five sections. When you finish all the work, you'll have several new elements that you'll pull into your final compositions in later chapters. In the process of creating these elements, you'll create and adjust several intermediate components, some of which you'll render before adding them to other compositions. This not only keeps your work area efficient, it speeds up the rendering process for the final project. Rendering now also makes it more likely that you'll discover any unwanted results right away, when it's easiest to correct them.

This entire lesson takes about two hours to complete. However, there are several natural stopping points indicated within the lesson where you can take breaks.

Getting started

Make sure that the following files are in the AE_CIB job folder on your hard drive, or copy them from the *After Effects Classroom in a Book* CD now.

- In the _psd folder: Squares.psd and SingleBox.psd
- In the Sample_Movies folder: Squares01_final.mov, LensFlare_final.mov, and BoxLightsLine_final.mov from the Sample Movies/Lesson02 folder on the CD
- In the Finished_Projects folder: Boxes02_finished.aep

Refer to "Note: (Windows only) If you do not see the Prefs file, be sure that the Show all files option is selected for Hidden files on the View tab of the Folder Options dialog box." on page 4 for the copying procedure, if necessary.

Note: It is important to use the folder structure described in "Setting up a folder structure" on page 4 for your files. This organization becomes increasingly important as your project gets more complex, so always take the time to place files in the appropriate folders before you start working. Rearranging files later can cause linkage problems and create extra work for you.

Open and play the sample movies—Squares01_final.mov, LensFlare_final.mov, and BoxLightsLine_final.mov—to see what you'll create in Lesson 2. When you finish viewing the movies, you can either delete them to save space on your hard drive, or leave them there for the duration of the lesson so that you can compare your results with the samples.

You'll do this entire lesson in a single project, so your first job is to create that project.

1 Start After Effects 5.0, if it is not already running.

2 Choose File > New > New Project.

3 Choose File > Save As.

4 In the Save Project As dialog box, find and open the _aep folder in your AE_CIB job folder.

5 In Name, type **Boxes02_work.aep**, and then click Save.

Note: In this book, the names of the project files include the lesson numbers, so that you can easily find the procedures associated with each lesson. The number 02 in the name Boxes02_work simply reminds you that you did the work in Lesson 2. The numbering does not mean that there is another file named Boxes01_work—there's not.

Creating the first element: dancing squares

In this segment you'll create an element to be used in the background of your final piece. To play the sample finished version, double-click the Squares01_final.mov file in the Sample_Movies folder.

In this section, you begin with an image of a single white box with rounded edges. You'll use the image to animate a number of these squares that read as "dancing" squares.

Importing source files for the dancing squares

This project uses a source file created in Adobe Photoshop. You copied the file into the _psd folder earlier, so now you can import it.

1 Choose File > Import > File.

2 Open the _psd folder inside the AE_CIB job folder and select the SingleBox.psd file.

3 Click Open (Windows) or Import (Mac OS).

4 In the Interpret Footage dialog box, leave the Straight – Unmatted option selected, and click OK. The file appears in the Project window.

5 Choose File > New > New Folder to create a new folder in the Project window.

6 Type **psd files** as the folder name, and press Enter or Return.

7 Drag the SingleBox.psd file into the psd files folder. Then expand the folder so that you can see the file nested inside it.

When you select the SingleBox.psd file, the thumbnail image appears at the top of the Project window. A white square appears against a black background, which is the After Effects default color for the transparent area of the alpha channel.

💡 *To see a larger view of the image, double-click the filename to open it in the Footage window. You can adjust the window size and magnification as needed. When you finish, close the Footage window.*

Creating the Square Grid Comp

You're ready to start your project again, beginning with the now-familiar task of creating a new composition.

1 Choose Composition > New Composition, or press Ctrl + N (Windows) or Command + N (Mac OS) to create a new composition. The Composition Settings dialog box opens.

2 In Composition Name, type **Square Grid Comp**.

3 On the Basic settings tab, adjust the settings as follows:

• In both Width and Height, type **440**.

• Make sure that the Pixel Aspect Ratio is Square Pixels.

• In Frame Rate, set **29.97**.

• (Optional) For Resolution, select Half (or lower), as needed for your system.

• Make sure the Start Timecode is 0;00.

• In Duration, type **500**, to specify five seconds, and then click OK.

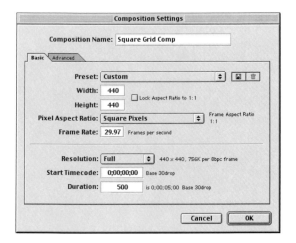

Placing and sizing squares

Now that your composition is ready, you'll place, duplicate, and resize a square in preparation for creating the first block of dancing squares.

1 In the Project window, select the SingleBox.psd and drag it into the Composition window.

2 Choose Edit > Duplicate four times, or press Ctrl + D (Windows) or Command + D (Mac OS) four times. The Timeline window should now show five layers in the composition, all named *SingleBox.psd*.

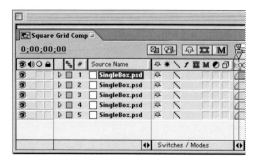

Note: The image in the Composition window doesn't change because all the layers are stacked directly above each other.

3 Choose Edit > Select All, or press Ctrl + A (Windows) or Command + A (Mac OS) to select all five layers.

4 Press S to display the Scale properties for all layers.

5 Click one of the underlined Scale values and type **85**. Then press Enter or Return. All five Scale settings are 85% and the image shrinks in size.

6 Press S again to hide the Scale property. Save your work.

Creating guides

To help you align the squares in a precise array, you create guides. You create guides by dragging them into position from the Rulers in the same way as in many other Adobe software products.

1 If necessary, choose Edit > Select All, or press Ctrl + A (Windows) or Command + A (Mac OS) to select all five layers.

2 Choose Layer > Quality > Best to set the Quality switch so that you have maximum accuracy for aligning your layers. Or, you can drag the pointer down the column of Quality switches. As you drag, the switches in each layer change from Draft to Best (✓).

Note: *If the Modes panel is open instead of the Switches panel, click the toggle bar at the bottom of the panel to see the Switches panel.*

3 Choose View > Show Rulers. Rulers appear on the top and left edges of the Composition window, using pixels as the unit of measurement.

4 Choose View > Show Guides, if this command is available. (If it is already selected, the Hide Guides command appears instead of Show Guides.)

5 Drag down from any position along the top Ruler into the composition frame to create a guide, and place it about 10 pixels below the top edge of the composition frame.

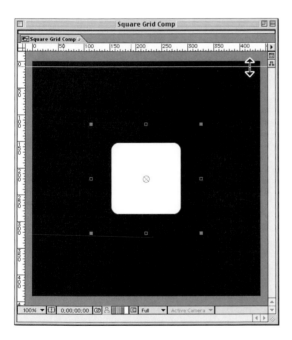

6 Repeat step 5, but this time drag the guide to about 10 pixels above the bottom edge of the composition frame.

7 Drag two more guides from the left Ruler, placing one about 10 pixels inside the left edge of the frame and the other about 10 pixels inside the right edge. Your composition frame now has four guides.

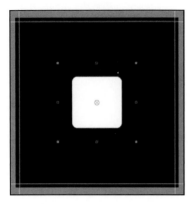

8 Drag a guide from the left Ruler and place it at about the 145 mark on the top Ruler.

9 Drag three more vertical guides from the left Ruler, placing them at about 155, 290 and 300.

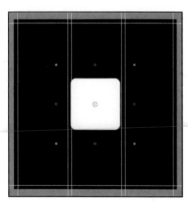

10 Drag four horizontal guides from the upper Ruler and set them at about 145, 155, 290, and 300 using the left Ruler as a position guide.

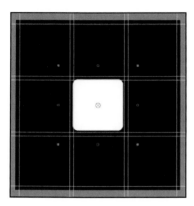

11 When all the guides are in place, choose View > Hide Rulers. Then choose Edit > Deselect All, and save the project.

For more information about guides, see "Using rulers and guides" in After Effects online Help.

Animating the dancing squares

Next, you'll animate the squares so that they shift positions within the grid every 15 frames.

1 Select Layer 1 in the Timeline window. In the Composition window, drag Layer 1 to the location shown in the diagram below, using the arrow keys to nudge it into place, as necessary. Then select each of the remaining four layers and drag each to its new location.

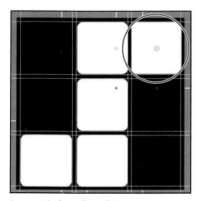

Layer 1 (selected) and Layers 2–5

Because you're trying to align elements with precision here, it's helpful to turn off the Dynamic Resolution preference in After Effects, which makes the image jagged as you drag. To maintain the image resolution, choose Edit > Preferences > Previews and then deselect Use Dynamic Resolution. Then click OK. Now the image resolution doesn't drop as you drag the layers. Because this requires a little more time to redraw, you can reselect this preference when you finish this procedure.

2 Set the current-time marker at 0:00, choose Edit > Select All, and press P to open the Position properties on all five layers.

3 Press Alt + P (Windows) or Option + P (Mac OS) to set Position keyframes for all five layers.

4 Choose Edit > Deselect All, and then move the current-time marker to 0:15.

5 Drag one of the squares either vertically or horizontally into any open slot, pressing Shift after you start dragging to constrain the movement either vertically or horizontally. (It doesn't matter which square you choose or in which direction it moves, but do not move it over other squares.) A new Position keyframe appears at the fifteenth frame.

6 Select a different square and drag it to another available slot.

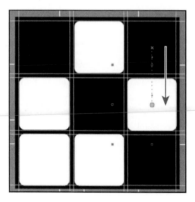

7 Without moving the remaining three layers, click the keyframe check boxes to set a checkmark in each one. These layers will hold their original positions for these 15 frames.

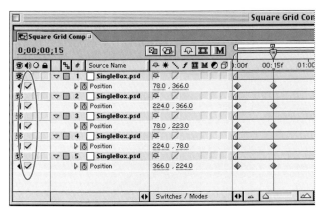

Keyframe check boxes

8 Move the current-time marker to 1:00 and drag any three squares into new positions, keeping them aligned with the guides. Again, do not move the squares over one another.

9 Select the keyframe check boxes to set keyframes for the other two layers.

10 Continue to randomly move squares into different slots every 15 frames, ending at 3:00. Be careful to move the current-time marker each time and to select the keyframe check boxes for the squares that don't move. You now have a total of 35 Position keyframes.

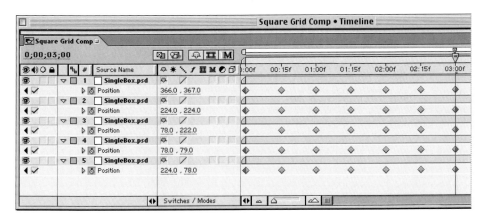

11 Press Home to move the current-time marker to 0:00. Then preview your work and save the project. Do not collapse the Position properties display in the Timeline window.

Maintaining straight-line motion

You may notice that some of the squares swerve as they move. When you select a layer, the motion path appears in the Composition window as a dotted line that runs from the original position of the square to its final position. If a square moves around a corner, the motion path curves slightly. You'll adjust the *keyframe interpolation* to restrain the motion and remove these curves.

1 Select all of the Position keyframes for all of the layers by drawing a marquee around them in the Timeline window.

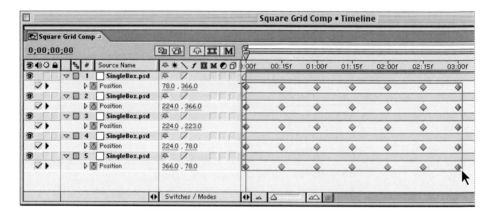

2 Choose Animation > Keyframe Interpolation to open the Keyframe Interpolation dialog box.

3 In Spatial Interpolation, select Linear, and then click OK.

The motion paths are now straight lines.

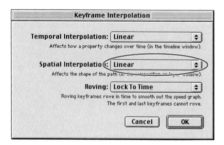

4 Press P to hide the Position properties.

5 Press Ctrl + Shift + A (Windows) or Command + Shift + A (Mac OS) to deselect all of the layers and keyframes.

6 Preview the animation and notice that the motion follows straight lines.

7 If you want to make any changes to the movements, do this now and then save your work.

For background information, see "Comparing interpolation methods" in After Effects online Help.

Resetting the work area for dancing squares

The *work area* is the portion of the composition that is included in previews. By limiting the work area to a portion of the composition, you can preview just the frames you need to see, without waiting for After Effects to create a RAM preview of the entire composition. A gray bar just above the timeline indicates the duration of the work area. By default, the work area is the same as the length of the composition.

1 Move the current-time marker to 3:00.

2 Press N. The work-area duration bar now ends at 3:00.

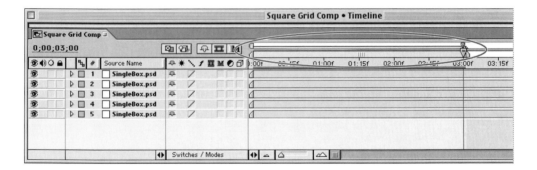

3 Choose File > Save.

4 Make sure that either the Timeline window or the Composition window is active and choose File > Close to close the Square Grid Comp. Or, you can click the close box on the Square Grid Comp tab.

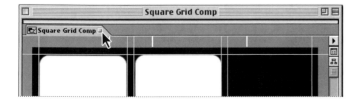

Reusing the composition in a new one

To complete the dancing-squares element, you'll create a new composition and use six Square Grid Comp animations in a long strip. The first task is to define the composition so that it has the right size.

1 Choose Composition > New Composition.

2 In Composition Name, type **Squares01 Comp**.

3 On the Basic tab, specify the following:

• In Width, type **2640**.

• In Height, type **440**.

• In Duration, type **400**, to specify four seconds.

3. Make sure the other settings match the illustration below, and then click OK.

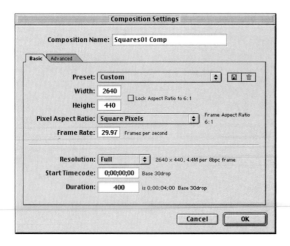

The new composition is many times wider than others you've worked on in these lessons, so it probably extends beyond your view. Resize the Composition window by dragging the corner until it fits within your screen.

💡 *You can simultaneously increase or reduce the magnification and size of the Composition window with keyboard shortcuts that use the plus or minus signs on the main keyboard (not the keypad). Pressing Ctrl + plus sign (+) (Windows) or Command + plus sign (+) (Mac OS) increases the magnification and size. Pressing Ctrl + minus sign (–) (Windows) or Command + minus sign (–) (Mac OS) reduces the magnification and size. The Composition window must be selected when you use the shortcut.*

Placing the Square Grid animations

You'll now add, duplicate, rename, and move the Square Grid Comp within the new composition.

1 In the Project window, select the Squares Grid Comp and drag it into the Composition or Timeline window.

2 Press Ctrl + D (Windows) or Command + D (Mac OS) five times to duplicate the layer so that a total of six layers appears in the Timeline window.

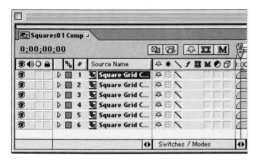

3 In the Timeline window, select Layer 1 and press Enter or Return. The layer name becomes active.

4 Type **Square Grid 1**, and press Enter or Return to enter the new name.

5 Repeat steps 3 and 4 to rename each of the other five layers, naming them according to their position in the layer stack: **Square Grid 2**, **Square Grid 3**, and so forth.

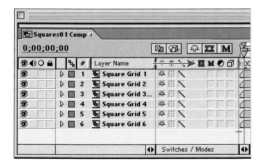

6 In the Timeline window, select Square Grid 1 and drag it to the far left edge of the Composition window, at approximately the 220, 220 coordinates.

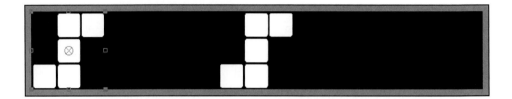

7 Move Square Grid 2 to the right of Square Grid 1, at approximately 660, 220.

8 Move each of the remaining layers until they line up approximately as shown:

- Square Grid 3: 1100, 220

- Square Grid 4: 1540, 220

- Square Grid 5: 1980, 220

- Square Grid 6: 2420, 220

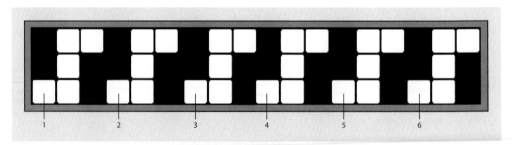

Layers 1–6 positions

Adjusting the opacity of some layers

To add variety and texture, you'll change the opacity of two layers.

1 In the Timeline window, select the Square Grid 1 layer and press T to open its Opacity property.

2 Scrub or type **50%** as the Opacity value, and press Enter or Return. Then press T again to close the Opacity property.

3 Select the Square Grid 4 layer and repeat this process, but this time change the Opacity value to **80%**.

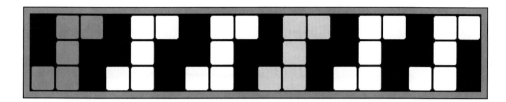

4 Save your work.

Rotating layers

To give this element a slightly less uniform appearance, you'll randomize the orientations. Because you created the original animation composition as a perfect square, you can simply rotate a few of the duplicates. This varies the movement within the overall composition, creating the impression that you've done a lot more work than you actually did. Your last task before rendering is to limit the work area.

1 Choose Edit > Select All or press Ctrl + A (Windows) or Command + A (Mac OS) to select all layers.

2 Press R to open the Rotation properties for all of the layers.

3 Choose Edit > Deselect All or press Ctrl + Shift + A (Windows) or Command + Shift + A (Mac OS) to deselect all layers, leaving the Rotation properties open.

4 Scrub or type to enter Rotation values for the layers, as follows:

- Square Grid 1: 0° (No change.)

- Square Grid 2: **90°**.

- Square Grid 3: **180°**.

- Square Grid 4: **–90°**.

- Square Grid 5: 0° (No change.)

• Square Grid 6: **90°**.

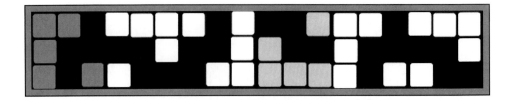

5 Move the current-time marker to 3:00 and press N to set the work area to end at 3:00.

6 Press Home to move the current-time marker to 0:00, and then preview the animation.

The squares randomly shift as they shuffle themselves in the Composition window. If you want to make adjustments, do so now.

7 Save the project.

Rendering the dancing squares

You've finished working with this element, so it's time to render the movie.

1 Close the Composition and Timeline windows, and then select the Squares01 Comp in the Project window.

2 Choose Composition > Make Movie, or press Ctrl + M (Windows) or Command + M (Mac OS).

3 In the Output Movie To dialog box, locate your _mov folder in the AE_CIB job folder and type **Squares01.mov** in Name.

4 In the Render Queue window, choose Best Settings for the Render Settings.

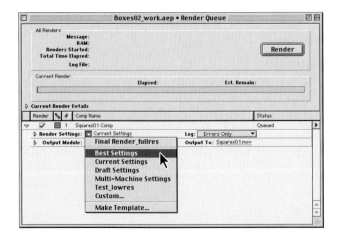

5 Click the underlined words *Best Settings* to open the Render Settings dialog box.

6 Make sure that Time Span is set to Work Area Only and that the work area indicated starts at 0:00 and ends at 3:00. Click OK to close the Render Settings dialog box.

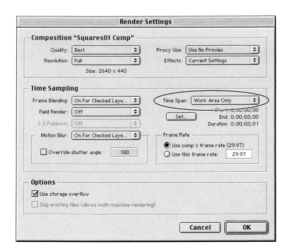

7 For the Output Module, choose Custom to open the Output Module Settings dialog box, and do all the following:.

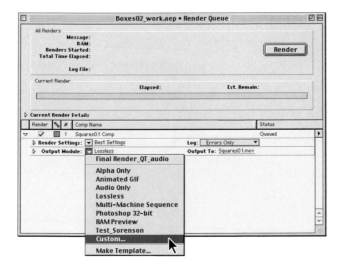

- In Format, choose QuickTime Movie.
- Select the Import into Project When Done option.

• Click Format Options to open the Compression Settings dialog box.

8 Choose Animation and Millions of Colors+, and then click OK to close the dialog box.

9 Make sure that Channels is set to RGB + Alpha, and then click OK to close the Output Module Settings. You'll use the alpha information when you composite this layer into your final piece in a later lesson.

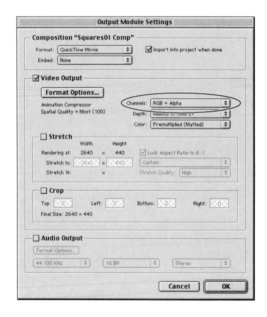

10 Choose File > Save, as a precaution.

11 Click the Render button.

When rendering is complete, close the Render Queue window. The Squares01.mov now appears in the Project window because of the option you selected in step 7.

Playing the Squares01 movie

You can now play the movie you've just rendered.

1 Press Alt (Windows) or Option (Mac OS) as you double-click the Squares01.mov to open it in the Footage window, and then reduce the size of the window as needed so that it fits on your screen.

Note: Pressing Alt or Option when you open the movie gives you access to the Magnification menu and shortcuts. If the movie fits on your screen as is, you do not need to use the Alt or Option key.

2 Play the movie. It should look just like it did in the final Preview before rendering.

3 When you are finished, close the Footage window, save your work, and close the project.

If you need to take a break, this is a good place to do so.

Creating pulsating strips of squares

In this section, you start to create a second squares-based element that will become part of the overall project. The first component of this element is made up of three different compositions: a strip of squares that moves into view from the left; a strip of squares that moves into view from the right; and a strip of squares that is not animated. Using transfer modes, you'll make these subcomponents interact with each other so that you see strips of squares that appear to pulsate, growing wider and then narrower in an apparently random fashion.

Importing a layered source file

For this composition, you use a layered Photoshop source file. When you import this kind of file into After Effects, you can either ignore the layering structure and use the Photoshop file as a single flat image or you can preserve the integrity of the Photoshop layers so that you can use them separately. To keep the layers, you'll import the file as a composition. The dimensions of the Photoshop layers determine the size of the After Effects composition.

You'll continue your work within the Boxes02_work.aep project you created at the beginning of this chapter. If it is not already open, find that file in the _aep folder in your AE_CIB job folder and open it now.

1 Choose File > Import > File. The Import File dialog box appears.

2 In the _psd folder in your AE_CIB job folder, select the Squares.psd file.

3 In Import As, select Composition.

Note: This option is available only when you select a file that contains layers.

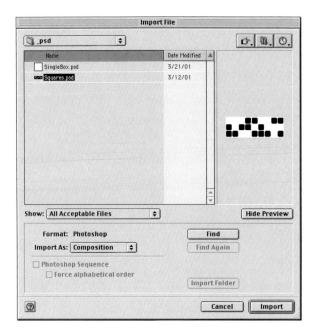

4 Click Open (Windows) or Import (Mac OS).

Two new elements appear in the Project window: a composition file and a folder, both named Squares.psd.

5 Double-click the composition to open it in the Composition and Timeline windows. In the Timeline window, you see the three layers created in Photoshop. Each layer retains all the Photoshop settings assigned to it.

Note: If you can't see the entire image in the Composition window, resize the window and then use the magnification menu in the lower left corner of the Composition window to reduce the zoom. Or, press Ctrl + minus sign (–) (Windows) or Command + minus sign (–) (Mac OS).

6 Close the Composition and Timeline windows, and then expand the Squares.psd folder in the Project window so that you see the three layers created in Photoshop.

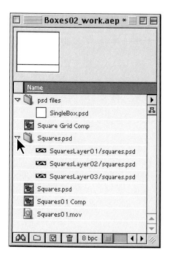

You can click any of these layers to see their thumbnail images in the top of the Project window. Because you imported the source file as a composition, you can also use each of these layers independently within your compositions. For more information about importing layered files, see After Effects online Help.

Note: In After Effects, this composition inherits the most recently used Duration and Frame Rate settings.

Creating a composition for pulsating squares

For this section, you begin with a new composition.

1 Choose Composition > New Composition, or press Ctrl + N (Windows) or Command + N (Mac OS). The Composition Settings dialog box opens.

2 In Composition Name, type **Moving Right Comp**.

3 On the Basic tab of the dialog box, set the following options:

• In Width, type **860**, and deselect Lock Aspect Ratio.

• In Height, type **300**.

• Make sure that the Pixel Aspect Ratio is Square Pixels.

• In Frame Rate, set **29.97**.

• (Optional) In Resolution, select Half or lower, as needed for your system.

• Make sure the Start Timecode is 0:00.

• In Duration, type **500**, to specify five seconds.

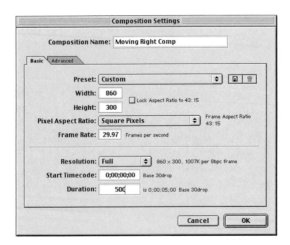

4 Click OK. The new composition appears in the Squares.psd folder in the Project window if that folder was selected when you started this task.

5 Drag the Moving Right Comp out of the Squares.psd folder and place it on the top level of the Project window hierarchy. (If necessary, enlarge the Project window so that you can drag the composition to an empty area at the bottom of the window.)

Note: You created this composition at a size (860 by 300 pixels) that is at least as large as you will ever need for your final animation. By building elements at larger-than-needed sizes, you accomplish two things. First, you give yourself maximum flexibility because you can always shrink the image later by reducing the Scale property. Second, you maintain image quality, which would be compromised if you scaled it up beyond 100%. This practice is a good general rule to follow—but there are exceptions to it, as you'll see later in this lesson.

Creating and animating the first layer

In this composition, you'll use just one of the Photoshop layers to animate squares that travel from left to right. You'll create this in a way that makes it easier for you later when you set it to loop (play seamlessly, without any apparent beginning or end).

1 Press Home to set the current time to 0:00, if it's not already there, and then reduce the magnification of the Composition window so that you can see a larger area of the pasteboard.

2 In the Project window, select SquaresLayer02 (in the Squares.psd folder) and drag it into the Composition window.

3 Press P to open the Position property and then drag the layer into the Composition window so that it is just outside of the left edge of the composition frame (about -430, 150).

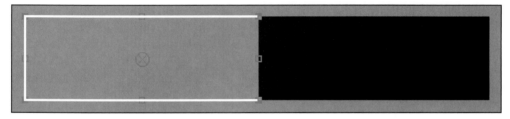

Starting position of Layer 1 on the Composition window pasteboard

4 Click the stopwatch (⏱) to set a Position keyframe. Or, press Alt + P (Windows) or Option + P (Mac OS).

5 Move the current-time marker to 4:01.

6 Drag the SquaresLayer02 layer to the center of the composition frame, or start dragging and press Ctrl + Shift (Windows) or Command + Shift (Mac OS) to snap the layer into the center. A second Position keyframe automatically appears at 4:01.

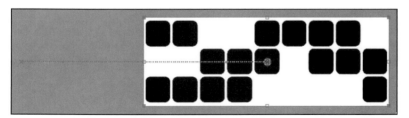

Final position of Layer 1 in the composition frame

7 Press Home to set the current time to 0:00.

8 Press the spacebar or 0 (zero) on the numeric keypad to preview or RAM preview the animation, and then save the project.

Note: If RAM preview doesn't show the entire clip, see "Allocating RAM to After Effects" on page 2 for tips about working around RAM limitations on your computer.

Duplicating and modifying the first layer

Next, you'll create a second layer that is almost identical to the first, using the same source footage and moving in the same direction. The difference is that Layer 2 begins at a position that snugs up to the end of Layer 1, so the two move in tandem, like two cars of a train, without any gap between them. Rather than recreating everything for a new layer, you can re-use and modify Layer 1.

1 Select Layer 1 and choose Edit > Duplicate, or press Ctrl + D (Windows) or Command + D (Mac OS). A new layer appears, having the same position keyframes as the original.

2 Select Layer 2 and press P to open the Position property, if it's not already open.

3 Draw a marquee around both Position keyframes to select them. Or, click the word *Position* in Layer 2.

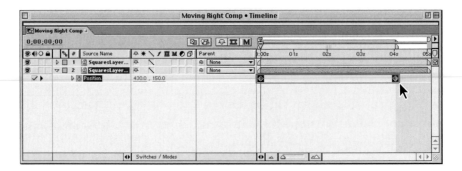

4 Move the current-time marker to 0:00.

5 In the Composition window, drag Layer 2 to the right so that the layer is positioned in the center of the Composition window. As you drag, press Ctrl + Shift (Windows) or Command + Shift (Mac OS) to snap the layer to the center of the composition. Notice that both of the layer keyframes (shown as small *X*'s) move with the layer as you drag.

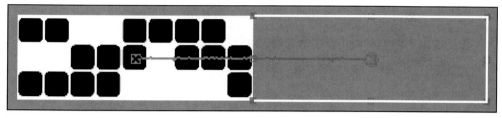

Layer 2 at 4:01 (left) and at 0:00 (right)

6 Press P to hide the Position property.

7 Preview the animation. The two layers now move in tandem from left to right, from 0:00 to 4:01.

8 Save the project.

When you moved Layer 2 and its keyframes, the center of the Composition window became the Position value for the first keyframe. Because you also selected the second keyframe, the two moved as a unit, maintaining their relative positions. When the composition starts, Layer 2 is at the center of the composition, filling the frame, and Layer 1 is out of view on the left side of the frame. At the end of the motion, Layer 1 has moved in to fill the frame and Layer 2 has passed out of the frame to the right.

Note: *If you don't see the X's representing the layer keyframes, open the Composition window menu and make sure that Layer Keyframes is selected.*

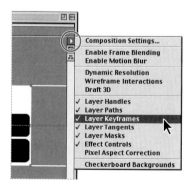

Adjusting the work area for pulsating squares

You'll take steps now that set up the animation to be easier to preview and better looking, so you won't have a "stutter" in the motion.

The first and last frames of this animation are identical, so the animation would stall for one frame each time it loops. Use the keyframe navigation arrows on the far left of the Position property to see this by jumping back and forth between the first keyframe and the last, or by pressing J and then K.

You fix the stutter by removing one of the two identical frames. You do this by redefining the work area, limiting it to the area in which Position keyframes occur.

1 Move the current-time marker to 4:00 (one frame *before* the second keyframe).

2 Press N to set the end of the work area at the current time. Or, drag the handle at the right end of the work-area bar, watching the display in the Info palette until it reads 4:00. You can press Shift as you drag to snap the work-area handle to the position of the current-time marker.

The work-area bar now ends at 4:00, and the background color of the timeline beyond the work area changes to a darker shade of gray.

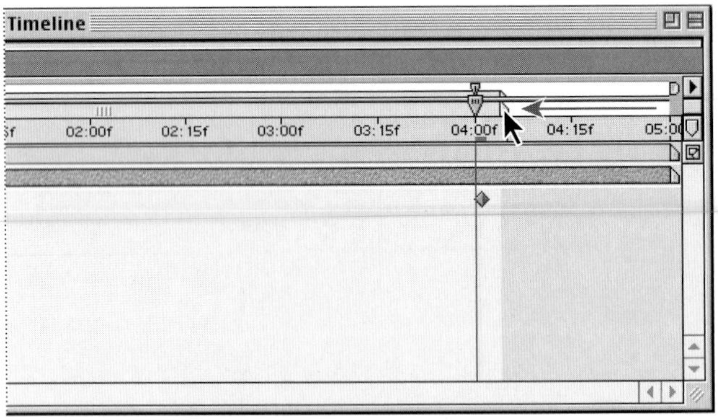

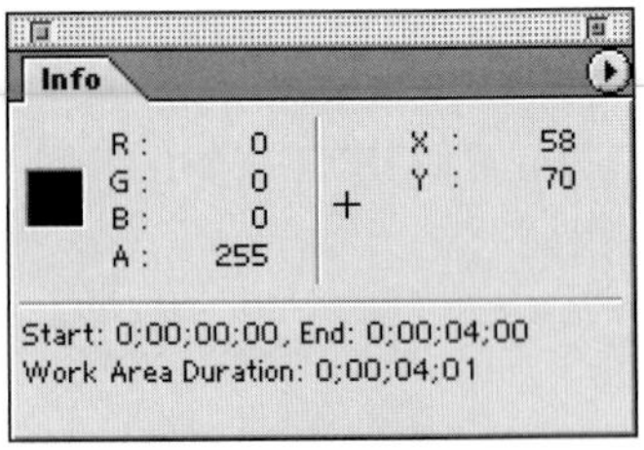

3 In the Time Controls palette, click the RAM Preview (▮▮▶) button. The RAM preview now plays back only those frames that are within the work area.

4 Save the project and close the Timeline and Composition windows.

When you render this composition, you'll select a setting so that it renders only the work area rather than the entire length of the composition.

Creating a second composition for pulsating squares

Next, you'll create a composition similar to the one you just made except for three details: you give the composition a different name, you use different artwork, and the new layer travels from right to left. Consequently, you do this procedure using the same steps as before, so this is a good time to see how much you can do on your own. You can refer to the instructions for creating the Moving Right Comp as your guide, beginning with "Creating a composition for pulsating squares" on page 87, but be careful to include all the following differences:

• Create the new composition, but this time name it **Moving Left Comp**. Otherwise, use the same composition settings you used for the Moving Right Comp.

• Add a layer to the composition, but this time use the SquaresLayer03.psd from the layered Photoshop footage file.

• Animate Layer 1, but this time set the 0:00 Position keyframe at the coordinates 1290, 150 (just outside the frame on the right). Then, set the 4:01 Position keyframe at the center of the composition frame.

• Create Layer 2 by duplicating Layer 1 and set the current-time marker at 0:00.

• Select both the Layer 2 Position keyframes, and drag Layer 2 to the center of the composition frame.

• Set the work area to end at 4:00.

When you finish your work on Moving Left Comp, check your work and preview the animation. Make sure you've used the Moving Left Comp name, the SquaresLayer03.psd footage file, and that the layers travel from right to left. Then close the Composition and Timeline windows.

Creating an all-inclusive composition for pulsating squares

You're ready to bring the different parts of your composition together: the two animations you've made so far and another Photoshop layer that won't be animated. The first task is to create the composition that will combine all these resources.

1 Choose Composition > New Composition, or press Ctrl + N (Windows) or Command + N (Mac OS). The Composition Settings dialog box opens.

2 In Composition Name, type **Squares02 Comp**.

3 On the Basic tab of the Composition Settings dialog box, set the following options:

- In Width, type **860**, and deselect Lock Aspect Ratio option if it is selected.

- In Height, type **300**.

- Make sure that the Pixel Aspect Ratio is Square Pixels.

- Set Frame Rate to **29.97**.

- (Optional) In Resolution, select Half or lower, as needed for your system.

- Make sure the Start Timecode is 0:00.

- In Duration, type **500**, to specify five seconds.

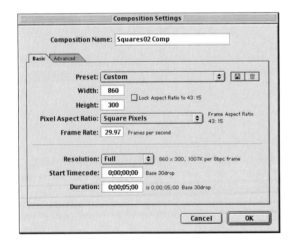

4 Click OK.

Adding compositions as layers

Next, you'll add the Moving Left and Moving Right compositions into the Squares02 Comp.

1 Press Home to set the current time marker at 0:00.

2 In the Project window, select and drag each of the following into the Composition window, centering each one in the composition frame:

- SquaresLayer01 (in the Squares.psd folder)

- Moving Left Comp

- Moving Right Comp

Notice how the image in the Composition window changes each time you add a new layer.

Note: In the Timeline window, make sure that the SquaresLayer01 is in the lowest (Layer 3) position in the layer stack. If it is not, select it and drag it to that position.

Applying transfer modes and adjusting the work area

Transfer modes are a familiar concept to Adobe Photoshop users, but you can also use them in After Effects. With transfer modes, the layer appearances affect each other, based on the luminance and color properties of the individual layers. Using transfer modes with moving footage creates interesting interactions among the layers. Your next task is to apply the Screen transfer mode to two of the layers.

1 If the Modes panel is not open in the Timeline window, do one of the following:

• Click the Switches/Modes toggle bar.

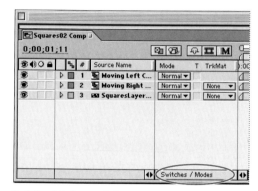

Switches/Modes toggle bar

• On the Timeline window menu, choose Panels > Modes.

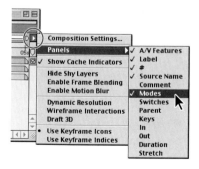

2 In the Modes panel for Layer 1 (the Moving Left Comp), select Screen on the pop-up menu. Notice the change in the composition.

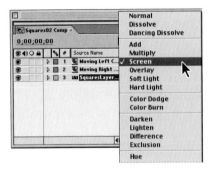

3 Repeat step 2 for Layer 2 (the Moving Right Comp). Leave Layer 3 (SquaresLayer01) in Normal transfer mode.

4 Move the current-time marker to 4:00, and press N to define that time as the end of the work area.

5 Save your work and preview the animation. The squares interact as they pass over each other to create pulsating shapes.

6 Close the Composition and Timeline windows.

The result of using Screen transfer mode is comparable to superimposing different film negatives and printing (exposing and developing) the result on paper. White always produces white in Screen transfer mode. Black superimposed on white—or any other color—has no effect.

Rendering the pulsating squares

All that remains for this section is to render the composition as a movie, going through the same steps that you followed when you rendered the Squares01 element.

1 In the Project window, select Squares02 Comp, and then choose Composition > Make Movie.

2 In File Name, type **Squares02.mov** and designate the _mov folder in your AE_CIB job folder. Click Save.

The Render Queue opens with the Squares02 Comp as item number one in the queue.

3 In the Render Settings pop-up menu, choose Best Settings to set Quality to Best and Resolution to Full. These settings override any settings that were left in the Composition and Timeline windows.

4 Click the words *Best Settings* to open the Render Settings dialog box.

5 Make sure that Time Span is set to Work Area Only, the Start is 0:00, and the End is 4:00.

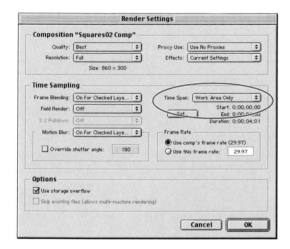

6 Click OK to close the Render Settings dialog box.

7 On the Output Module pop-up menu, choose Custom. The Options Settings dialog box opens.

8 On the Format pop-up menu, choose QuickTime Movie.

9 Select the Import into Project When Done option.

10 Click Format Options to open the Compression Settings dialog box and make sure that Animation and Millions of Colors are selected.

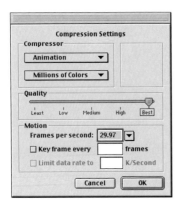

11 Click OK to close the Compression Settings and the Output Module Settings dialog boxes. You can expand the Output Module in the Render Queue to review your settings again before rendering.

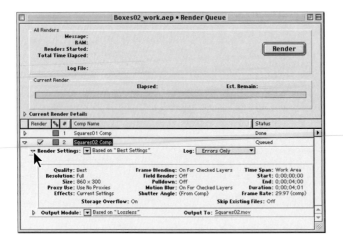

12 Save the project again.

13 Click Render.

Playing your pulsating-squares movie

After rendering, the Squares02.mov appears in the Project window. You can now play the movie.

1 Double-click the Squares02.mov to open it in the Footage window. If you need to resize the player window, hold down Alt (Windows) or Option (Mac OS) as you double-click to open it in the After Effects player, and then use the Magnification menu.

2 Click the Play button. The movie should look just as it did in the final Preview before rendering.

3 When you finish, close the Footage window.

4 Choose File > Save.

You'll use this movie later in this chapter as a component of another composition. Later, that composition will become an element you'll render and use in the overall project.

If you need to pause before you continue, this is a good time to take a break. Be sure that you have saved your work.

Creating a lens flare

In the previous section, you created a movie of pulsating squares. In this section, you'll create a lens-flare movie. Both of these movies will be components of an element that you'll bring together and render in the later sections in this lesson.

The lens-flare component requires no footage files, so there's nothing to import.

Creating a composition for the lens flare

You start by creating a new composition within the Boxes02_work.aep project file. You need a black background color while you work, so this task includes the procedure for changing this setting.

1 Choose Composition > New Composition.

2 In the Composition Settings dialog box, type **Lens Flare Comp** as the name.

3 In the Preset pop-up menu, select NTSC D1 Square Pix, 720 x 540. This option automatically enters the following settings:

- Width: 720

- Height: 540

- Pixel Aspect Ratio: Square Pixels

- Frame Rate: 29.97

4 (Optional) In Resolution, select Half or lower, as needed for your system.

5 In Duration, type **400** to specify four seconds, and then click OK to close the Composition Settings dialog box. The Lens Flare Comp appears in the Project, Composition, and Timeline windows.

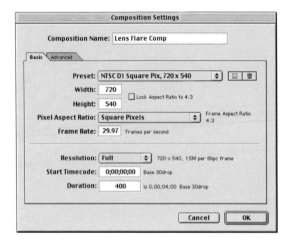

6 Choose Composition > Background Color to open the Background Color dialog box.

Note: *If the background in the Composition window is already black, you do not have to do steps 6 and 7.*

7 Do one of the following:

• Click the color swatch to open the color picker, and select black. Then click OK.

• Click the eyedropper and then click any available black area on the screen to select a black sample. Then click OK.

Creating a solid layer for the lens flare

After Effects includes many effects that you can apply to your work to create complex images quickly. But effects cannot exist by themselves; you must have at least one layer first and then apply the effects to the layer. In this task, you'll create the layer without placing any footage. This layer is simply a solid color.

1 Choose Layer > New > Solid, to open the Solid Settings dialog box.

2 In Name, type **Lens Flare Solid**.

3 In Width, scrub or type **720**.

4 In Height, scrub or type **540**.

5 Using either the eyedropper or the color swatch, select black.

6 Click OK to close the Solid Settings dialog box.

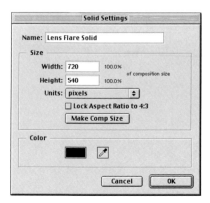

The Lens Flare Solid appears in the Timeline window as Layer 1 in the Lens Flare composition. The Composition window looks the same as it did before you did this task because both the solid and the background color are black.

Applying the Lens Flare effect

The Lens Flare effect creates areas of brightness on screen as if an intense light is shining directly on the camera lens and creating reflections of itself. You'll set properties and keyframes for the effect in a way that is closely similar to the way you set transformation properties and keyframes.

1 With the Lens Flare Solid layer selected, choose Effect > Render > PS+Lens Flare.

2 In the Lens Flare dialog box, do the following:

• In Flare Brightness, type **10**.

• In Lens Type, select 35mm Prime. Then click OK. A new window, the Effect Controls window, appears on your screen, with the PS+Lens Flare effect listed on the Lens Flare Solid tab.

3 In the Effect Controls window, in Flare Center, scrub or type **–20, 270**, being careful to make the first number negative. Leave Blend With Original set at zero.

4 In the Timeline window, make sure that the current-time marker is at 0:00.

5 In the Effect Controls window, click the stopwatch next to the Flare Center option to set a keyframe.

6 Click the stopwatch next to Flare Brightness to set a keyframe for that option.

7 Move the current-time marker to 1:08, and change the Flare Center coordinates (in the Effect Controls window) to **360, 270**. Then change the Flare Brightness value to **150**.

8 Move the current-time marker to 3:29. Change the Flare Center coordinates to **740, 270** and the Flare Brightness value to **10**.

9 Preview the animation and then save your work.

The effect adds not only a main light but also haloes and echoes of that light. Because of the keyframes you set, the lens flare travels across the composition frame, first growing brighter and then dimming back to its original level of brightness.

Duplicating and adjusting the lens flare

To make the light movement more complex, you'll add a second lens flare. You can move some of the keyframes to different points on the timeline simply by selecting them and dragging. Then you'll adjust the settings for the moved keyframes so that the two lens flares have some variety.

1 Select the Lens Flare Solid layer and press Ctrl + D (Windows) or Command + D (Mac OS) to duplicate the layer. Or, choose Edit > Duplicate.

2 Press Shift + click to select both layers, and press U. The layer outlines open, showing you all the keyframes you set in the original layer, which now also exist in the duplicate layer.

3 Click the empty area of the Timeline window below the layers to deselect both layers.

4 On Layer 1, drag a marquee around the two middle keyframes (at 1:08) to select them.

5 Drag the selected keyframes to 2:08, using the display on the Info palette as your guide.

6 In the Timeline window, move the current-time marker to 2:08 and change the Layer 1 Flare Brightness value to 100, which changes the value of the existing Flare Brightness keyframe.

7 Click the Modes/Switches toggle bar in the bottom of the Timeline window to open the Modes panel, and select Screen transfer mode for Layer 1. Leave Layer 2 in Normal transfer mode. The two Lens Flares now overlap and interact as they pass over each other.

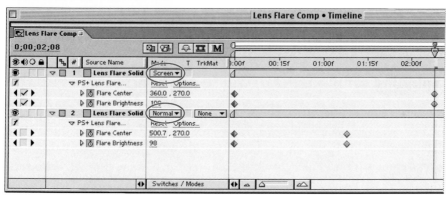

8 Preview the animation and save the project.

Rendering the lens flare

For easiest working convenience, you'll render the lens flare before combining it with the pulsating-squares movie that you created earlier in this lesson.

1 Close the Lens Flare Comp in the Composition, Timeline, and Effect Controls windows.

2 In the Project window, select the Lens Flare Comp and choose Composition > Make Movie.

3 In the Output Movie To dialog box, type **LensFlare.mov** in Name and specify the _mov folder inside the AE_CIB job folder. Then click Save. The Render Queue window opens.

4 In the Render Settings pop-up menu, select Best Settings.

5 In the Output Module pop-up menu, select Custom to open the Output Module Settings dialog box, and select the following settings:

• In Format, select QuickTime Movie.

• Select the Import into Project When Done option.

6 Click Format Options to open the Compression Settings dialog box, and select Animation and Millions of Colors. Then click OK to close this dialog box.

7 In the Output Module Settings dialog box, click OK to close it.

8 Save the project one more time and then click Render.

When rendering is complete, close the Render Queue. The LensFlare.mov appears in the Project window. This movie is now ready to be combined with the pulsating squares.

If you want to take a break before you continue, be sure to save your work first.

Combining components to create box lights

This section continues your work on the second element for the final animation. Your plan is to combine the LensFlare.mov that you just created with the Squares02.mov that you rendered earlier in this lesson. (You'll use the LensFlare.mov again in another part of the final composition.) The lights of the lens flares will shine through the boxes, creating additional visual texture to the element. Your first step is to create a new composition.

1 With the Boxes02_work.aep project open, choose Composition > New Composition.

2 In the Composition Settings dialog box, type **Box Lights Comp** in Name.

3 In Preset, select NTSC D1 Square Pix, 720 x 540.

4 (Optional) In Resolution, select Half or lower, as needed for your system.

5 In Duration, type **400** to specify four seconds, and then click OK.

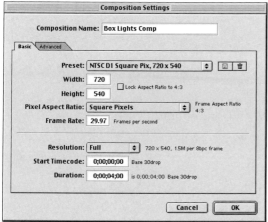

The Box Lights Comp appears in the Project, Composition, and Timeline windows.

Combining and adjusting two components

You're now ready to add the LensFlare.mov and the Squares02.mov to the new composition.

1 With the current-time marker at 0:00, drag both the LensFlare.mov and the Squares02.mov from the Project window to the Timeline window. Make sure that the LensFlare.mov is Layer 2 in the layer stack.

2 With only Layer 2 (LensFlare.mov) selected, press S to open the Scale property value, and then scrub or type **170%**.

Note: Because this layer is a blurred, soft image in the composition, the loss of resolution created by scaling up the image isn't a problem.

3 Select Layer 1 (Squares02.mov) and make the following changes to that layer:

• Choose Effect > Channel > Invert to reverse the RGB channels. Instead of black squares on a white background, you see white squares against a black background.

• In the Modes panel, select Multiply. The composition frame appears entirely black.

4 Preview the animation to see the lens-flare lights appear inside the boxes. Then save the project.

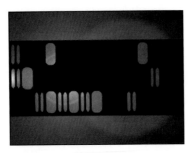

By inverting the channels in the Squares02.mov, you make the light shine through the squares instead of in the background around them. Multiply transfer mode combines areas of overlapping color in the two layers. Unless one of the colors is white, Multiply always creates darker colors. In this case, the white squares do not change the colors of the lens flare, but the black background around the squares completely blocks the view of the flare.

Rendering the box lights

That's all the work needed for this combined composition, so it's time to render it.

1 Close the Box Lights Comp in the Composition, Timeline, and Effect Controls windows.

2 In the Project window, select the Box Lights Comp and choose Composition > Make Movie.

3 In the Output Movie To dialog box, type **BoxLights.mov** in Name and specify the _mov folder inside the AE_CIB job folder. Then click Save.

4 In the Render Queue, in Render Settings, select Best Settings.

5 In Output Module, select Custom to open the Output Module Settings dialog box, and select the following settings:

• In Format, select QuickTime Movie.

• Select Import into Project When Done.

6 Click Format Options to open the Compression Settings dialog box and select Animation and Millions of Colors. Then click OK.

7 Click OK to close the Output Module Settings dialog box, and then save the project again.

8 Click Render.

When rendering is complete, close the Render Queue. The BoxLights.mov appears in the Project window. Double-click the movie to preview it in the Footage window. If necessary, you can make changes to the Box Lights Comp and render the movie again to create a new movie.

Because you've finished rendering a component, this is a natural opportunity to take a break from your work, if needed.

Creating the second element: a line of box lights

You're not finished with the box lights composition yet. You're going to make it wider and more complex by duplicating it in a new composition. Then, you'll move the layers into different positions in the composition frame so that they overlap each other, creating more visual interactions among the layers. By adjusting the In points so layers appear at different times, you create even more variety. The rendered version of this composition, along with the Squares01.mov, will eventually be imported into the final overall project.

Creating a new composition and adjusting settings

You'll begin by creating a new, wide composition that can accommodate several instances of the box lights. If it is not already open in the Project window, open the Boxes02_work.aep project now.

1 Choose Composition > New Composition.

2 In the Composition Settings dialog box, type **BoxLights Line Comp** in Name.

3 In Width, type **1720**.

4 In Height, type **300.**

5 Make sure that Pixel Aspect Ratio is set to Square Pixels and Frame Rate to 29.97.

6 In Duration, type **1100**, and then click OK.

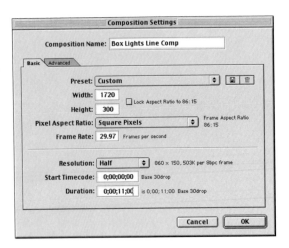

7 In the Project window, select the BoxLights.mov and drag it into the Timeline window.

8 In the Modes panel, select Screen for the BoxLights.mov layer.

Duplicating and placing the box lights

You'll now create many instances of the box lights and position them differently in time and space. Before you start, make sure that you can see the entire composition frame by adjusting the Composition window size and magnification.

1 With the BoxLights.mov layer selected, choose Ctrl + D (Windows) or Command + D (Mac OS) 12 times to create a total of 13 layers. Then select Layer 2.

2 In the Composition window, drag the selected layer to the left side of the composition frame, holding down Shift as you drag so that the layer moves only horizontally, not vertically.

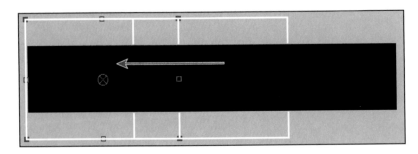

3 Using the same process, drag Layer 3 to the right side of the composition frame.

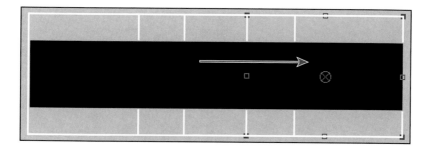

4 Continue to select each layer and drag it so that the layers overlap at various positions in the composition frame: left, right, center, left-middle, right-middle, and so forth. The exact position coordinates are not important.

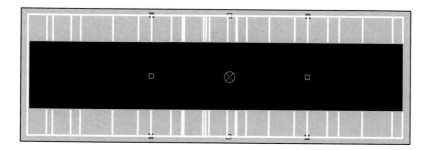

5 Change the In points for the layers so that they enter the composition at different times between 0:00 and 7:00, using either of the following techniques:

• Drag the duration bars (being careful to drag the colored area of the bar, not its ends) while watching the In point display in the Info palette.

• Open the In/Out panel in the Timeline window and type In values for each layer.

The sample movie used the In point settings shown in the illustration below, but you do not have to match these exactly.

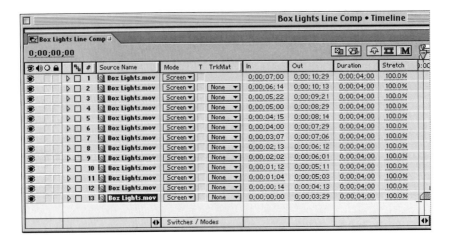

6 In the Modes panel, make sure that Screen is selected for each of the 13 layers.

7 Preview the animation and save the project.

Rendering the BoxLightsLine movie

Now you are ready to render the long line of box lights.

1 Close the BoxLights Line Comp in the Composition, Timeline, and Effect Controls windows.

2 In the Project window, select the BoxLights Line Comp and choose Composition > Make Movie.

3 In the Output Movie To dialog box, type **BoxLightsLine.mov** in Name and specify the _mov folder inside the AE_CIB job folder. Then click Save. The Render Queue opens, with BoxLights Line Comp as the fifth item in the queue, following the other four components you rendered in this lesson.

4 In Render Settings, select Best Settings.

Note: If you reset the work area for this composition, be sure to select Length of Comp in Time Span.

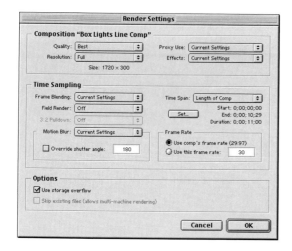

5 In Output Module, select Custom to open the Output Module Settings dialog box, and select the following settings:

• In Format, select QuickTime Movie.

• Select Import into Project When Done.

6 Click Format Options to open the Compression Settings dialog box and select Animation and Millions of Colors; then click OK.

7 Click OK to close the Output Module Settings dialog box, and then save the project again.

8 Click Render.

When rendering is complete, close the Render Queue. The BoxLightsLine.mov appears in the Project window. Press Alt (Windows) or Option (Mac OS) and double-click the movie to open it in the After Effects Player. Then press 0 (zero) on the numeric keypad to RAM preview, or press the spacebar to play the rendered movie.

You now have three more movie files (elements) that you'll use in the final composition: the Squares01.mov, the LensFlare.mov, and the BoxLightsLine.mov, all of which are stored in your _mov folder. In the final project, these elements will serve as subtle textural elements in the background, helping to suggest the high-technology environment of the client's product line.

Congratulations—you have completed Lesson 2!

Note: *To save storage space, you can now delete the sample files for this lesson from the Sample_Movies and Finished_Projects folders in your AE_CIB job folder. Your own work is safely stored in other folders in your AE_CIB job folder. You'll need those files later, so be sure that you delete only the sample files, not the source files or the files you created.*

Lesson 3

3 | Animating Circles

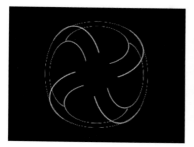 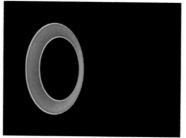 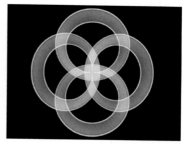

This is your chance to work with more new features in After Effects 5.0: drawing masks right in the Composition window and creating expressions by a simple trick of dragging. Expressions define relationships between layer properties that make it incredibly easy to program synchronized movements and transformations, so you get great-looking results with very little effort.

In this lesson, you'll learn to do the following:

- Use mask tools to create paths

- Resize masks

- Apply and animate the Stroke effect

- Create different types of lines by adjusting effect properties

- Create and animate a null object

- Use the pick whip to create simple expressions

- Apply the Basic 3D effect to make objects appear to swivel in 3D

- Duplicate and replace entire compositions

- Render multiple compositions in one session

This lesson takes a little over one hour to complete, plus the amount of time required to render the compositions. At the end of this lesson you'll have three individual QuickTime elements of ring images that you'll use in the final piece.

Getting started

Make sure that the following files are available in folders within your AE_CIB job folder on your hard drive, or copy them from the *After Effects Classroom in a Book* CD now:

- In the _psd folder: Ring.psd

- In the Sample_Movies folder: Rings_final.mov, LineCircles_final.mov, and DotCircles_final.mov from the Sample_Movies/Lesson03 folder on the CD

- In the Finished_Projects folder: Circles03_finished.aep

Refer to "Note: (Windows only) If you do not see the Prefs file, be sure that the Show all files option is selected for Hidden files on the View tab of the Folder Options dialog box." on page 4 for the copying procedure, if necessary.

Open and play each of the three sample movies to see the work you'll create in Lesson 3. When you finish, quit the QuickTime player. You can delete the sample movies to save storage space, if necessary.

You'll create the three circle movies within a single project. Your first task is to create that project.

1 Start After Effects if it is not already running.

2 Choose File > New > New Project.

3 Choose File > Save As.

4 Type **Circles03_work.aep** to name the project, and set the location as the _aep folder in your AE_CIB job folder. Then click Save.

Creating line circles

The first component is an animation of a set of circle outlines that draw over a four-second period. You'll create the circles within After Effects using the mask tools and the Stroke effect. The only prepared footage file you'll use is an image that serves as a reference for drawing the masks. Eventually, you'll incorporate this component into a multiple-rings image and use the result to create a QuickTime movie.

Importing the footage file

The source file that you'll work with in this project is a ring image, created as a single-layered Photoshop file with an alpha channel.

1 Choose File > Import > File.

2 Open the _psd folder inside your AE_CIB job folder and select the Ring.psd file. Then click Open (Windows) or Import (Mac OS).

3 In the Interpret Footage dialog box, choose Straight – Unmatted, and then click OK.

Organizing the project

As in earlier lessons, you'll organize the footage items in the Project window by file type. Because you're importing only one footage file for this project, you need only one folder. Although this project is quite simple, it's important to consistently practice good habits of organization so that they become second nature to you.

1 Choose File > New > New Folder to create a new folder in the Project window.

2 Type **psd files** for the folder name.

3 Drag the Ring.psd file into this folder and then expand the folder so that you can see the Ring.psd file inside it.

Create a new composition

Next, you'll create and define settings for the line circles composition.

1 Choose Composition > New Composition, or press Ctrl + N (Windows) or Command + N (Mac OS).

2 In Composition Name, type **Line Circles Comp**.

3 On the Basics tab of the Composition Settings dialog box, enter the following options:

• In both Width and Height, type **800**.

• In Duration, type **600** to specify six seconds.

• Make sure the following options are set: that Pixel Aspect Ratio is Square Pixels, Frame Rate is 29.97, and Start Timecode is 0:00. Lock Aspect Ratio should *not* be selected.

- (Optional) In Resolution, select Half or lower, as needed for your system.

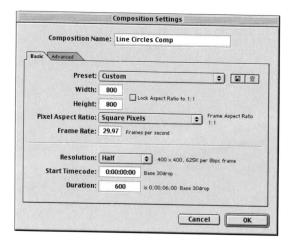

4 Click OK. Composition and Timeline windows open for the Line Circles Comp.

5 If your Background Color is not black, change it now by choosing Composition > Background Color and selecting black in the color picker.

Placing layers in the composition

Your next task is to place the Ring.psd file in the new composition and create a new solid layer. In After Effects, you need to have a layer before you can apply an effect. A little later, you'll use the solid layer with the Stroke effect to draw the circles.

1 Press Home to move the current-time marker to 0:00, if necessary.

2 Drag Ring.psd from the Project window into the Timeline window. The image automatically centers itself in the composition frame.

3 Choose Layer > New > Solid.

4 In the Solid Settings dialog box, use the following settings:

- Type **Circles Solid** to name the solid.

- Click the Make Comp Size button to automatically set the dimensions of the solid as the composition size: 800 x 800 pixels. Or, you can type **800** in both Width and Height.

• For Color, select black, using the eyedropper or the color swatch. Then check all your settings and click OK to close the Solid Settings dialog box.

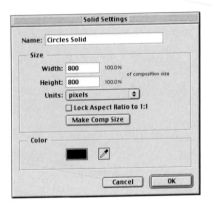

A new layer named Circles Solid appears in the Timeline window, and the composition frame is filled with a solid black layer, blocking your view of the Ring.psd layer. The color of the solid will not be visible in the final output because you'll use it as a mask. However, it cannot be white or you won't be able to see the reference Ring.psd layer underneath it while you draw the mask. Black provides the best view of the Ring.psd layer.

Setting a transfer mode

You need to see the Ring.psd layer so that you can draw the masks. You'll apply Screen transfer mode to make the Ring.psd visible behind the solid.

1 Select the Circles Solid layer.

2 In the Timeline window, open the Modes panel, if it is not already open, by clicking the bottom of the Switches/Modes panel. Or, right-click (Windows) or Control + click (Mac OS) the heading of any Timeline window panel to open the contextual menu, and then choose Panels > Modes.

3 Select Screen as the transfer mode for the Circles Solid layer.

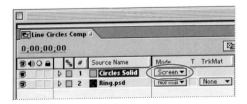

The Ring.psd layer is now visible behind the Circles Solid layer.

Creating the paths using masks

In After Effects 5.0, you can create masks directly in the Composition window. This is essential to the next task, because you'll need to see the Ring.psd layer behind the paths so that you can make the dimensions match.

The Stroke effect applies a stroke to an existing path. A path can be created in a number of ways, including the method you'll use here: creating two circular paths using the After Effects masking tools, and then applying the Stroke to that path.

1 Select the Circles Solid layer, if it is not already selected.

2 In the Tools palette, select the oval mask tool. It may be behind the rectangle mask tool, depending upon which one was used most recently.

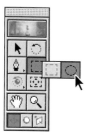

Note: *If the oval mask tool is not available, open the Composition window menu (by clicking the arrow button above the vertical scroll bar in the Composition window) and choose Layer Masks.*

3 Place the cross hairs in the center of the Composition window, using the center of the Ring.psd layer as your guide. Start dragging and then press Ctrl + Shift (Windows) or Command + Shift (Mac OS) to draw the circle from its center and to constrain it to a perfect circle. Continue dragging until the yellow circle you're drawing matches the outer edge of the Ring.psd reference image (shown as a heavy white line).

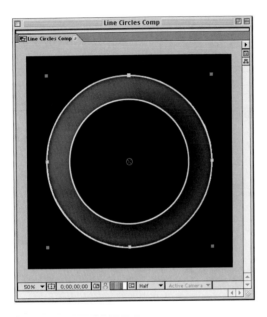

4 Repeat step 3 to draw a second circle, but draw this one smaller, so that it matches the inner edge of the ring in the Ring.psd layer.

5 On the Tools palette, select the selection tool (↖), and then save the project.

Now two Mask Shape properties appear under the Circles Solid layer in the Timeline window: Mask 1 and Mask 2. You can show these by selecting the layer and pressing the M key. To hide them, press M again.

Applying the Stroke effect

Next, you'll apply the Stroke effect to the Circle Solid layer and use the Effect Controls window to set qualities for the Stroke.

1 Select the Circles Solid layer and choose Effect > Render > Stroke.

2 In the Effects Controls window, use the following Stroke-effect settings:

• Select the All Masks option to apply the stroke to both masks.

- Deselect the Stroke Sequentially option.

- In Color, select white.

- In Brush Size, scrub or type **3** to specify the breadth of the stroke.

- In Brush Hardness, scrub or type **30%** to specify the edge quality of the stroke.

- Make sure that Opacity is 100%.

- Make sure that Start is 0%.

- In End, scrub or type **0%**. (You'll set other keyframes later, so that the circle appears gradually.)

- In Spacing, scrub or type **10%** to specify the gaps between stroke segments.

- In Paint Style, select On Transparent.

You won't see any change in the Composition window because both the Start and End are set at 0%; that means the circle hasn't started to appear.

Animating the Stroke effect

You'll now set keyframes for the End value to animate the drawing of the stroke. These settings can be made in the Timeline window by expanding all the necessary properties, but it's more convenient to set them in the Effect Controls window. Either way, the settings you specify appear in both places.

1 Move the current-time marker to 0:00, if it is not already there.

2 In the Effect Controls window, click the End stopwatch (ŏ) to set a keyframe. You won't see the keyframe yet, but the hands in the stopwatch assure you that you've set it correctly.

3 Move the current-time marker to 3:29.

4 Change the Stroke-effect End value to **100%** to set a second keyframe. The strokes may be difficult to see over the Ring.psd image.

5 With the Circles Solid layer selected in the Timeline window, press E to open the Effects, and then click the arrow to expand the Stroke properties. Confirm that two keyframes are in place at 0:00 and 3:29.

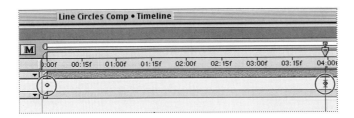

Note: *The icons representing the keyframes on the Stroke level (before you expand it) have a different appearance (⊛) than keyframes you've set in earlier lessons. The circular keyframe icons merely indicate the points at which some effects are animated, but not which controls are keyframed or what interpolation methods are in use. The keyframes shown at the End level are the familiar diamond shape (◇).*

6 Press E again to hide the Effects, and then close the Effect Controls window.

Removing the reference artwork and finishing up

You've finished drawing the masks, so you no longer need the Ring.psd layer, which served only as a reference. You'll remove that file now, so that your composition contains only the line circles.

1 Select the Ring.psd layer in the Timeline window, and press Delete. Now you see just the two circular strokes in the Composition window.

2 Move the current-time marker to 0:00 and press 0 (zero) on the numeric keypad to preview the animation.

3 Save the project and then close the Timeline and Composition windows.

In the preview, you see the stroke appearing along a circular mask shape over a period of four seconds.

Note: If the preview does not show the entire animation, then the amount of RAM required is greater than the amount available. You can make adjustments to your Quality or Resolution settings in order see the entire animation. For more information, see "Allocating RAM to After Effects" on page 2.

Creating dot circles

You'll now use the composition you just created to create a second circle component, which will closely resemble the Line Circles Comp. By duplicating the first composition and changing a few details, you save yourself the work of repeating all the steps required to create the original composition.

Duplicating the original composition

The first task is to create the new composition.

1 In the Project window, select the Line Circles Comp.

2 Press Ctrl + D (Windows) or Command + D (Mac OS) to duplicate the Line Circles Comp. The duplicate appears in the Project window with an asterisk (Line Circles Comp*), indicating that it is a copy.

3 Choose Composition > Composition Settings, or press Ctrl + K (Windows) or Command + K (Mac OS) to open the Composition Settings dialog box.

4 Type **Dot Circles Comp** in Composition Name, and click OK. Do not change any other settings.

Resizing the masks

In the final project, the circular lines and the dotted ones you're about to create will appear close to each other. In this task, you'll make them slightly different sizes so that you can see both types of strokes. You'll use the Photoshop file of the rings for reference when you adjust the sizes.

1 In the Project window, double-click the Dot Circles Comp to open it in the Composition and Timeline windows.

2 Make sure that the current-time marker is at 0:00. Then drag the Ring.psd footage file from the Project window to the Timeline window, so that it centers itself in the Composition window.

3 In the Timeline window, move the current-time marker to 3:29 and select the Circles Solid layer.

4 Press M to reveal both Mask Shapes (Mask 1 and Mask 2) under the Circles Solid layer.

5 Select Mask 1 and press Ctrl + T (Windows) or Command + T (Mac OS). The Mask transform handles appear in the Composition window.

6 Move the selection tool over one of the corner transform handles until the pointer changes to a diagonal double-headed arrow (↖), and then drag toward the center of the ring so that the edge of the mask moves a small distance inside the outer edge of the reference image.

7 Move the pointer to the opposite corner transform handle and repeat step 6. When you finish, the mask is again a perfect circle, centered on the reference image.

8 Press Enter (Windows) or Return (Mac OS) to deactivate the Mask transform handles.

9 Repeat steps 5 through 8, but this time selecting Mask 2 instead of Mask 1, and making Mask 2 just slightly smaller than the inner edge of the reference image.

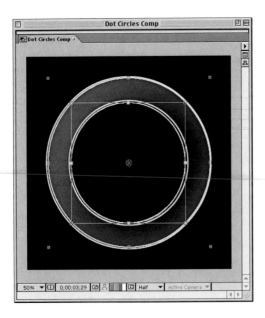

When you finish, press M to hide the Mask Shape property.

10 Select the Ring.psd layer and press Delete to remove the reference image.

Changing solid lines into dotted lines

Your final task is to change the Stroke-effect settings so that dotted lines form the circle instead of solid ones.

1 In the Timeline window, select the Circles Solid layer and choose Effect > Effect Controls, or press F3 to open the Effect Controls window.

2 In the Effect Controls window, change the following Stroke-effect settings:

• In Spacing, scrub or type **86%**, Or, you can expand the Spacing setting and then use the slider to change the value.

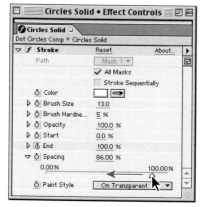

Dragging the Spacing slider

• In Brush Size, scrub or type exactly **13**. (Precision is important here because it affects the spacing of the dots at the Start and End points of the circle.)

• In Brush Hardness, scrub or type **5%**.

3 In the Timeline window, move the current-time marker to 0:00 and deselect the Circles Solid layer.

4 Preview the animation. If necessary, reduce the resolution in the Composition window.

5 Save the project and close the Composition, Timeline, and Effect Controls windows.

Creating the first element: multiple rings

You'll now start creating your own version of another element that you previewed at the beginning of this lesson, the Rings_final.mov sample movie.

You'll animate the ring elements using a null object and simple expressions to control the scale and swivel amounts of each ring. Although you can read more about what null objects and expressions are in After Effects online Help and other resources, seeing the features in action is a powerful way to get a sense of how they work and what they can do, even without a thorough understanding. Try going through the procedures first and then read more about null objects, parenting, and expressions.

Beginning to build the multiple-rings composition

You'll begin by creating a new composition and placing the artwork in it.

1 With the Circles03_work.aep project open in the Project window, choose Composition > New Composition.

2 In the Composition Settings dialog box, use the following settings:

• Type **Multiple Rings Comp** for the Composition Name.

• Type **800** in both Height and Width.

• Type **600** in Duration.

• Make sure that all the following are selected: Square Pixels for Pixel Aspect Ratio, 29.97 for Frame Rate, and 0:00 for Start Timecode.

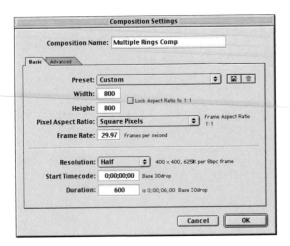

3 Click OK to close the Composition Settings.

4 Drag the Ring.psd file to the Timeline window. It appears centered in the Composition window.

Creating a null object

Next, you'll create a null object. A *null object* is an invisible layer that contains almost all of the same layer properties as any other layer. The exception is Opacity: The default opacity of a null object is 0%. You'll use the null object to control the movement of the ring layers. Start this procedure with the Multiple Rings Comp open in the Timeline and Composition windows.

1 Choose Layer > New > Null Object. Null 1 appears as Layer 1 in the Timeline window and Ring.psd is now Layer 2. In the Composition window, Null 1 appears as a small square outline with an anchor point in its upper left corner, which is the default anchor-point position for null objects.

2 Select Layer 1 (the Null 1 layer) and press T to open the Opacity property. Then change the Opacity value to **100%** so that the null object appears as a small white square in the Composition window.

3 Double-click the Null 1 layer to open it in the Layer window.

4 Click the right-pointing arrow button above the vertical scroll bar to open the Layer window menu, and choose Anchor Point Path if it is not already selected.

5 In the Layer window, drag the anchor-point marker to about the center of the square (the position doesn't need to be precise).

6 Close the Layer window.

Adding an expression

In this task, you'll use the pick whip feature to create an expression so that the vertical position of the null object controls the scale of the Ring.psd layer. Expressions are based on the standard JavaScript language and are used to create relationships between two layer properties.

1 In the Timeline window, select the Null 1 layer, and press P to open the Position property.

2 Select the Ring.psd layer and click the arrows to expand it so that you can see its Transform properties. If necessary, resize the Timeline window so that you can see all these properties.

3 Under the Ring.psd layer, select the word *Scale*.

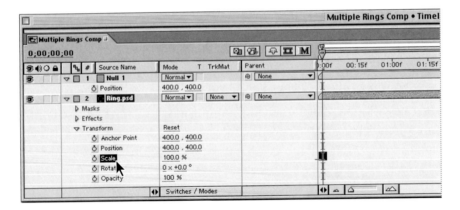

4 Choose Animation > Add Expression.

5 Under the Ring.psd Scale property, select the Expression: Scale pick whip (⊚) and drag it to the Y Position coordinate of the Null 1 layer. When you release, an expression appears under the Ring.psd layer duration bar.

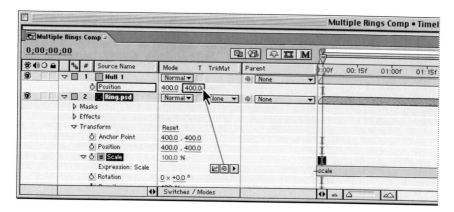

Note: Be careful not to drag the pick whip to the X Position coordinate because linking to that value would not maintain the aspect ratio of the layer while it scales.

6 In the Timeline window, select the Null 1 layer. Then, in the Composition window, drag the Null 1 layer up near the top of the window. The ring image enlarges and shrinks, depending on the vertical position of Null 1. To get more perspective on the interaction, try reducing the magnification in the Composition window so that you can see the outline of the Ring.psd image on the pasteboard as it resizes in response to the Null 1 position.

The Y Position coordinate of the Null 1 layer and the scale of the layer are now linked by the expression.

Adding the Basic 3D effect and a second expression

Next, you apply the Basic 3D effect to the Ring.psd layer so that you can make it appear to pivot in three-dimensional space. Then, you'll use expressions again so that the X Position coordinate of the null object controls the Swivel property of the rings.

1 In the Timeline window, select the Ring.psd layer and choose Effect > Perspective > Basic 3D.

2 Press E to reveal the Basic 3D effect for the Ring.psd layer in the Timeline window.

3 Expand the Basic 3D properties, and select the word *Swivel*.

4 Choose Animation > Add Expression.

5 In the Timeline window, drag the Expression: Swivel pick whip (⦿) to the X Position coordinate value of the Null 1 layer.

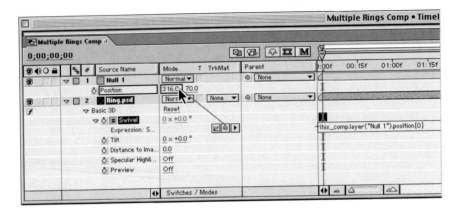

6 In the Composition window, select the Null 1 layer and drag it from left to right to see the Ring.psd layer swivel back and forth on its vertical axis as you drag.

7 Close the Effect Controls window.

8 Choose Edit > Select All, and then press accent grave (`) to collapse all the layer properties. Save the project.

Now, the Ring.psd layer swivels as the null object moves right or left. As the X Position coordinate of the Null 1 layer increases, so does the amount of swivel.

Positioning multiple rings in the composition

In this task, you'll duplicate the Ring.psd layer to create four overlapping rings. Because both of the expressions you created earlier are copied in the duplicate layers, all four rings are linked to the null object. You'll make each ring swivel in a unique way around either a horizontal or vertical axis by setting different Rotation values for the individual ring layers. You'll also specify the Screen transfer mode, which creates interactions among the overlapping ring layers.

1 In the Composition window, drag the Null 1 layer so that the Ring.psd layer is flat rather than swiveled (at about 360, 50, as shown in the Info palette as you drag).

2 Select the Ring.psd layer and drag it to the right side of the composition frame (at about 520, 400).

3 Press Ctrl + D (Windows) or Command + D (Mac OS) to duplicate the Ring.psd layer.

4 Press R to open the Rotation property for Layer 2 and set the Rotation value to **180°**.

5 Drag Layer 2 to the left side of the composition frame (at about 280, 400).

6 Select Layer 3 (the original Ring.psd layer) and duplicate it two more times.

7 Select Layers 3 and 4 and press R to open their Rotation properties. Then deselect both layers.

8 Scrub or type to set the Layer 3 Rotation value to **-90°** and the Layer 4 Rotation value to **90°**.

9 In the Composition window, drag Layer 3 to the center of the top half of the composition frame (at about 400, 280) and Layer 4 to the center of the bottom half of the composition frame (at about 400, 520). Be careful to confirm that you're dragging the right layer by referring to the selection in the Timeline window.

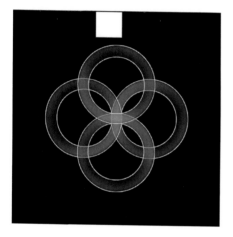

10 In the Timeline window Modes panel, select Screen as the transfer mode for each of the four Ring.psd layers.

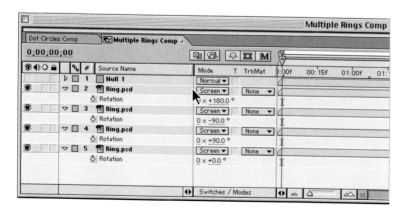

11 Choose Edit > Select All and press accent grave (`) twice to collapse the layer properties.

Now when you drag the Null 1 layer around the Composition window, all the rings change size when you drag up or down and swivel on their respective axes when you drag left or right.

Note: The four circles should maintain a cloverleaf formation and swivel symmetrically around the center of the frame. If your results are different, you may have mixed up the layers when you dragged them into position. To confirm this, reopen the Rotation properties for the four Ring.psd layers. Select each layer in the Timeline window and notice its position in the Composition window. Compare the positions and rotation values with the following settings:

- The ring at the top of the frame is set at -90° rotation.

- The ring on the right is set at 0° rotation.

- The ring on the bottom is set at 90° rotation.

- The ring on the left is set at 180° rotation.

If your settings are different, fix them by changing the values. It is easier to change the rotation numbers than to drag the layers into different positions in the Composition window.

Rotation and swivel

Two kinds of turning take place here. Rotation refers to the orientation of the layer in two-dimensional space. Within the Basic 3D effect, the word swivel refers to the amount that an object pivots around a vertical axis. Therefore, if you rotate a layer 90°, the axis becomes horizontal instead of vertical (in two-dimensional space). If you then swivel the layer by 90°, it pivots a quarter-turn around that axis (in three-dimensional space).

Animate the null object

Next, you set keyframes to animate the null object. As the null object moves, all of the ring layers respond by scaling and swiveling because of the expressions linking them.

1 Press Home to move the current-time marker to 0:00.

2 Select the Null 1 layer and press P to open its Position property.

3 Drag, scrub, or type to set the Position coordinates to **-93, -4.**

Note: This position is outside the composition frame on the pasteboard. To see these Null 1 positions, reduce the magnification in the Composition window, if necessary.

4 Click the Position stopwatch to set the first keyframe.

5 Move the current-time marker and change the Position coordinates to set the following additional keyframes for the Null 1 layer:

- At 0:23, set **-14, 48.**

- At 1:20, set **57, 70.**

- At 2:22, set **127, 45.**

- At 4:05, set **5, 242.**

- At 5:00, set **-31, 310.**

6 Press P to hide the Null 1 layer properties.

7 In the Timeline window A/V Features panel (far left side of the Timeline window, by default), turn off the Video switch (👁) for the Null 1 layer so that the null object no longer appears in the Composition window.

8 With the current-time marker still at 5:00, press N to set the end of the work area here.

9 Move the current-time marker to 0:00 and preview the animation, reducing the Resolution if necessary.

10 Close the Composition and Timeline windows, and save the project.

Creating more elements: multiple lines and multiple dots

You've created all the components, so it's time to bring them together into two more pieces that will become QuickTime elements for the overall job. You'll use the two components you created earlier in this lesson (the Line Circles Comp and the Dot Circles Comp) to replace the Ring.psd footage in the Multiple Rings Comp, but the layers retain all the properties, transfer modes, and expressions that you applied to the Ring.psd layers.

You've already had experience replacing one footage file with another in Lesson 1. The only difference is that this time, you'll replace entire layers in a composition with other compositions.

1 In the Project window, select the Multiple Rings Comp.

2 Choose Edit > Duplicate or press Ctrl + D (Windows) or Command + D (Mac OS).

3 Choose Composition > Composition Settings or press Ctrl + K (Windows) or Command + K (Mac OS) to open the Composition Settings dialog box.

4 Type **Multiple Lines Comp** to rename the composition, and then click OK. (Do not change any other composition settings.)

5 In the Project window, double-click the Multiple Lines Comp to open it.

6 In the Timeline window, press Shift and click to select all four Ring.psd layers. (Leave the Null 1 layer unselected.)

7 In the Project window, select the Line Circles Comp. Then press Alt (Windows) or Option (Mac OS) and drag the Line Circles Comp into the Timeline window. The Line Circles Comp replaces each of the Ring.psd layers.

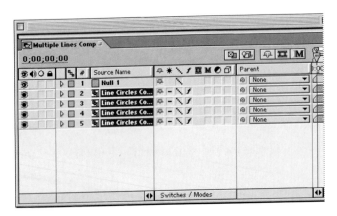

8 Preview the animation. Then close the Composition and Timeline windows.

9 Repeat steps 1-8 to create another duplicate of the Multiple Rings Comp, but this time rename the composition **Multiple Dots Comp**, and replace the four Ring.psd layers with the Dot Circles Comp instead of the Line Circles Comp.

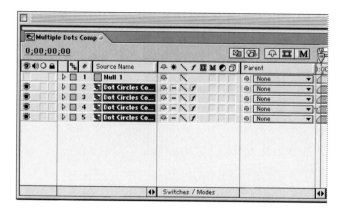

10 Save the project and close the Timeline and Composition windows.

Rendering the three elements

Now you're ready to render the three circle elements. You'll add all three compositions to the Render Queue, adjust the settings, and then set them all to render in one render session. This process will probably take longer than the renders you did in earlier lessons, so plan accordingly.

1 In the Project window, press Ctrl (Windows) or Command (Mac OS) and click to select the three compositions: Multiple Rings Comp, Multiple Lines Comp, and Multiple Dots Comp.

2 Choose Composition > Add to Render Queue. The Render Queue window opens and all three items appear in the queue. Leave all three items selected.

3 In the Render Settings pop-up menu for any one of the selected compositions, select Best Settings to set this option for all three. Then click an empty area of the Render Queue window to deselect the compositions.

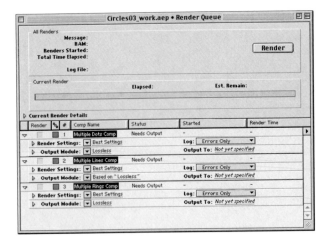

4 Select the first composition in the queue and set the following options. (Settings for each composition must be done separately.)

• For Output Module, select Custom, which opens the Output Module Settings dialog box.

• For Format, select QuickTime Movie.

• Select the Import into Project When Done option.

• Click Format Options to open the Compression Settings dialog box, and under Compressor, select Animation and Millions of Colors+. Then click OK to return to the Output Module Settings dialog box.

• Make sure that Channels is set to RGB + Alpha, Depth to Millions of Colors+, and Color to Premultiplied (Matted). Then click OK to return to the Render Queue.

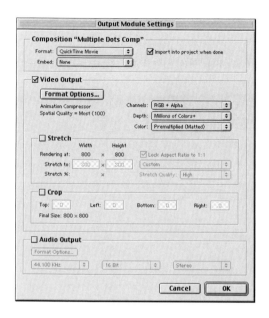

5 Select the second composition in the queue and apply the same settings described in step 4.

6 Select the third composition and again apply the settings from step 4.

7 For each of the three compositions, set the Output To filename and location as follows:

• Click the words *Not Yet Specified*.

• Navigate to the _mov folder in the AE_CIB job folder.

• Type **Rings.mov, LineCircles.mov,** or **DotCircles.mov,** corresponding to the name of each composition, and click Save.

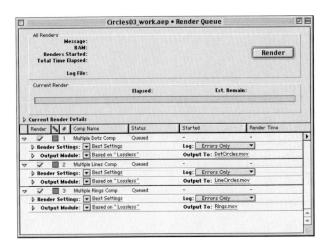

8 Save the project—just in case—and then click Render.

💡 *If it's not convenient for you to render the project now, you can do it later. After you add these items to the Render Queue and save the project, you can close the Render Queue and continue working in this or any other project. When you are ready to render them, you can return to the Render Queue. To do this, choose Window > Render Queue. Then make sure that all the settings are correct and do step 8 (above).*

When After Effects finishes rendering the three QuickTime movies, they appear in the Project window. Double-click each one to preview it in the Footage window. If you want to make any changes, you can go back into the original compositions and make those adjustments. However, you must re-render the composition to create an updated version of the movie.

You have now completed this lesson making three circle elements to be used in the final project. They are saved in the _mov folder within your AE_CIB job folder and will remain there until you import them for use in a later lesson.

Lesson 4

4 | Building Star-like Elements

 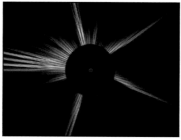 

This lesson takes you into one of the most fun features in the After Effects treasury of tools: playing with the output graph for an audio file to create an animated graphic. You'll also use a transition effect to create another animated graphic. Both of these elements challenge you to dream up your own innovative ways of using After Effects features, tools, and effects to create fresh looks in animated design.

In this lesson, you'll learn to do the following:

• Import multiple files

• Import and work with audio files

• Create images from audio layers

• Apply the Audio Spectrum effect to a path

• Apply the Radial Blur effect

• Apply the Stencil Alpha transfer mode

• Apply the Iris Wipe effect and use it in a non-traditional way

• Set keyframes in the Effect Controls window

In this lesson, you'll build two star-like elements. You'll render each of these as a QuickTime movie and eventually use them both in the final composite.

This lesson takes about one hour to complete, plus the amount of time your system requires to render the movies.

Getting started

Make sure that the following files are in the AE_CIB job folder on your hard drive, or copy them from the *After Effects Classroom in a Book* CD now.

• In the _audio folder: Soundtrack.aif

• In the _ai folder: Starburst.ai

• In the Sample_Movies folder: Starburst_final.mov and Lightrays_final.mov from the Sample_Movies/Lesson04 folder on the CD

• In the Finished_Projects folder: Starshapes04_finished.aep

Refer to "Note: (Windows only) If you do not see the Prefs file, be sure that the Show all files option is selected for Hidden files on the View tab of the Folder Options dialog box." on page 4 for the copying procedure, if necessary.

Open and play the two sample movies to see the elements you'll be creating in this lesson. When you finish, quit the QuickTime player. You can delete the sample movies now to save storage space, if necessary.

You'll create both of these elements within a single project. Your first task is to create that project.

1 Start After Effects 5.0, if it is not already running.

2 Choose File > New > New Project.

3 Choose File > Save As.

4 In the Save Project As dialog box, find and open the _aep folder in the AE_CIB job folder you created earlier.

5 Type **Starshapes04_work.aep** to name the project, and then click Save.

Creating the first element: an audio starburst

The first component begins with an audio file, the sound track for the final piece. By applying an effect, you create a visual display of the audio file, which pulsates in perfect synchronization with the sound track. When you add an Adobe Illustrator file, the pulsating starburst appears through the transparent areas of this image.

Importing the footage file

Although the footage files are an Adobe Illustrator and an audio file, the process is the same as for any of the footage files you've imported for earlier lessons. However, this time you'll use the Import Multiple Files command, which requires fewer mouse actions than using the File > Import > File command, especially when you import many files.

1 Choose File > Import > Multiple Files to open the Import Multiple Files dialog box. Or, press Ctrl + Alt + I (Windows) or Command + Option + I (Mac OS).

2 Select the Starburst.ai file in your _ai folder, and click Open (Windows) or Import (Mac OS). The dialog box disappears momentarily.

3 When the Import Multiple Files dialog box reappears, go to your _audio folder and select Soundtrack.aif. Then click Open (Windows) or Import (Mac OS).

4 When the dialog box reappears, click Done.

Note: The Starburst.ai file contains a labeled alpha channel, which already contains the interpretation information After Effects needs. Because of this, the Interpret Footage dialog box does not appear during the import process.

Both items appear in the Project window, and they are currently selected. Click any empty area of the Project window to deselect them.

Examining the footage files

You can use the Footage windows to review footage files without placing them in compositions. The Starburst.ai file image is large and appears as black-on-black, so you'll use techniques that make it easily visible. Also, you'll play the audio file in the Footage window.

1 In the Project window, double-click the Starburst.ai file.

2 Press Ctrl + - (hyphen) (Windows) or Command + - (hyphen) (Mac OS) to reduce both the magnification and window size so that you can see the entire image area. You may need to press this keyboard shortcut combination more than once.

Note: Be sure to use the hyphen key in this shortcut, not the minus sign on the numeric keypad.

3 Click the alpha-channel button at the bottom of the Footage window so that you can see the shape of the artwork. When you are ready to continue, close the Footage window.

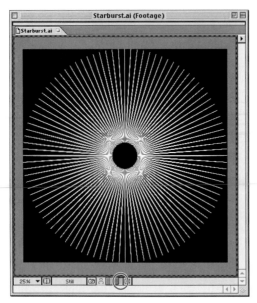

Alpha-channel button

4 In the Project window, double-click the Soundtrack.aif file. The Footage window opens as a small playbar.

Footage window for audio

5 Press the play button (▶) in the Footage window to hear the audio, which starts quietly and then grows louder. When you are ready to continue, close the window.

💡 *If you cannot hear the audio or if it is too loud, click the Footage window volume button (◐) and then drag the slider up or down to adjust the volume. Also, check the audio settings for your system.*

Organizing the project

Although this project uses only two source files, you'll practice good habits of organization that can help when you do complex projects of your own. This means creating folders for the Project window.

1 Choose File > New > New Folder, or click the folder icon (▢) at the bottom edge of the Project window.

2 Type **ai files** for the name, and press Enter or Return.

3 Drag the Starburst.ai file into the ai files folder and expand the folder so that you can see the item inside. Make sure that nothing is currently selected.

4 Choose File > New > New Folder again.

5 Type **audio files** to name the new folder, and press Enter or Return.

6 Drag the Soundtrack.aif file into the audio files folder and expand the folder so that you can see the item inside.

Note: If you accidentally create one folder inside another one, you can drag the folders to organize them at the same level. To avoid doing this in the future, be sure to deselect all items in the Project window before you create a new folder.

Creating a composition

You'll use a preset option to set options quickly for this composition.

1 Choose Composition > New Composition.

2 Type **Starburst Comp** in Composition Name.

3 For Preset, select NTSC D1 Square Pix, 720 x 540 in the pop-up menu. After Effects automatically fills in the next four settings:

• Width: 720

• Height: 540

• Pixel Aspect Ratio: Square Pixels

• Frame Rate: 29.97

4 (Optional) In Resolution, select Half or lower, as needed for your system.

5 In Duration, type **800** to specify eight seconds, and then click OK.

Adding footage to the composition

Next, you'll add the audio file to the composition and preview it within the composition. You'll also change the default audio-preview time limitation.

1 Move the current-time marker to 0:00, select Soundtrack.aif in the Project window and drag it into the Timeline window.

2 Choose Composition > Preview > Audio Preview (Here Forward) to preview the audio, or press the decimal key (.) on the numeric keypad. The audio preview plays to 4:00 and then stops.

3 Choose Edit > Preferences > Previews to open the Preview Preferences dialog box.

4 Under Audio Preview, type **800** in Duration to change it from four seconds to eight seconds. Then click OK.

5 Press the decimal key to preview again. You can now hear audio for the entire length of the composition.

Note: If you don't hear the audio, look in the A/V Features panel in the Timeline window (to the far left of the layer, by default) and make sure that the Audio switch(◄) is turned on. You can click this switch to toggle the audio layer off and on, but make sure that it's turned on now.

Create a new solid and add a mask

Next, you'll create a new solid layer and add a circular mask to this solid. You'll use the results in the next procedure to apply an effect.

1 If necessary, choose Composition > Background Color, select black, and click OK.

2 Choose Layer > New > Solid.

3 In the Solid Settings dialog box, choose the following settings:

• Type **Audio Spectrum** in Name. (This is also the name of one of the two effects that you'll apply to this layer.)

• Click Make Comp Size, or type **720** in Width and **540** in Height.

• Under Color, click the color swatch to open the color picker and select black. Or, select the eyedropper tool and click any black item in the After Effects interface.

4 Click OK to close the Solid Settings dialog box.

5 In the Timeline window, select the Audio Spectrum layer.

6 In the Tools palette, select the oval mask tool. You may have to press the rectangular mask tool and drag to select the oval mask tool from the pop-up display.

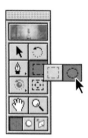

7 Beginning approximately at the center of the solid, start to drag and then press Ctrl + Shift (Windows) or Command + Shift (Mac OS) to draw from the center and constrain the shape to a circle. Drag without releasing the mouse button until the circle is approximately one-eighth the size of the composition (about 90 pixels).

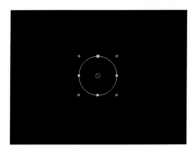

Applying the Audio Spectrum effect

You'll now generate an animated element with the Audio Spectrum effect. This is a visual effect that links a graphical representation of sound frequencies to a path. You'll use the path you drew in the previous procedure so that lines representing the sound radiate in and out from a single point on the path.

1 With the Audio Spectrum layer selected, press M to reveal the Mask Shape property.

2 Expand the Soundtrack.aif layer outline by clicking the arrows next to the layer name, Audio, and Waveform. The graphic representation of the audio levels appears in the timeline.

💡 *To increase the vertical proportion of the waveform display, move the pointer to the faint white line below the lower waveform until it turns into a double-headed arrow (↕). Drag downward to stretch the waveform display, as shown below.*

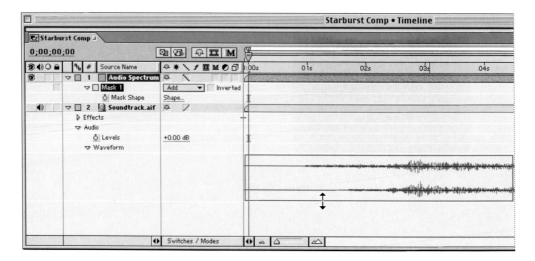

3 In the Switches panel, click the Quality switch for the Audio Spectrum layer to set it at Best (╱).

4 Set the current time to about 5:00. (The audio is loud at this point, making it easier to see the results as you apply the effect.)

5 Make sure that the Audio Spectrum layer is still selected and then choose Effect > Render > Audio Spectrum.

6 In the Effect Controls window, change only the following settings:

• For Audio Layer, select Soundtrack.aif in the pop-up menu. A row of vertical green lines appears in the Composition window, representing the frequencies of the audio layer.

• For Path, select Mask 1. The green lines now radiate from the circular path.

• For Start Frequency, scrub or type **1.0**.

• For End Frequency, scrub or type **5667**.

• For Frequency Bands, scrub or type **117**.

• For Maximum Height, scrub or type **31000**.

• For Audio Duration (Milliseconds), scrub or type **180**.

• For Thickness, scrub or type **6**.

- For Softness, scrub or type **100%**.

- For both Inside Color and Outside Color, select white.

- Select Blend Overlapping Colors.

- Deselect both Dynamic Hue Phase and Color Symmetry.

- For Display Options, select Analog Lines and notice the changes in the image.

7 Make sure that the following remain at the default settings:

- Start and End Point (values are irrelevant in this case).

- Audio Offset (at 0).

- Hue Interpolation (at 0).

- Side Options (Side A & B).

- Duration Averaging (not selected).

- Composite on Original (not selected).

8 When all other options are set, select Use Polar Path (near the top of the list of options) so that the display radiates from one point along the circular path.

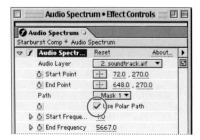

9 Collapse the Audio Spectrum effect.

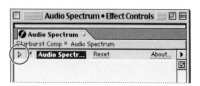

10 In the Timeline window, close the waveform for the Soundtrack.aif layer, set the Quality switch for the Audio Spectrum layer back to Draft, and create a RAM preview.

Note: Depending on the amount of RAM available to After Effects, you may also need to drop the resolution of the composition to see the entire RAM preview in close to real time.

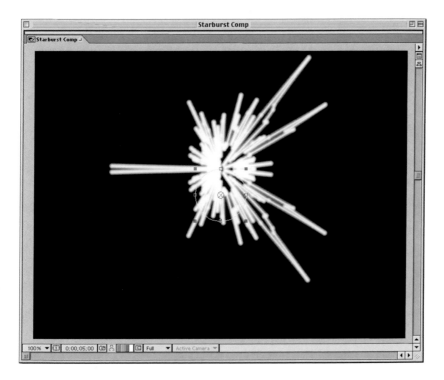

11 Save the project.

You have now created a graphical representation of the audio frequencies in the Soundtrack.aif layer. As a result, you have an animated image (the Audio Spectrum layer) synchronized with the audio. At the beginning, the layer image is small but it increases in size and intensity as the audio grows louder and more complex.

Some of the settings for the Audio Spectrum effect determine how After Effects calculates the lines for the display. Other settings determine visual properties of the lines themselves. For a description of each of these controls, see the Effects documentation available on the *After Effects 5.0 Classroom in a Book* CD and on the Adobe Web site for After Effects, in the in-depth section under After Effects product information. For general information and sample images showing examples of the Audio Spectrum effect in action, see After Effects online Help.

Applying the Radial Blur effect

You'll now apply another effect to the Audio Spectrum layer. The Radial Blur effect creates smoother lines by blurring the graphic image of the audio. In this procedure, you'll also learn how to override the size limitation of a slider in the Effect Controls window by setting that option in the Timeline window.

1 With the current-time marker at about 5:00, select the Audio Spectrum layer, if it is not already selected, and press E to open the Effects properties in the Timeline window.

2 Choose Effect > Blur & Sharpen > Radial Blur. The Radial Blur effect is now listed below the Audio Spectrum effect in the Effect Controls window.

3 Expand the Radial Blur effect in both the Timeline and Effect Controls windows so that you can see the Amount value in both windows. In the Effect Controls window only, expand the Amount to see the graphical preview and slider. You can drag the slider only as high as 118, but you can set higher values in the Timeline window.

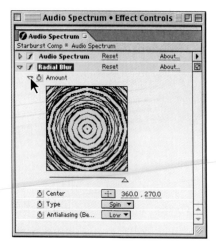

4 In the Timeline window, type or scrub to set the Amount value at **160**. (Notice that in the Effect Controls window, the arrow points beyond the right end of the slider.)

5 For Type, select Zoom to create a blur that pulls into the center.

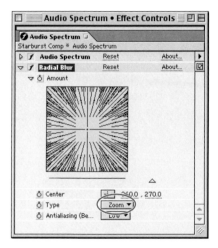

Do not change the Center coordinates or the Antialiasing (Best Quality) option, which is set at Low by default.

6 In the Switches Panel, set the Quality switch to Best (╱).

7 In the Composition window, set the Resolution to Full to see the layer with full antialiasing so that you can see the results of the blur.

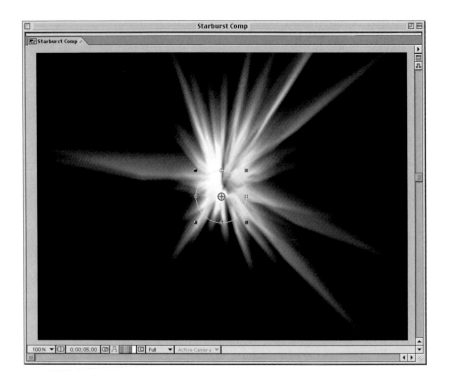

8 Lower the Resolution and Quality settings, if necessary for your system, and then preview the animation.

9 Close the Effect Controls window. In the Timeline window, click the arrow to collapse the layer-properties outline. Save the project.

Note: After Effects uses a large amount of RAM when it calculates these effects, so you may notice a slowdown in workflow at this point, especially if you are working on a slower system or one with the minimum required RAM. For information about using RAM, see "Allocating RAM to After Effects" on page 2.

Moving the mask

Next, you'll nudge the mask into position in the center of the Audio Spectrum image. If you drew the Mask 1 path so that it is centered in the composition frame, this procedure is not required. However, you should try this in any case, to learn how to move the mask within the layer instead of moving the entire layer.

1 Move the current-time marker to about 5:00, so you can see rays representing the audio track.

2 Select the Audio Spectrum layer.

3 Press M to open the Mask 1 Mask Shape property. The yellow path appears in the Composition window.

4 In the Timeline window, select Mask 1. Four solid-yellow handles appear, representing the path points.

5 Using the selection tool (▶), click one of the yellow handles or anywhere along the yellow line and then drag the path to the approximate center of the frame. It is not necessary to be precise. When you finish, press M to hide the Mask property.

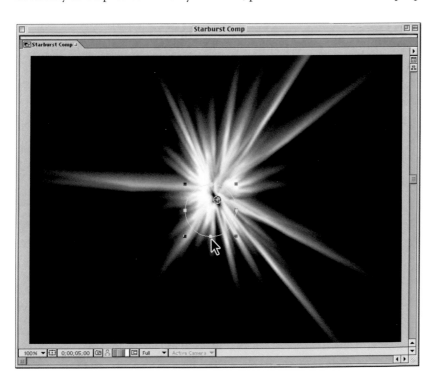

Adding the starburst image and applying a transfer mode

You're now ready to add the Adobe Illustrator file to the composition. You'll use a transfer mode so that the graphic display of the audio appears through the alpha channel of the starburst image.

1 Move the current-time marker to 0:00.

2 In the Project window, select the Starburst.ai file, drag it to the Timeline window, and place it in the Layer 1 position. If it appears at some other layer number, you can drag it by its name to the top of the layer stack.

Note: This image is black artwork with an alpha channel, so you won't see its shape in the Composition window when you add it to the composition. It will also cover the Audio Spectrum layer, so you won't see that layer until you set the transfer mode.

3 Move the current-time marker to approximately 3:00 (where the Audio Spectrum layer would not be completely black), so that you'll be able to see it behind the Starburst.ai layer when you set the transfer mode.

4 Click Switches/Modes at the bottom of the panel in the Timeline window to open the Modes panel. Or, choose Panels > Modes in the Timeline window menu.

5 In the Modes panel, choose Stencil Alpha for the Starburst.ai layer to set the transfer mode.

6 Move the current-time marker to 0:00, preview the animation, and then save the project.

Audio Spectrum layer (left), alpha channel of the Starburst.ai layer (center), and Stencil Alpha transfer mode applied to relate the Audio Spectrum layer and Starburst.ai layer (right)

The Starburst.ai layer now acts like the holes in a stencil: You can see the Audio Spectrum layer only through the transparent areas of the Starburst.ai layer alpha channel.

Rotating the starburst image

You'll now set Rotation keyframes for the starburst image so that it spins as the Audio Spectrum layer pulsates behind it, seen through the starburst alpha channel.

1 In the Timeline window, move the current-time marker to 0:00 and select the Starburst.ai layer.

2 Press S to open the Scale property, and then scrub or type **50%** to reduce the image size by half.

3 Press R to open the Rotation property.

4 Make sure that the Rotation value is set to 0° and then click the Rotation stopwatch (⏱) to set a keyframe.

5 Press End to move the current-time marker to 7:29.

6 Change the Rotation value to 90°. A second keyframe is added.

7 Move the current-time marker back to 0:00 and preview the animation. Then save the project.

Rendering the starburst element

You have finished building the starburst element, so it's time to render the composition.

Note: This composition is more complex than other compositions you have rendered in these lessons. Consequently, the rendering process will take longer than your earlier sessions. For example, if you've been rendering earlier movies in a minute or two, this one may take between 15 minutes and half an hour, depending on your operating system, hardware, and available RAM.

1 Close the Composition, Timeline, and Effect Controls windows for Starburst Comp.

2 In the Project window, select Starburst Comp and then choose Composition > Make Movie.

3 In the Output Movie To dialog box, type **Starburst.mov** in Name and specify the _mov folder in the AE_CIB job folder. Then click Save.

4 In the Render Queue, click the underlined words *Current Settings* to open the Render Settings dialog box.

5 Use the following Render Settings:

• For Quality, select Best.

- For Resolution, select Full.

- For Time Span, select Length of Comp. Then click OK to close the Render Settings dialog box.

6 In the Output Module pop-up menu, choose Custom to open the Output Module Settings dialog box, and set the following options:

- For Format, select QuickTime Movie.

- Select Import into Project When Done.

- Click Format Options.

7 In the Compression Settings dialog box, select Animation and Millions of Colors+, and then click OK.

8 In the Output Module Settings dialog box, review the settings: Channels is now set to RGB + Alpha, indicating that this item will be rendered with an alpha channel. Depth is set as Millions of Colors+, and Color is set as Premultiplied (Matted). When you are ready to continue, click OK.

Note: You'll render this composition as a silent movie, so do not select options for audio output. The sound track will be added to the final project at a later stage.

9 Save the project one more time, and then click Render.

When the rendering process is complete, close the Render Queue and double-click Starburst.mov in the Project window to view the rendered movie.

If you need to make any changes, reopen the Starburst Comp and make those adjustments. Remember to save those changes and render the composition again, using the same render settings.

Creating the second element: light rays

The next element will serve as a rotating star. To do this, you'll apply and animate a transition effect to create the star image. Transition effects are typically used to phase out one layer and phase in another, but in this case you'll use the effect in an non-traditional way that creates the animation you want in very little time.

Building the composition

Your first task is to create a new composition in the Starshapes04_work project. This time, you'll learn another method of starting this process.

1 Click the New Composition icon (⊡) at the bottom of the Project window to create a new composition. Or, choose Composition > New Composition.

2 Type **Light Rays Comp** to name the composition.

3 In Preset, select NTSC D1 Square Pix, 720 x 540. The following settings are automatically entered:

• Height at 540

• Width at 720

• Pixel Aspect Ratio at Square Pixels

• Frame Rate at 29.97

4 (Optional) In Resolution, select Half or lower, as needed for your system.

5 For Duration, type **400** to specify four seconds, and then click OK.

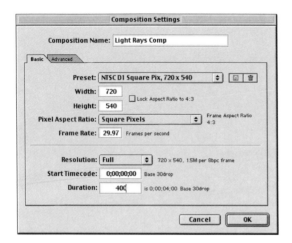

Adding a solid

You'll be creating the light rays by applying an effect, so you need a layer to start the process. You'll do this by creating a black solid layer. You'll set the background to white so that you can see the results later, after you apply the effect.

1 Choose Composition > Background Color. Then specify white in the color picker and click OK to close the Background Color dialog box.

2 Move the current-time marker to 0:00, and choose Layer > New > Solid. Or, press Ctrl + Y (Windows) or Command + Y (Mac OS).

3 In the Solid Settings dialog box, set the following options. When you finish, click OK.

• In Name, type **Light Rays Solid**.

• Click Make Comp Size to automatically set the dimensions at the same size as the composition. Or, in Width, type **720** and in Height, type **540**.

- In Color, select black, and then click OK.

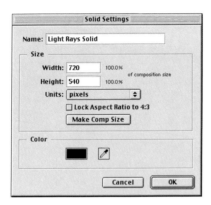

The Composition window appears with the black solid filling the composition frame.

Applying the Iris Wipe effect and setting keyframes

Next, you'll create the star image by applying a transition effect to the new solid layer. You'll also use the Effect Controls window to set keyframes, because it is more convenient in this case.

1 Select the Light Rays Solid layer (if it is not still selected).

2 Choose Effect > Transition > Iris Wipe.

3 In the Effect Controls window, change the following Iris Wipe settings:

- For Iris Points, scrub or type **18** to create a nine-pointed star shape.

- For Outer Radius, scrub or type **13**.

- Select the Use Inner Radius option.

- For Feather, scrub or type **12** to give the star shape a soft edge.

4 Make sure that the following are at the default settings, as indicated:

- Iris Center at 360, 270, which is the center of the Composition window.

- Inner Radius at 0.

- Rotation at 0°.

5 Move the current-time marker to 0:00 and click the following stopwatches in the Effect Controls window to set keyframes:

- Outer Radius.

- Inner Radius.

- Rotation.

Note: *Up to this point, you won't see any change in the Composition window.*

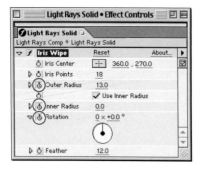

6 Move the current-time marker to 3:00 and change the following Iris Wipe settings to set new keyframes:

- For Outer Radius, scrub or type **640**.

- For Inner Radius, scrub or type **30**. The nine-ray star now appears in the Composition window.

7 Press End to move the current-time marker to 3:29 and change the following settings in the Effect Controls window:

- For Outer Radius, scrub or type **0**. The star disappears again.

- For Inner Radius, scrub or type **0** so that the star maintains its shape as it shrinks in size.

- For Rotation, scrub or type **180°** so that the shape rotates by a half turn over the length of the composition.

The Outer Radius of the Iris Wipe determines the length of the star rays, from center to tip. The Inner Radius determines where the rays join together at the base. When the Outer Radius and the Inner Radius are equal, the star becomes an equilateral shape—as close to a sphere as it can be. When either radius is set at zero, the star disappears because the rays have no width.

💡 *The U shortcut (which stands for Uber) expands the selected layer outline to show all properties with keyframes or expressions. To try this, select the Light Rays Solid layer and then press U. All the animated Iris Wipe effect properties and keyframes now appear in the Timeline window.*

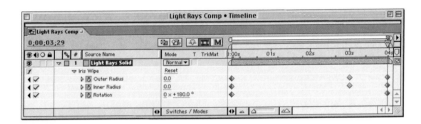

Preview the animation and save the project.

For more information and sample images showing the Iris Wipe effect in action, see After Effects online Help and the Effects documentation (PDF files) available both on the *After Effects 5.0 Classroom in a Book* CD and on the Adobe Web site in the in-depth section under After Effects product information.

Render the Light Rays element

The element is complete and ready for rendering. This is a simpler composition than the Starburst Comp, so rendering will take considerably less time.

1 Close the Composition, Timeline, and Effect Controls windows for Light Rays Comp.

2 In the Project window, select Light Rays Comp and then choose Composition > Make Movie.

3 In the Output Movie To dialog box, type **LightRays.mov** in Name and specify the _mov folder inside the AE_CIB job folder. Then click Save. The Light Rays Comp appears as the second item in the Render Queue, under the Starburst Comp that you rendered earlier in this lesson.

4 Click the underlined words *Current Settings* to open the Render Settings dialog box.

5 Use the following Render Settings, and then click OK to close the Render Settings dialog box:

• For Quality, select Best.

• For Resolution, select Full.

- For Time Span, select Length of Comp.

6 In the Output Module pop-up menu, select Custom to open the Output Module Settings dialog box, and set the following options:

- For Format, select QuickTime Movie.

- Select Import into Project When Done.

- Click Format Options.

7 In the Compression Settings dialog box, select Animation and Millions of Colors+, and then click OK.

8 In the Output Module Settings dialog box, review the settings: Channels is now set to RGB + Alpha, indicating that this item will be rendered with an alpha channel. Depth is set as Millions of Colors+, and Color is set as Premultiplied (Matted). When you are ready to continue, click OK.

9 Save the project one more time, and then click Render.

When the rendering process is complete, close the Render Queue and double-click LightRays.mov in the Project window to view the rendered movie.

If you wish to make any changes, reopen Light Rays Comp and make those adjustments. Remember to save your changes and then render the composition again, using the same render settings.

You have now completed Lesson 4! You have two more elements ready for use in your final piece.

Lesson 5

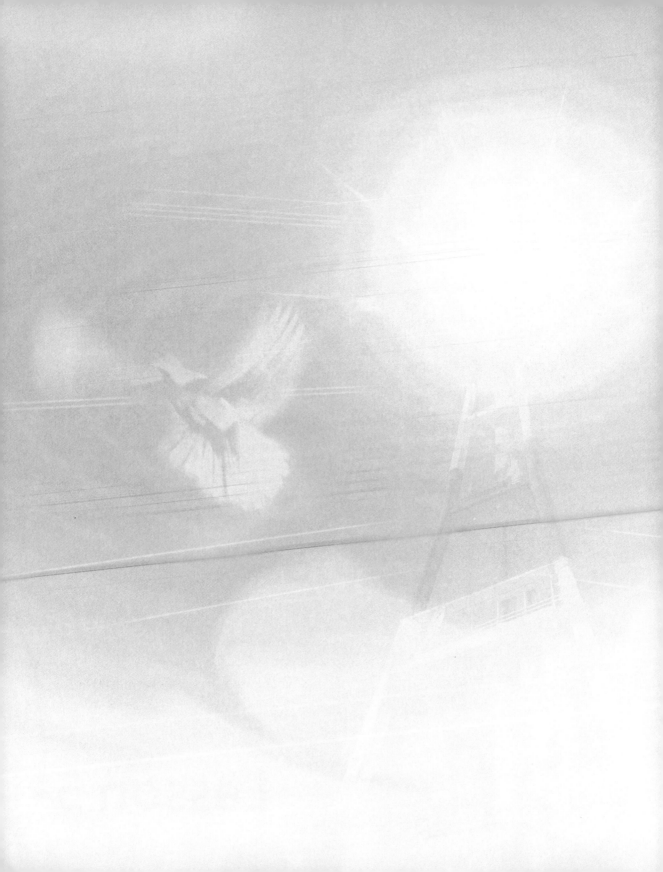

5 | Working with Text and Numbers

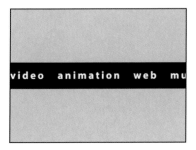
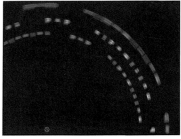

Even text and numbers can add visual excitement with the right design ideas and After Effects features. In this lesson, you'll practice a number of techniques for using blur to simulate the look of smooth, continuous motion in fast-moving text. Then you'll crank up the tempo with random numbers that flash in and out of view in a busy visual staccato.

In this lesson, you'll learn to do the following:

- Apply, format, and animate the Basic Text effect

- Apply, format, and animate the Path Text effect

- Apply, format, and animate the Numbers effect

- Add Motion Blur to fast-moving layers

- Apply the Fast Blur effect

- Edit expressions that you apply

- Apply the Easy Ease In keyframe assistant

Your next job is to build two text compositions and one numbers composition that you'll render separately as elements for the final composite in a later lesson.

This lesson takes about an hour to complete, not including the time required to render the elements.

Getting started

Make sure the following files are available in your AE_CIB job folder on your hard drive, or copy them from the *After Effects Classroom in a Book* CD now.

- In the Sample_Movies folder: TextLine_final.mov, TextCircles_final.mov, and Numbers_final.mov from the Sample_Movies/Lesson05 folder on the CD

- In the Finished_Projects folder: Text05_finished.aep

Refer to "Note: (Windows only) If you do not see the Prefs file, be sure that the Show all files option is selected for Hidden files on the View tab of the Folder Options dialog box." on page 4 for the procedure, if necessary.

This lesson does not use any footage files. However, it does use specific fonts, which are included in the Fonts folder on the *After Effects Classroom in a Book* CD. If these fonts are not already installed on your computer, copy these fonts files to your local drive and follow the standard procedure for installing fonts on your operating system. See the online Help for your Windows or Mac OS system for specific instructions.

Open and play the sample movies to see the work you'll be creating in this lesson. When you finish, quit the QuickTime player. You can delete the sample movies now to save storage space, if necessary.

You create all three elements within a single project. Your first task is to create that project.

1 Start After Effects 5.0, if it is not already running.

2 Choose File > New > New Project.

3 Choose File > Save As.

4 In the Save Project As dialog box, find and open the _aep folder in your AE_CIB job folder.

5 Type **Text05_work.aep** to name the project, and then click Save.

Creating the first element: a line of text

You saw the results of the first composition when you played the TextLine_final.mov. This element is a line of text that begins as a dot in the center of the screen and then expands outward. You'll create this element entirely within After Effects using a solid and the Basic Text effect, without importing source files.

Creating a composition

You'll begin building the first text element by creating a new composition. The dimensions you'll use create an element that is short but so wide that it will not fit on your screen at actual size (100%).

1 Choose Composition > New Composition.

2 Type **Text Line Comp** as the composition name.

3 Set the following options:

• In Width, type **2000**.

• In Height, type **50**.

• In Pixel Aspect Ratio, select Square Pixels.

• In Frame Rate, type **29.97**.

4 In Resolution, select Half or lower, so that the Composition window automatically opens at 50%.

5 In Duration, type **200** to specify two seconds. Then review your settings and click OK.

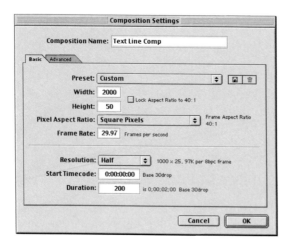

Creating a new solid

Next you'll create a new solid layer that is the size of the composition. You need this layer as the basis for the first text effect.

1 If the Background Color of the composition is not set to black, choose Composition > Background Color, click the color swatch, and select black in the color picker. Or, use the eyedropper to select black in any area in the interface. Click OK to close the Background Color dialog box.

2 Choose Layer > New > Solid.

3 In the Solid Settings dialog box, type **Text Solid** to name the solid.

4 Click Make Comp Size to automatically enter the Width as 2000 and the Height as 50.

5 Using the color swatch or eyedropper, select black. Then click OK.

Adding and formatting a line of text

Now that you have a layer, you can apply the Basic Text effect to it. Using this effect, you'll create a long line of type and apply simple text formatting.

1 In the Timeline window, select the Text Solid layer and choose Effect > Text > Basic Text.

2 In the Basic Text dialog box, set the following options:

- In Font, select Myriad.

- In Style, select Bold.

- Under Direction, select Horizontal, and under Alignment, select Center.

3 Still in the Basic Text dialog box, type the following seven words, adding three spaces after each word to separate them:

film video animation web multimedia dvd television

Be sure to type three spaces after the word *television*.

4 Select the text, including all the spaces, and press Ctrl + C (Windows) or Command + C (Mac OS) to copy the text.

5 Move the cursor to the end of the text (after the final three spaces) and press Ctrl + V (Windows) or Command + V (Mac OS) to paste the copied text so that you have a total of 14 words.

6 If you want to preview the font and style before closing the dialog box, select the Show Font option, if it is not already selected. When you are ready to continue, click OK.

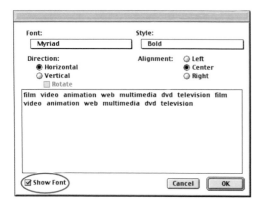

In the Composition window, a line of red type now appears across the solid layer.

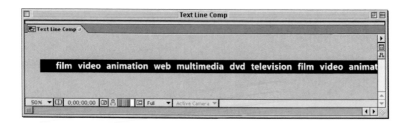

💡 *If you need to edit the text after you close the Basic Text dialog box, click the underlined word Options in the Effect Controls window, next to the name Basic Text. Then you can make any adjustments to the options. Click OK when you are satisfied with the text appearance.*

Setting properties for text along a line

Next, you'll apply more changes to the text, adjusting the color and other settings for appearance and placement. You'll make these changes in the Effect Controls window, which opens as soon as you close the Basic Text dialog box and contains all the Basic Text controls. You won't change the Position because the default setting (the center of the layer) is what you want to use.

1 In the Effect Controls window for Basic Text, expand Fill and Stroke controls by clicking the small arrow next to the words *Fill and Stroke*.

2 In Display Options, select Fill Only.

3 In Fill Color, use the color picker or eyedropper to select white.

4 In Size, scrub or type **20**. This is smaller than the default setting, so the text shrinks in the Composition window.

5 In Tracking, scrub or type –**40**, being careful to include the minus sign.

Because the tracking value is negative, the text squeezes together at the center of the layer.

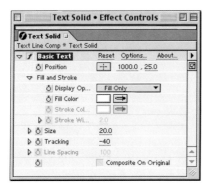

As you change settings in the Effect Controls window, After Effects updates the view in the Composition window so that you see the results immediately.

Animating the text line by setting keyframes

The next task is to animate the Basic Text effect settings so that the type grows outward from the center of the layer. You do this by setting Tracking keyframes in the Effect Controls window, but you'll examine the resulting keyframes in the Timeline window. As a finishing touch, you'll apply the Easy Ease In keyframe assistant. This feature slows down the movement of the text as it nears the final Tracking keyframe.

1 With the current-time marker at 0:00, click the Tracking stopwatch in the Effect Controls window to set a keyframe with the current Tracking value.

2 In the Timeline window, select the Text Solid layer and press E to open the effect applied to that layer: Basic Text. Expand the Basic Text properties so that you can see the keyframe for Tracking at 0:00.

3 Press End to move the current-time marker to 1:29.

4 In the Effect Controls window, scrub or type **30** to set Tracking. The type expands to the length of the Text Solid layer.

5 Press the spacebar or 0 on the numeric keypad to preview the animation. The type grows outward from the center of the layer as the Tracking value increases.

6 In the Timeline window, select the Tracking keyframe at 1:29, making sure that it is the only selected keyframe. Then choose Animation > Keyframe Assistant > Easy Ease In. The keyframe itself changes shape, indicating a change in keyframe interpolation.

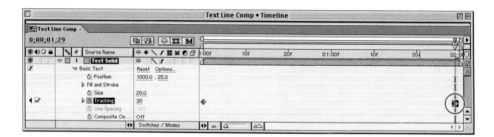

7 Preview the animation again. The type now slows down slightly as it reaches its fully expanded state. When you are ready to continue, save the project.

If you want to see the results of applying the Easy Ease In, look at the velocity graph in the Timeline window. To do this, expand the Tracking property under Basic Text. By default, the graph is a straight line, representing a constant rate of change. After you use Easy Ease In, the velocity line curves, flattening out as it approaches the second keyframe to indicate deceleration of the Tracking change. For more information about keyframe assistants and keyframe interpolation, see topics listed under "Fine-tuning Animation" in After Effects online Help.

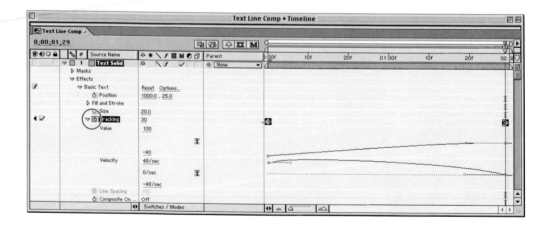

Adjusting opacity

Next you'll set Opacity keyframes to dissolve the text solid in two ways. First, you have the text fade in at the beginning of the animation. Then, as the characters reach full expansion and begin to move off screen, you'll make them dissolve again and disappear. This creates a smoother animation.

1 With the current-time marker at 0:00 in the Timeline window, select the Text Solid layer and press Shift + T to open Opacity without closing the Basic Text effect properties.

2 For the Opacity value, scrub or type **0** (zero).

3 Click the Opacity stopwatch to set a keyframe.

4 Move the current-time marker to 0:04 and change the Opacity to 100%. You have created a four-frame dissolve.

5 Move the current-time marker to 1:16 and set another 100% Opacity keyframe by clicking the keyframe check box in the A/V Features panel. The Opacity stays at 100% from 0:04 to 1:16.

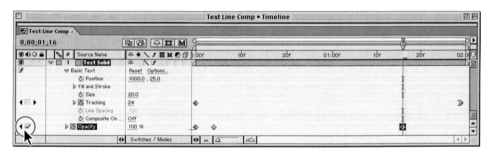

Keyframe check box

6 Press End to move the current-time marker to 1:29, and change Opacity to 0% to create a 14-frame dissolve.

7 Preview the animation. The text now fades up as it begins to expand and fades out as it reaches its full length. When you are ready to continue, save the project.

Adding motion blur

To add a finishing touch to this text animation, you'll turn on the Motion Blur switch for the text layer. Motion blur simulates a realistic camera blur based on a shutter angle (set on the Advanced tab of the Composition Settings dialog box) and the speed of the moving layer.

💡 *As you work, you can use the Enable Motion Blur button (the button on the right of the group of five buttons above the panels in the Timeline window) to make the results visible in Composition window previews. However, leaving this option selected can dramatically slow down After Effects performance, so it's best to deselect this button after you preview.*

1 In the Timeline window, select the Text Solid layer.

2 Click the Switches/Modes bar to open the Switches panel if it is not already open, and select the Motion Blur switch. A checkmark appears, indicating that motion blur will be applied to the layer when you render this composition.

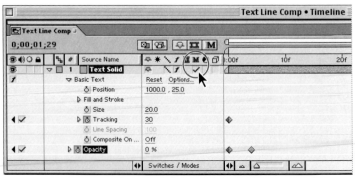

Motion Blur switch

3 Select the Enable Motion Blur button to display the motion blur in the Composition window.

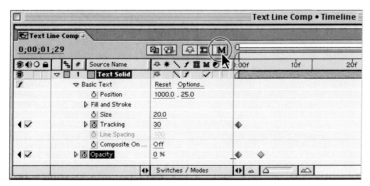

Enable Motion Blur button

4 Preview the animation, using Best quality, Full resolution, and 100% magnification, if possible—even if this means you see only a small part of the composition. The motion blur is not visible in the Composition window at lower quality or resolution settings.

5 Deselect the Enable Motion Blur button and save the project.

Motion blur is especially helpful to the appearance of this element because the text layer is moving so quickly. As you set up the rendering process, you'll choose the appropriate settings for the motion blur.

Rendering the text line element

You have finished building the first text element, so it's time to render the composition. This render takes only a few seconds on most systems.

1 Close the Composition, Timeline, and Effect Controls windows for the Text Line Comp.

2 In the Project window, select the Text Line Comp, and then choose Composition > Make Movie.

3 In the Output Movie To dialog box, type **TextLine.mov** as the name and specify the _mov folder in the AE_CIB job folder. Then click Save.

4 In the Render Queue, click the underlined words *Current Settings* to open the Render Settings dialog box, and then set the following options:

• In Quality, select Best.

• In Resolution, select Full.

• In Time Span, select Length of Comp.

• Under Time Sampling, in Motion Blur, select On For Checked Layers to render motion blur for any layers with checkmarks for the Motion Blur switch.

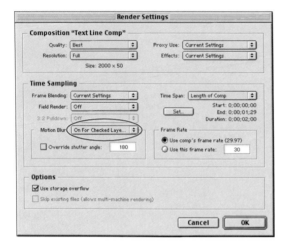

5 Click OK to return to the Render Queue.

6 In the Output Module pop-up menu, select Custom to open the Output Module Settings dialog box, and then set the following options:

• In Format, select QuickTime Movie.

• Select Import into Project When Done.

• Click Format Options.

7 In the Compression Settings dialog box, select Animation and Millions of Colors+. Make sure that the slider is set to Best, and then click OK.

8 In the Output Module Settings dialog box, review the settings: Channels is now set to RGB + Alpha, indicating that this item will be rendered with an alpha channel. Depth is set to Millions of Colors+, and Color is set as Premultiplied (Matted). When you are ready to continue, click OK.

9 Save the project one more time, and then click Render.

When the render is complete, close the Render Queue and double-click TextLine.mov in the Project window to view the rendered movie.

💡 *Because this element is so wide, press Alt (Windows) or Option (Mac OS) as you double-click the movie to open it in the After Effects Player window rather than the QuickTime Player window. Then you can use the magnification controls to resize the window to fit your screen.*

If you need to make any changes, reopen the Text Line Comp and make those adjustments. Remember to save those changes and render the composition again, using the same render settings.

Creating the second element: text circles

The next element is the circular text element you previewed in the TextCircle_final.mov sample movie. This element is made up of three rings of text that expand, rotate, and then fade into dots. You'll create this element using several solid layers and the Path Text effect. You'll do the entire composition without any source files, so you don't need to import anything.

Building the composition

The first step in building this element is to create a new composition.

1 In the Project window, click the New Composition icon (▣).

2 In the Composition Settings dialog box, type **Text Circle Comp** to name the composition.

3 In both Width and Height, type **800**.

4 In Pixel Aspect Ratio, select Square Pixels.

5 In Frame Rate, type **29.97**.

6 (Optional) In Resolution, select Half or lower, as needed for your system.

7 In Duration, type **500** to specify five seconds, and then click OK.

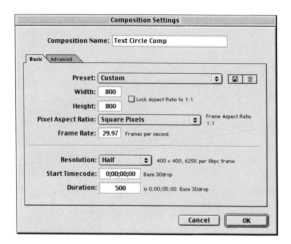

Creating a solid for circle text

Next you'll create a new black solid layer.

1 With the current-time marker at 0:00, choose Layer > New > Solid.

2 In the Solid Settings dialog box, type **Circle Text Solid** to name the solid.

3 Click Make Comp Size to automatically set the Width and Height at 800.

4 Use the color swatch or the eyedropper to select black, if necessary. Then click OK.

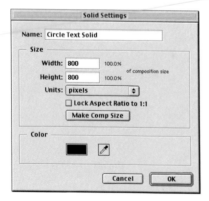

The layer appears as a black square in the Composition window frame, and is listed as Circle Text Solid in the Timeline window layer stack.

Adding and formatting circle text

Applying the Path Text effect to the Circle Text Solid is similar to the work you did with the text lines element: You'll enter the text and apply basic text formatting.

1 In the Timeline window, select the Circle Text Solid layer, and choose Effect > Text > Path Text.

2 In the Path Text dialog box, type the same seven words you used earlier, making sure to add three spaces after each word:
film video animation web multimedia dvd television

3 In Font, select Myriad.

4 In Style, select Bold, and then click OK.

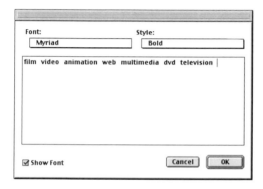

The text appears in red, starting along a curved path.

Note: In this composition, seven words are all you want so you do not copy and paste the text as you did with the Text Line Comp.

Setting text properties for text in circles

In the following steps, you'll adjust the Path Text effect controls to create the desired path shape, path size, text color, and character spacing.

1 In the Effect Controls window for Path Text, expand Path Options to see those controls.

2 In Shape Type, select Circle. In the Composition window, the type now runs along a circular path.

3 In the Effect Controls window, expand the Control Points properties.

4 In Tangent, scrub or type **188** and **578**.

5 In Vertex, scrub or type **400** and **400**.

6 Select the Reverse Path option to align the type from left to right along the interior edge of the circle.

7 Expand Fill and Stroke, and then in Options select Fill Only.

8 In Fill Color, select white, using either the eyedropper or the color picker.

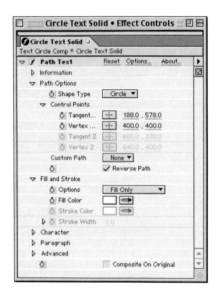

For more information about Path Text controls, see "Path Text" in After Effects online Help and the effects PDF files on the After Effects application CD.

Animating the text circle by setting keyframes

Next, you'll animate the size and spacing of the text by setting Size and Tracking keyframes.

1 Move the current-time marker to 0:00.

2 In the Effect Controls window under Path Text, expand the Character properties and scrub or type to set both Size and Tracking to **0**. The type disappears.

3 Click the stopwatches for Size and for Tracking to set keyframes.

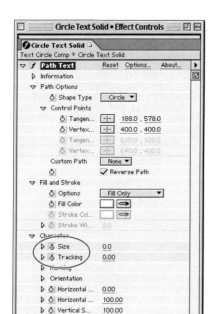

4 Move the current-time marker to 2:15.

5 In the Effect Controls window, scrub or type to set Size at **21** and Tracking at **18**. The type appears larger and evenly spaced (tracked) along the circular path. After Effects creates a second pair of Size and Tracking keyframes when you change the values.

6 Move the current-time marker to 3:29.

7 In the Effect Controls window, change Size to **0** and Tracking to **100**. The type expands along the path as the characters shrink in size to small dots and then disappear.

8 With the Path Text layer still selected in the Timeline window, press U to reveal all the keyframes. Review the keyframes and then collapse the layer properties again.

9 Save the project and preview the animation.

Reduce Quality and Resolution if you have trouble seeing all of the frames in a RAM preview. For more information, see "Allocating RAM to After Effects" on page 2.

Now you have a line of type that expands to form a circle over the duration of the composition. Once the circle is complete, the type rotates more quickly as the characters reduce and dissolve.

Duplicating the text layer and adjusting layer In points

You'll now add two more layers of circular type to your composition. Rather than redoing all the previous steps to create the new layers, you do this the easy way: by duplicating the layer you have just created and changing a few settings in each new layer. In this procedure, you'll also change the In points so that each layer begins at a different frame in the composition timeline.

1 In the Timeline window, select the Circle Text Solid layer and choose Edit > Duplicate twice, or press Ctrl + D (Windows) or Command + D (Mac OS) twice. You now have three identical layers in the stack.

2 Move the Layer 2 In point to 0:15 by doing one of the following:

• Drag the layer duration bar (being careful to select the shaded area, not either of the end points) so that the left end is at 0:15, using the Info palette as your guide.

• Click the double-arrow button (◆) at the bottom of the Timeline window to open the In/Out panel and then type **15** for the Layer 2 In point value.

• Select Layer 2, move the current-time marker to 0:15, and press [(left bracket key).

3 Select Layer 1 and set its In point to 1:00 using one of the methods described in step 2.

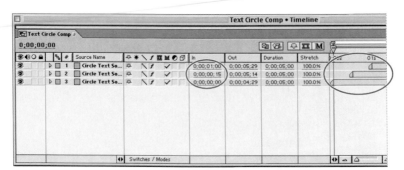

Text layer In points

You have three text layers that enter the composition at 15-frame intervals.

Changing the Path Text keyframes

Currently, the three layers are positioned directly on top of one another in the composition. Now, you'll separate the layers in space by increasing the diameters of the circle paths in the duplicated layers. You'll also adjust the Size and Tracking keyframes to make each layer animation slightly different from the other two.

1 With Layer 2 selected, press F3 to open the tab for that layer in the Effect Controls window.

2 Expand both Path Options and Control Points (if necessary), and then scrub or type to set the Tangent coordinates at **168, 613**. This path is now slightly larger than the path in Layer 1. Leave Layer 2 selected.

3 Press U to open all the effect keyframes for Layer 2.

4 In the Timeline window, move the current-time marker to 3:00 and change both Size and Tracking to **22** for Layer 2. Because the current-time marker is positioned over existing keyframes when you do this, you are setting new values for these keyframes.

5 Move the current-time marker to 4:14 and make sure that the Size value is 0 and the Tracking value is 100.

6 Repeat the process described in steps 1-5 for Layer 1, but use the following settings:

• Set the Tangent coordinates at **140, 645**.

• For step 4, move the current-time marker to 3:15 and set both Size and Tracking to **24**.

• For step 5, move the current-time marker to 4:29.

7 Preview the animation and save the project.

Now you should see three animated rings of text that expand in succession and then speed up as they shrink into dots. For more information on the Path Text effect, see After Effects online Help and the Effects.pdf file on your After Effects 5.0 applications CD.

Applying motion blur to all text circle layers

You'll apply motion blur to these layers, as you did for the Text Line element earlier in this lesson. Motion blur adds a realistic blur to the Circle Text layers as they spin; it is most noticeable when they speed up towards the end of the composition.

1 Press Ctrl + A (Windows) or Command + A (Mac OS) to select all three text circle layers.

2 In the Switches panel, select a Motion Blur switch for any layer to turn on all three switches, indicated by checkmarks.

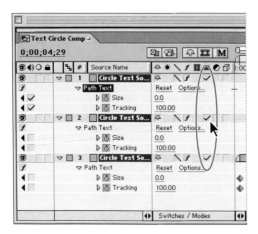

3 Select the Enable Motion Blur button.

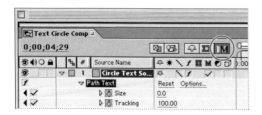

4 Preview the animation, using Full resolution, Best quality, and 100% magnification—even if you can only see a small section in the Composition window. The motion blur is not visible at lower quality and resolution settings.

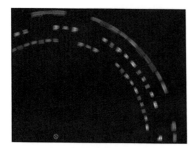

5 Deselect the Enable Motion Blur button, and then save the project.

Rendering the Text Circle Comp

The element is complete and ready for rendering. On most systems, this rendering takes only a few minutes.

1 Close the Composition, Timeline, and Effect Controls windows for the Text Circle Comp.

2 In the Project window, select the Text Circle Comp, and then choose Composition > Make Movie.

3 In the Output Movie To dialog box, type **TextCircle.mov** as the name and specify the _mov folder inside the AE_CIB job folder. Then click Save. The Render Queue opens with the Text Circle Comp set as the second item in the Queue (the Text Line Comp rendered earlier is the first item).

4 Under Text Circle Comp, click the words *Current Settings* to open the Render Settings dialog box and then set the following options:

• In Quality, select Best.

• In Resolution, select Full.

• In Time Span, select Length of Comp.

• Under Time Sampling, in Motion Blur, select On For Checked Layers to render motion blur for any layers with checkmarks for the Motion Blur switch.

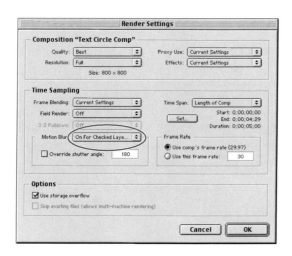

5 Click OK to return to the Render Queue.

6 In the Output Module pop-up menu, select Custom to open the Output Module Settings dialog box, and then set the following options:

• In Format, select QuickTime Movie.

• Select Import into Project When Done.

• Click Format Options.

7 In the Compression Settings dialog box, select Animation and Millions of Colors+. Make sure that the slider is set to Best, and then click OK.

8 In the Output Module Settings dialog box, review the settings: Channels is now set to RGB + Alpha, indicating that this item will be rendered with an alpha channel. Depth is set to Millions of Colors+, and Color is set as Premultiplied (Matted). When you are ready to continue, click OK.

9 Save the project one more time, and then click Render.

When the render is complete, close the Render Queue and double-click the TextCircle.mov item in the Project window to view the rendered movie.

Press Alt (Windows) or Option (Mac OS) when you double-click the item to open it in the After Effects Player window rather than the standard QuickTime Player window. Then you can use the magnification controls to reduce the size of the window to fit your screen.

If you need to make any changes, reopen the Text Circle Comp and make those adjustments. Remember to save those changes and render the composition again, using the same render settings.

Creating the third element: numbers

The last element is the one you previewed in the Numbers_final.mov sample movie. It consists of several layers of flashing numbers that you'll create with the Numbers effect. You'll then apply the Fast Blur effect and use simple expressions to increase the blurring of the numbers as they appear to get closer to the camera. You'll build this element entirely within After Effects so you don't need to import any source files.

Building the composition

You start by creating a new composition.

1 Choose Composition > New Composition.

2 In the Composition Settings dialog box, type **Numbers Comp** to name the composition.

3 In Preset, select NTSC D1 Square Pix, 720 x 540. After Effects automatically fills in the next four settings:

- Width: 720

- Height: 540

- Pixel Aspect Ratio: Square Pixels

- Frame Rate: 29.97

4 (Optional) In Resolution, select Half or lower, as needed for your system.

5 In Duration, type **600**, for six seconds, and then click OK.

Creating a solid for the Numbers effect

Next you'll create a new solid layer that is black and the same dimensions as the composition. Later, you'll apply the Numbers effect to this layer.

1 Move the current-time marker to 0:00 and choose Layer > New > Solid.

2 In the Solid Settings dialog box, select the following settings for your solid:

- Type **Numbers 1** to name the solid.

- Click Make Comp Size to automatically set Width to 720 and Height to 540.

- Under Color, select black, and then click OK.

A black solid layer appears in the Composition window and a Numbers 1 layer appears in the Timeline window.

Adding and formatting numbers

Now you're ready to apply the Numbers effect to the solid layer. The Numbers effect generates the random numbers that make up this element so you don't need to type any numbers but you do assign basic text characteristics to the numbers.

1 In the Timeline window, select the Numbers 1 layer and choose Effect > Text > Numbers.

2 In the Numbers dialog box, set the following options:

- In Font, select Myriad.

- In Style, select Roman.

- Leave Direction set to Horizontal.

- In Alignment, select Center, and then click OK.

Red numbers appear in the Composition window at the center of the solid layer.

Setting properties for the numbers

Again, you'll use the Effect Controls window to specify options for the numbers.

1 In the Effect Controls window, under Numbers, expand the Format controls, and change the following options:

- In Type, select Number (the default setting).

- Select the Random Values option.

- In Value/Offset/Random Max, scrub or type **1000**.

- In Decimal Places, scrub or type **10**.

2 Expand the Fill and Stroke controls, and change the following options:

- In Display Options, select Fill Over Stroke.

- For both Fill Color and Stroke Color, select white.

- In Stroke Width, scrub or type **1.5**.

- In Size, scrub or type **1000**.

3 In Tracking, scrub or type **86**.

4 Make sure that Proportional Spacing is selected.

Note: The number characters are very large at this point and may not be visible in the Composition window. They will reappear after you do more work with the numbers.

Animating the numbers by setting keyframes

You'll now set keyframes so that the numbers vary in size and spacing. This time, you'll use both the Effect Controls window and the Timeline window to do your work.

1 With the current-time marker at 0:00, click the Size and Tracking stopwatches in the Effect Controls window to set keyframes.

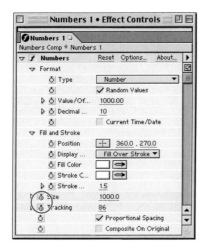

2 In the Timeline window, select the Numbers 1 layer. Press E and then expand the Numbers properties to see the keyframes.

3 Move the current-time marker about 10 to 20 frames forward on the timeline. The exact position is not important. Then scrub or type the Size and Tracking values, using arbitrary numbers. For example, you could set Size to 30 and Tracking to 150.

4 Continue moving the current-time marker forward along the timeline and changing the Size and Tracking values at about 10- to 20-frame intervals. Exact amounts are not important, but the more dramatic the change in values, the more interesting your animation will be. Continue adding keyframes until the end of the timeline (5:29).

5 Save the project and preview the animation. If you are not satisfied, make adjustments to the Size and Tracking keyframes and preview the animation again. When you are ready to continue, save your changes again.

Now you have a randomly generating line of numbers in your Composition window. The rapid change in Size and Tracking creates the flashing appearance. This layer is the first of three that will make up this element.

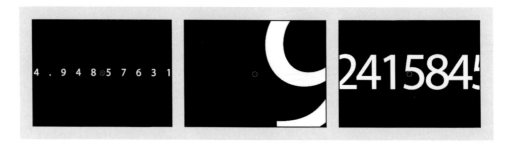

Applying the Fast Blur effect and creating an expression

In the sample movie, you saw the numbers get more blurry as they grew larger. To create this look, you'll apply a blur effect to the numbers layer. You'll also apply a simple expression to link the amount of blur to the number size. Because the automatically generated expression creates too much blur, you'll then edit the expression to reduce the blur.

1 In the Timeline window, select the Numbers 1 layer, and then choose Effect > Blur & Sharpen > Fast Blur. In the Effect Controls and Timeline windows, the Fast Blur effect appears below the Numbers effect.

2 In the Timeline window, expand the Fast Blur and Numbers properties. You may need to scroll or resize the window to see all the properties.

3 Under Fast Blur, select the word *Blurriness*, and then choose Animation > Add Expression.

4 In the Timeline window, drag from the Blurriness pick whip (⊚) to the Numbers effect Size value. When the dark rectangle appears around the word *Size*, release the mouse button. The expression appears under the timeline with an active cursor after the final parenthesis.

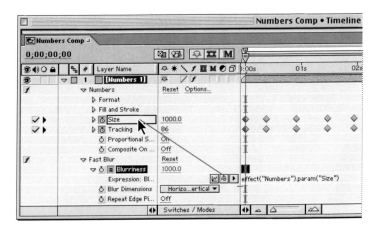

5 Being careful not to leave any spaces, type **/10** in the expression to indicate that this value will be divided by 10. The entire expression is now:

effect("Numbers").param("Size")/10

6 Click anywhere outside the expressions text box and then collapse the properties outline for the Numbers 1 layer.

7 Preview the animation and save the project.

You won't turn on the Motion Blur switch because the expression will create all the blur you need for this composition.

Duplicating and renaming the numbers layer

Next, you'll duplicate the Numbers 1 layer to create two more numbers layers for this element. After Effects duplicates all the original keyframes and the expression in the new layers.

1 Select the Numbers 1 layer and press Ctrl + D (Windows) or Command + D (Mac OS) twice to create a total of three identical layers.

2 In the Timeline window, select Layer 2 and press Enter (Windows) or Return (Mac OS) and type **Numbers 2** for the name. Then press Enter (Windows) or Return (Mac OS) to enter the new name.

3 Select Layer 3, and rename it **Numbers 3**, using the same process as in step 2.

Randomizing the number display

Now you'll shuffle the keyframes you created earlier for Size and Tracking. This makes the layers change size and tracking at different times and in different orders.

1 Choose Edit > Select All, or press Ctrl + A (Windows) or Command + A (Mac OS) to select all three numbers layers.

2 Press U to open all of the layer properties that have keyframes or expressions. The Size, Tracking, and Blurriness controls appear under each layer. All of the layer keyframes also appear and are at the same time positions because these layers are duplicates.

3 For Layer 2, draw a marquee around one pair of the Size and Tracking keyframes and drag them to another point on the timeline. It doesn't matter which pair of keyframes you select or where you drag them on the timeline. For example, you might select the Size and Tracking keyframes at 2:00 and drag them to 5:00.

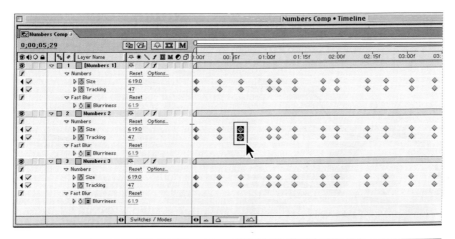

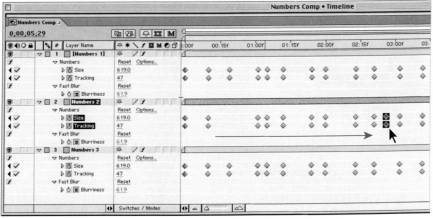

Drawing a marquee to select keyframes (above) and dragging keyframes (below)

4 Repeat step 3 for most (or all) the Size and Tracking keyframes for the Numbers 2 layer, creating an arrangement that is distinctly different from the original set (in Layer 1).

5 Select the Numbers 3 layer and repeat steps 3 and 4 to arrange the keyframes in a randomly different order than either of the other two layers. Refer to the illustration below as an example, but you do not need to match the times or values shown.

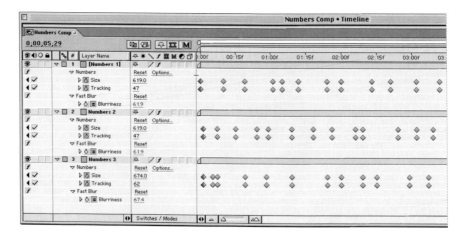

6 In the Time Controls palette, drag the Jog control (⊲⊪ ⊪⊳)to scrub through the composition to make sure that the three layers vary in size and blurriness. If necessary, continue to rearrange keyframes until you are satisfied with the results.

Preview the animation and save the project.

Varying the numbers displayed

To vary the actual numbers generated by the Numbers effect, you'll now change the Value/Offset/Random Max value for two of the numbers layers. The Value/Offset/Random Max control value limits the random number selections to a specific range.

1 In the Timeline window, set the current time to 0:00 and select the Numbers 2 layer.

2 Press F3 to open the Numbers 2 tab in the Effect Controls window.

3 Expand both the Numbers effect and the Format properties underneath Numbers. With the Value/Offset/Random Max value set at 1000, click the stopwatch for this control to set a keyframe.

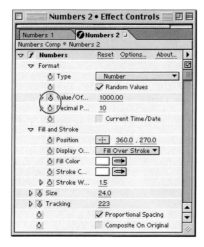

4 In the Timeline window, select the Numbers 3 layer and repeat steps 2 and 3 for this layer.

5 Press End to move the current-time marker to 5:29.

6 Select the Numbers 2 layer and press F3, if necessary. In the Effect Controls window, for Value/Offset/Random Max, scrub or type **750**.

7 Select the Numbers 3 layer and repeat step 6, this time scrubbing or typing **500**.

8 Preview the animation and save the project.

Render the Numbers element

You have completed work on this element so it is ready for rendering. This rendering process is more complex and takes longer than either of the other two. For example, if you rendered the Text Circle Comp in a couple of minutes, this one may take as long as 15 minutes.

1 Close the Composition, Timeline, and Effect Controls windows for the Numbers Comp.

2 In the Project window, select the Numbers Comp, and then choose Composition > Make Movie.

3 In the Output Movie To dialog box, type **Numbers.mov** as the name and specify the _mov folder inside the AE_CIB job folder, and then click Save. The Render Queue opens with the Numbers Comp as the third item in the Queue (the Text Line Comp and Text Circle Comp rendered earlier are the first and second items).

4 Under Numbers Comp, click the words Current Settings to open the Render Settings dialog box, and then set the following options:

- In Quality, select Best.

- In Resolution, select Full.

- In Time Span, select Length of Comp, and then click OK to return to the Render Queue.

5 In the Output Module pop-up menu, select Custom to open the Output Module Settings dialog box, and then set the following options:

- In Format, select QuickTime Movie.

- Select Import into Project When Done.

- Click Format Options.

6 In the Compression Settings dialog box, select Animation and Millions of Colors+. Make sure that the slider is set to Best, and then click OK.

7 In the Output Module Settings dialog box, review the settings: Channels is now set to RGB + Alpha, indicating that this item will be rendered with an alpha channel. Depth is set to Millions of Colors+, and Color is set as Premultiplied (Matted). When you are ready to continue, click OK.

8 Save the project one more time, and then click Render.

When the render is complete, close the Render Queue and double-click the Numbers.mov item in the Project window to view the rendered movie.

If you need to make any changes, reopen the Numbers Comp and make those adjustments. Remember to save those changes and render the composition again, using the same render settings.

You have now completed Lesson 5. You have created three text elements that you'll use in your final composite.

Lesson 6

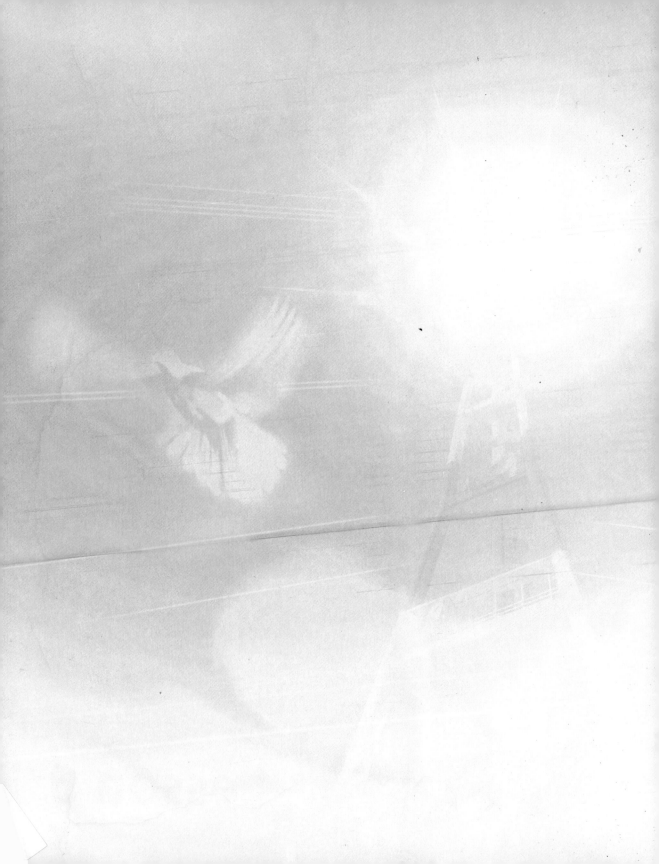

6 Building 3D Hexagon Elements

  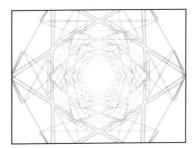

The big news in this lesson is working in true 3D with a virtual camera to control the view. When you arrange layers in 3D space and then move the camera around, the viewer sees only what the camera sees. Because you set up your layers in a tube-like arrangement of spinning hexagon rings, watching one of these elements is like riding through a tunnel with moving geometric walls.

In this lesson you learn to do the following:

- Move and orient layers in 3D space

- Use orthogonal views for 3D layers

- Define keyboard shortcuts for 3D views

- Add a camera layer

- Set keyframes to move a camera in 3D space

- Duplicate compositions and replace layers to create new elements

- Render multiple compositions in one session

Unlike the Rings.mov element you built in Lesson 3—which you made appear to swivel by applying a 3D *effect*—this lesson involves real 3D layers that have rotation and position coordinates in all three directions. This 3D involves a camera, so that you place the individual layers in space and then move the camera around them, pointing it at them from different distances and from various angles.

This chapter takes about an hour and a half to complete, plus the amount of time required to render the compositions on your computer. When you finish this lesson, you will have two additional elements to add to your final composite.

Getting started

Make sure that the following files are in the AE_CIB job folder on your hard drive, or copy them from the *After Effects Classroom in a Book* CD now:

- In the _ai folder: 3DHexagon01.ai and 3DHexagon02.ai

- In the Sample_Movies folder: 3DHexagons_final.mov and 3DHexLines_final.mov from the Sample_Movies/Lesson06 folder on the CD

- In the Finished_Projects folder: 3DHexagons06_finished.aep

Refer to "Note: (Windows only) If you do not see the Prefs file, be sure that the Show all files option is selected for Hidden files on the View tab of the Folder Options dialog box." on page 4 for the procedure, if necessary.

Open and play the sample movies to see the elements you'll create in Lesson 6. When you finish, quit the QuickTime player. You can delete the sample movies now to save storage space, if necessary.

You create both of these elements within a single project. Your first task is to create that project.

1 Start After Effects 5.0, if it is not already running.

2 Choose File > New > New Project.

3 Choose File > Save As.

4 In the Save Project As dialog box, find and open the _aep folder in the AE_CIB job folder you created earlier.

5 Type **3DHexagons06_work.aep** to name the project, and then click Save.

Creating the first element: 3D hexagons

In this lesson, you'll create two elements with hexagons that appear to move in three-dimensional space. This first element includes solid-fill hexagonal shapes. You'll create the element using a single source file.

Importing and organizing the source file

You'll start by importing the hexagon illustration.

1 Choose File > Import > File.

2 Locate the _ai folder inside of your AE_CIB job folder and select the 3DHexagon01.ai file.

3 Click Open (Windows) or Import (Mac OS). The file is added to the Project window.

4 Choose File > New > New Folder to create a new folder in the Project window.

5 Type **ai files** to name the folder.

6 Drag the 3DHexagon01.ai file into the ai files folder. Expand the folder so that you can see the file inside it.

This file is an image of a solid black hexagon with a transparent background, so the thumbnail in the Project window is completely black. The file was created in Adobe Illustrator and contains a *labeled* alpha channel (that is, an alpha channel that After Effects can automatically interpret), so the Interpret Footage dialog box is not required and does not appear during the import process.

When you deselect the file (by clicking an empty area in the Project window), the thumbnail and file information no longer appear at the top of the window.

Creating a composition

Begin building the 3D hexagons element by creating a new composition.

1 Choose Composition > New Composition.

2 In the Composition Settings dialog box, type **Hexagon Ring Comp** in Composition Name.

3 In Preset, select NTSC D1 Square Pix, 720 x 540 to automatically set the Width, Height, Pixel Aspect Ratio, and Frame Rate to the appropriate selections.

4 (Optional) In Resolution, select Half or lower, as needed for your system.

5 In Duration, type **300** to specify three seconds, and then click OK.

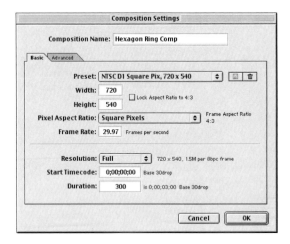

Note: If the In/Out/Stretch/Duration panel is still open, close it now by clicking the Expand or Collapse button (◄►), which is below the panel and to its right.

Adding the hexagons

Next you'll add the 3DHexagon01.ai to the composition. After adjusting its Opacity, you'll duplicate the layer. You'll use one layer for reference and make the other a 3D layer.

1 Move the current-time marker to 0:00, if it is not already there.

2 In the ai files folder in the Project window, select the 3DHexagon01.ai and drag it into the Timeline window. The layer automatically centers itself in the Composition window, but if the background is black, all you see are the layer selection handles.

3 Choose Composition > Background Color, and select white, using the color picker or eyedropper. The hexagon is now visible in the Composition window.

4 Press T to open the Opacity property, and scrub or type to set the Opacity value to **50%.** Press T again to close the Opacity property.

5 Duplicate the layer by pressing Ctrl + D (Windows) or Command + D (Mac OS). There are now two 3DHexagon01.ai layers in the Composition and Timeline windows.

6 In the A/V Features panel for Layer 2, select the Lock switch (⬤) so that you cannot accidentally select or change it. Layer 2 will act as a reference layer as you position the hexagons.

7 In the Switches panel for Layer 1, click the 3D Layer switch (⬚). A small cube appears, indicating that this is now a 3D layer.

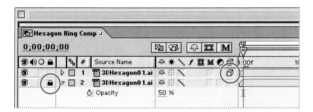

Now you have one 3D hexagon layer and one 2D reference layer in your composition.

Views

When working in 3D space it is helpful—and often necessary—to view the layers in the composition from more than one angle. You use the view pop-up menu to select the orthogonal view (Front, Left, Top, Back, Right, and Bottom) that you see as you work with your layers. You can also create and save up to three custom views at any angles and distances you want to use. For more information about 3D Views, see "Understanding 3D Views" in After Effects online Help.

Setting the orientation of the hexagon in 3D space

Next, you'll position hexagons in 3D space, using one orthogonal view. You begin by moving Layer 1 so that its center sits on one of the six sides of the reference hexagon. Then you rotate Layer 1 so that it is flush with that edge.

1 In the view pop-up menu at the bottom of the Composition window, select Front. Or, choose View > Switch 3D View > Front.

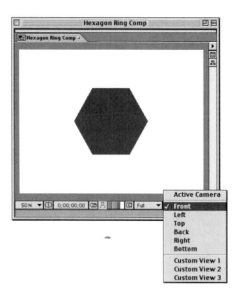

2 Select Layer 1 and drag it to the upper right quadrant of the frame in the Composition window. The exact position is not important now.

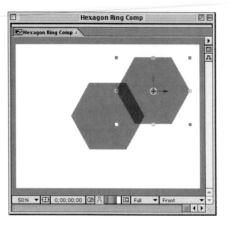

3 Press R to open Orientation and the Layer 1 X, Y, and Z Rotation properties.

4 In the Tools palette, select the rotation tool (○) and place the cross hairs in the Composition window over the red X-axis arrow so that the pointer changes to a small letter X inside the rotation symbol.

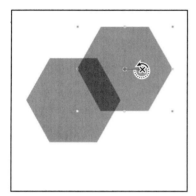

5 Drag downward. The layer begins tilting forward as it rotates on its X axis in 3D space. Continue dragging until the layer is reduced to a thin line and the Orientation values in the Timeline window are 90°, 0°, 0°.

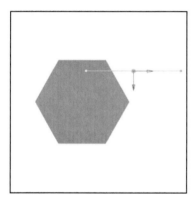

6 Move the cross hairs over the green Y-axis arrow (which appears as a green dot because it is pointing straight toward you) until the rotation pointer appears with a small letter Y.

7 Drag to the left until the layer is parallel to the upper right side of the reference hexagon and the Orientation values are 90°, 60°, 0°.

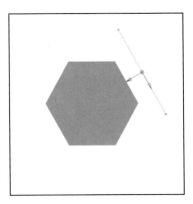

💡 *You can also type or scrub to enter any of these values or to correct values you change accidentally.*

8 In the Tools palette, click the selection tool (➤).

9 Move the pointer over the blue Z-axis arrow so that the pointer becomes an arrow with a small letter Z, and then drag down and to the left (in the direction the blue arrow is pointing) until the layer is flush with the upper right side of the reference hexagon.

Note: Dragging the layer by one of its colored axis line or arrow constrains the motion so that it moves only back and forth along that axis.

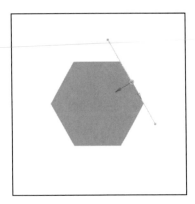

10 Place the selection tool over the red X-axis arrow and drag the layer so that the layer is roughly centered on the upper right side of the reference hexagon. (You'll position it more precisely later.)

11 Press R to hide the Orientation and Rotation properties.

Duplicating the layer and setting more orientations

Now you'll duplicate the layer several times and move each new layer around the reference hexagon to create a tunnel-like arrangement. In each case, you'll point the Z axis toward the center of the reference hexagon.

1 With Layer 1 still selected, choose Edit > Duplicate, or press Ctrl + D (Windows) or Command + D (Mac OS). A new layer appears above the original as Layer 1 and is already selected.

2 Press R to open the Orientation and the X,Y, and Z Rotation properties for the selected layer.

3 Using the selection tool (▸), drag the layer by the blue Z axis until it is flush with the lower left side of the reference hexagon (directly opposite the first hexagon).

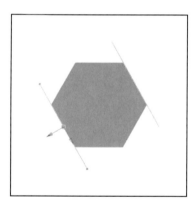

4 Select the rotation tool (⟳) and move the cross hairs over the Y-axis arrow (a green dot). Then drag to the left to turn the layer 180° so that the blue arrow points toward the center of the reference hexagon and the Orientation values are 270°, 300°, 180°.

💡 *As you rotate the layer, press Shift to snap to 45° increments.*

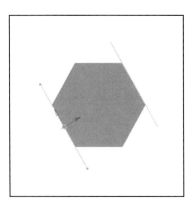

5 Repeat steps 1 through 4 four more times to create a total of six layers with the locations and orientations described in the list below. When you finish, each hexagon should be flush with a different side of the reference hexagon and all the blue Z-axis arrows should point toward the center. Remember to use the rotation tool to turn the layers so that they are parallel to the various sides of the reference hexagon and then use the selection tool to move them into position.

- Layer 1: Flush with the top side of the reference hexagon, rotated on Y axis to 90°, 0°, 0°.

- Layer 2: Flush with the bottom side of the reference hexagon, rotated on Y axis to 270°, 0°, 180°.

- Layer 3: Flush with the lower right side of the reference hexagon, rotated on Y axis to 270°, 60°, 180°.

- Layer 4: Flush with the upper left side of the reference hexagon, rotated on Y axis to 90°, 300°, 0°.

6 Select all the 3D hexagon layers and press the accent grave (`) key (above the Tab key) to close all the layer properties. In the Composition windows, all six layers are arranged around the reference layer with their blue Z-axis arrows pointing toward the center.

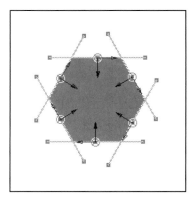

7 Deselect all layers and save the project.

You now have all six hexagon layers in approximate positions and correct orientations.

Preparing to align the hexagons

You'll align the hexagon positions, using guides, rulers, and a second reference hexagon to make the alignment precise. These positions are important in achieving the animation results you want.

1 Choose View > Show Rulers, or press Ctrl + R (Windows) or Command + R (Mac OS) to display the rulers in the Composition window.

2 At the bottom of the Composition window, click the Title-Action Safe button (⊞) to display the Title-Action Safe guides.

3 Choose View > Show Guides, if this command is not already selected.

4 Drag a vertical guide from the left ruler to the center of the Composition window, using the cross hairs in the center as your reference line. Then drag a horizontal guide from the top ruler to the center of the composition.

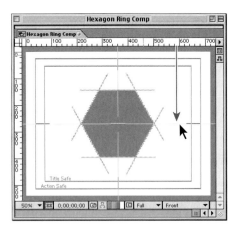

5 In the Timeline window, click the Lock switch ( ) for Layer 7 to unlock the layer, and then select it.

6 Press Ctrl + D (Windows) or Command + D (Mac OS) to duplicate the reference hexagon.

7 Press R to reveal the Rotation property for Layer 7, and then scrub or type to set the Rotation value at **30°**.

8 Press S to reveal the Scale property, and then scrub or type to set the Scale value at **86%**. Then press S to hide the Scale property.

9 Select the Lock switches for Layers 7 and 8 so that they cannot be selected or changed.

The points on the smaller reference hexagon now identify the centers of each side of the larger reference hexagon. You'll use them as a visual guide in the next procedure.

Aligning the hexagons precisely

Next you'll nudge the hexagon layers into exact positions and examine them from several views to make sure that everything is in alignment. After the hexagons are correctly positioned, you'll no longer need the items that helped you align them, so you'll remove that clutter from the Composition window.

1 Press Ctrl + A (Windows) or Command + A (Mac OS) to select all unlocked layers.

Note: Layer 7 and 8 are not selected because they are locked.

2 Press P to reveal the Position properties for the layers, and then press Ctrl + Shift + A (Windows) or Command + Shift + A (Mac OS) to deselect all layers.

3 Using the selection tool (▶), drag the Layer 1 axis arrows so that the base of the blue Z-axis arrow rests on the tip of the smaller reference hexagon and its tip points toward the center. The Position coordinates in the Timeline window should be 360, 144, 0.

If you can't drag the layer accurately to this position, try increasing the Composition window magnification. This makes it easier to see and also increases the sensitivity of your dragging motions. Or, you can scrub or type the exact values directly in the Timeline window.

4 Repeat step 3 for Layers 2-6. When all six hexagons are centered, make sure that the Position coordinates are as follows:

• Layer 2: 360, 393, 0.

• Layer 3: 466, 333, 0.

• Layer 4: 250, 208, 0.

• Layer 5: 250, 330, 0.

• Layer 6: 467, 205, 0.

5 Select Layers 1–6 and press P to hide the Position properties.

6 Choose View > Hide Rulers, and then choose View > Hide Guides to remove the ruler and guide displays in the Composition window.

7 At the bottom of the Composition window, click the Title-Action Safe button (⊞) to deselect it.

8 In the Timeline window, turn off the Lock switches (▪) for Layers 7 and 8. Then select these two layers and press Delete to remove them from the composition. Save the project.

Setting and using 3D-views shortcuts

After Effects reserves three keyboard shortcuts for 3D views: the F10, F11, and F12 keys. You can reassign these shortcuts to any view that is convenient for your project. In this composition, you'll use Front, Top, and Active Camera views, so those are the views you want to assign to the shortcuts.

1 In the Composition window, make sure that Front is selected in the views pop-up menu.

2 Choose View > Set 3D View Shortcut > Replace "*<currently assigned view>*" Shift+F10. (If the command already says Replace "Front" Shift+F10, you can skip this step.) The F10 key is now the shortcut for Front view.

3 In the Composition window views pop-up menu, select Top.

4 Press Shift + F11 to set Top view as the F11 key assignment. Or, choose View > Set 3D View Shortcut > Replace "*<currently assigned view>*" Shift+F11.

5 In the views pop-up menu, choose Active Camera.

6 Press Shift + F12 to set Active Camera view as the F12 key assignment.

7 Press F10 to set the View to Front. Compare the hexagon image with the illustration on the left, below step 8.

8 Press F11 and compare to the middle illustration, and then press F12 and compare to the illustration on the right.

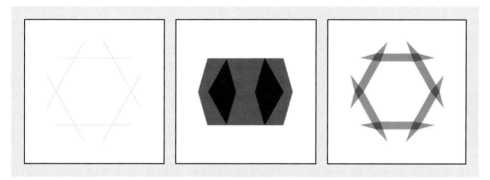

Views in the Composition window: Front view (left), Top view (center), Active Camera view (right)

9 If your composition image does not match the illustrations above, review the position settings in the previous procedure, "Aligning the hexagons precisely" on page 217, and make any necessary adjustments. Save the project.

For more information about 3D Views, see After Effects online Help.

Rotating the hexagon layers

Next you'll set keyframes for each hexagon layer so that they rotate on their X axes.

1 Make sure that the view is still set to Active Camera, or press F12 to make it so.

2 Select all layers, press R to reveal all the Orientation and Rotation properties, and then deselect all layers.

3 With the current-time marker at 0:00, click the stopwatch for the X Rotation property in each layer to set keyframes.

4 Move the current-time marker to 2:00 and select all layers again.

5 For one of the layers, click the X Rotation value, type **180°**, and press Enter. New X Rotation keyframes appear for each layer.

Note: You cannot change all the layer X Rotation values at once by scrubbing; you must type to do this.

6 Press R to hide the Orientation and Rotation properties for all layers, and then deselect all.

7 Move the current-time marker to 0:00 and preview the animation. Then save the project.

The hexagons now turn inward toward the camera (like a flower opening) and continue turning until they are again perpendicular to the camera. You have finished animating the individual hexagon layers.

Creating a second composition

Now you'll create a new composition. In it, you'll create a tunnel-like visual, using multiple copies of the Hexagon Ring Comp you just finished creating.

1 Set the current-time marker to 0:00 (if necessary).

2 Press Ctrl + N (Windows) or Command + N (Mac OS) to create a new Composition.

3 In the Composition Settings dialog box, type **Hexagon Tunnel Comp** as the Composition Name.

4 In Preset, select NTSC D1 Square Pix, 720 x 540 to automatically enter the appropriate settings for Width, Height, Pixel Aspect Ratio, and Frame Rate.

5 (Optional) In Resolution, select Half or lower, as needed for your system.

6 In Duration, type **300** to specify three seconds, and then click OK.

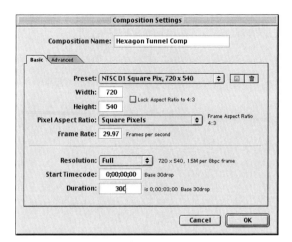

Adding and setting properties for the hexagon ring

Next you add the Hexagon Ring Comp so that you'll have a composition nested within a composition. You'll then duplicate the composition to create the number of layers required to build the tunnel. You'll also reduce the opacity so that the layers are semitransparent, and then switch them all to 3D layers.

1 Make sure that the current-time marker is still at 0:00.

2 In the Project window, select the Hexagon Ring Comp and drag it into the Timeline window.

3 With the layer still selected, choose Edit > Duplicate five times to create a total of six layers.

4 Choose Edit > Select All, and press T to open the Opacity property on all layers.

5 Click the Opacity value for one of the selected layers, type **50**, and press Enter. All the layers are set at 50% opacity.

6 In the Switches panel, click the 3D Layer switch (▱) for any one of the layers, being careful to keep all layers selected. A small cube appears in all six 3D switches, indicating that all are now 3D layers.

7 Save the project.

Creating the tunnel of hexagons

You are now ready to build the tunnel of hexagons. You'll position each of the Hexagon Ring layers in Z space to form a tunnel shape. After you change the view, you'll collapse transformations for the nested composition layers to preserve their 3D qualities.

1 Press the F11 key, or choose Top from the view pop-up menu in the Composition window. Now the entire composition appears as a thin horizontal line.

2 With all the Hexagon Ring Comp layers still selected, click the Collapse Transformations switch (✳) for one of the layers. All the layer transformations are collapsed and the Composition window appears as shown in the following illustration.

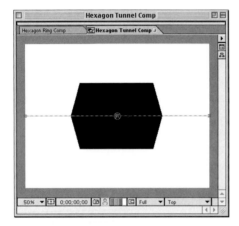

3 With all layers still selected, press P to reveal the layer Position property. Then deselect all layers.

4 Reduce the magnification in the Composition window to about 25% so that you can see the pasteboard area outside of the composition frame.

5 In the Timeline window, click the underlined Z Position coordinate (the third value) and change the setting for each layer in turn, using the values shown in the illustration below. Be careful to include the minus sign for the numbers that are negative.

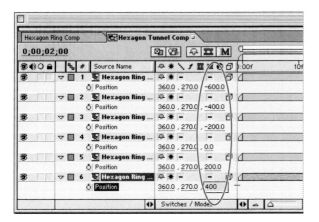

Note: *You can also move an individual layer manually by selecting it and dragging the blue Z-axis arrow until you reach the required coordinate. Use the Info palette or Timeline for reference as you drag.*

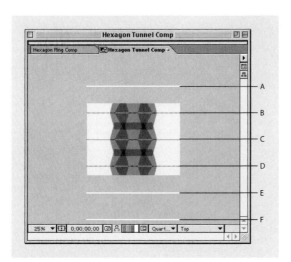

A. *Layer 6,* **B.** *Layer 5,* **C.** *Layer 4,* **D.** *Layer 3,* **E.** *Layer 2,* **F.** *Layer 1*

6 Select all the layers and press P to hide the Position property. Then save the project.

Now you have six layers positioned at increasing distances from the camera. You can see this because you're using Top view.

Adding the camera

Now you'll add a camera to your composition—as if you were filming real three-dimensional items and moving a physical camera around them in space. Your camera will travel through the center of the hexagon rings.

1 Move the current-time marker to 0:00, and choose Layer > New > Camera.

2 In the Camera Settings dialog box, for Preset, select 35mm. Leave the Name setting as Camera 1 and click OK.

The Camera 1 layer appears in the Timeline window, and the Camera appears in the Composition window.

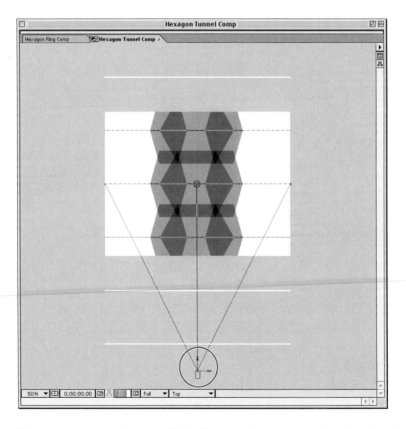

There are many settings available for creating cameras. By choosing the 35mm preset, you selected all the camera settings needed for this animation. For more information about working with Camera layers, see After Effects online Help.

Positioning the camera

Next you'll position the camera using the Active Camera view and the camera tools in the Tools palette. You'll animate the Camera Position so that it travels through the center of the hexagon layers. You'll use the track z camera tool to change the distance between the camera and the image layers.

1 Press F12 to select Active Camera view. The image in the Composition window now appears from the camera point of view.

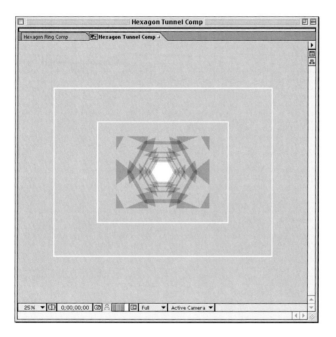

2 In the Timeline window, select the Camera 1 layer and press P to reveal its Position properties.

3 In the Tools palette, hold down the mouse button as you click the camera tool to see the three available camera tools: the orbit camera tool (◉), the track xy camera tool (◈) and the track z (◉) camera tool. Select the track z (◉) camera tool, which you can use to change the Z position of the camera, moving it closer to or farther from the image layers.

4 In the Composition window, click and drag downward to pull back (move away from the image layers). Watch the changing values in the Info palette or the Timeline window Camera 1 layer Position coordinates until the Z coordinate reaches –1000, and then release the mouse button. The camera is now positioned to look through the center of the hexagon layers.

Note: If the Composition window doesn't update as you drag the camera, choose Edit > Preferences > Previews and select Use Dynamic Resolution. You should see the outlines of the hexagon layers as the camera moves past them.

5 In the Timeline window, make sure that the current-time marker is at 0:00 and then click the Position stopwatch for Camera 1 to set a keyframe.

6 Move the current-time marker to 2:00 and drag the track z tool upward to change the Z Position coordinate to –16. A second keyframe appears.

7 Preview the animation. Then save the project.

Changing the camera velocity

For a subtle refinement on this camera move, you'll add a slight velocity change to soften the motion as the camera comes to rest at 2:00.

1 In the Timeline window, select the second Position keyframe at 2:00, making sure to select only that keyframe.

2 Choose Animation > Keyframe Assistant > Easy Ease In. You can expand the Position properties to display the graph, which now has a curved line.

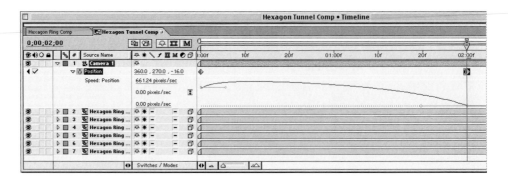

3 Press P to hide the Position property.

4 Preview the animation and save the project.

Note: If you have trouble seeing all the frames in a RAM preview, try setting your work area to begin at 1:15 and end at 2:15. To do this, move the current-time marker to 1:15 and press B (for beginning*); then move the current-time marker to 2:15 and press N to set the end of the work area.*

Rotating the camera and adjusting the rotation speed

As your last adjustment to this composition, you'll add rotation to the camera so that it spins as it moves through the hexagon layers.

For extra finesse, you also add a slight velocity change to the rotation as it comes to a stop at 2:00.

1 Move the current-time marker to 0:00 and select the Camera 1 layer (if it is not selected).

2 Press R to reveal the Orientation and Rotation properties for the camera. All the Rotation values are at 0°.

3 Click the Z Rotation stopwatch to set a keyframe for the Camera 1 layer.

4 Move the current-time marker to 2:00 and then scrub or type the Z Rotation value as **–180°** to set a second keyframe. Leave this keyframe selected.

5 Choose Animation > Keyframe Assistant > Easy Ease In, and then expand the Z Rotation property to see the velocity graphs, which now curve into the second keyframe.

6 Press R to hide the Rotation property.

7 Preview the animation and save the project. Then close the Composition and Timeline windows.

You have completed the first 3D hexagons element.

Creating the second element: 3D hexagon outlines

The second element is exactly the same as the first except that it uses a different source file. However, creating this element is much easier because you can duplicate the first compositions and then replace the source file. The replacement artwork is a hexagon outline instead of a solid hexagon.

Importing the second source file

First, you'll import the new source file into the 3DHexagons_work.aep project.

1 Choose File > Import > File, or press Ctrl + I (Windows) or Command + I (Mac OS) to open the Import File dialog box.

2 Open the _ai folder in your AE_CIB job folder, and select the 3DHexagon02.ai file.

3 Click Open (Windows) or Import (Mac OS).

4 In the Project window, drag the 3DHexagon02.ai file into the ai files folder, and then deselect the file.

Duplicating the compositions

Next, you'll duplicate and rename the Hexagon Ring Comp and Hexagon Tunnel Comp to create two new compositions.

1 In the Project window, select the Hexagon Ring Comp and choose Edit > Duplicate, or press Ctrl + D (Windows) or Command + D (Mac OS). The new composition name includes an asterisk, indicating that it is a copy.

2 With Hexagon Ring Comp* selected, press Ctrl + K (Windows) or Command + K (Mac OS) to open the Composition Settings dialog box.

3 Type **HexLines Ring Comp** for the name, and then click OK. (Do not change any other settings.)

4 In the Project window, select the Hexagon Tunnel Comp and repeat steps 1 through 3, typing **HexLines Tunnel Comp** for the new name.

Now you have two new HexLines compositions ready for artwork replacement.

Replacing the images in HexLines Ring Comp

In the first new composition, you'll select and replace the solid hexagons with hexagon outlines.

1 In the Project window, double-click the HexLines Ring Comp to open it in the Composition and Timeline windows.

2 Select all six 3DHexagon01.ai layers.

3 In the Project window, select the 3DHexagon02.ai file and press Alt (Windows) or Option (Mac OS) as you drag the file into the Timeline window. This image replaces all the original images, so all the layer names are now 3DHexagon02.ai.

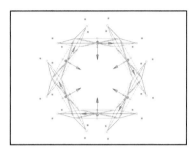

4 Preview the composition. The outline hexagons have replaced the solid hexagons. All the movement and 3D positioning that you set up remain in place. Save the project.

Replacing the images in HexLines Tunnel Comp

In the first element you created, Hexagon Tunnel Comp is made up of multiple copies of the Hexagon Ring Comp. In the same way, you'll use the HexLines Ring Comp for the layers in the HexLines Tunnel Comp. You'll replace all the Hexagon Ring Comp layers in the HexLines Tunnel Comp with the new HexLines Ring Comp.

1 In the Project window, double-click the HexLines Tunnel Comp to open it in the Composition and Timeline windows.

2 In the Timeline window, select the six Hexagon Ring Comp layers (all layers except the Camera 1 layer.)

3 In the Project window, select the HexLines Ring Comp, and press Alt (Windows) or Option (Mac OS) as you drag it into the Timeline window. All six layers are now listed as HexLines Ring Comp.

4 Preview the composition. The outline hexagon rings have replaced the solid ones in the tunnel animation.

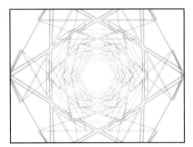

All the keyframes and properties in these compositions remain unchanged. By simply replacing the source file, you have created an additional element for use in your final piece.

Rendering both 3D hexagon elements

You have finished building both 3D hexagon elements. Now you'll render both final compositions. Together, rendering these two compositions takes approximately the same amount of time as rendering the Number Comp, which you did at the end of Lesson 5.

1 Close the Composition and Timeline windows for the HexLines Tunnel Comp and the Hexagon Tunnel Comp.

Rather than closing the Composition windows, you can press the Caps Lock key on your keyboard to prevent the Composition window from redrawing each frame as the composition is rendered—reducing render time.

2 In the Project window, press Ctrl + click (Windows) or Command + click (Mac OS) to select both the Hexagon Tunnel Comp and HexLines Tunnel Comp, and then choose Composition > Add to Render Queue. The Render Queue appears with both items in the queue.

3 In Output To for item number one (the Hexagon Tunnel Comp), click the words *Not Yet Specified* to open the Output Movie To dialog box. Type **3DHexagons.mov** and save it in the _mov folder inside your AE_CIB job folder.

4 Repeat step 3 for the HexLines Tunnel Comp, typing **3DHexLines.mov** for the name and saving it in the same location.

5 Under item 1, the Hexagon Tunnel Comp, click the words *Current Settings* to open the Render Settings dialog box, and then select the following Render Settings:

• In Quality, select Best.

• In Resolution, select Full.

• In Time Span, select Length of Comp, and then click OK to return to the Render Queue.

6 Repeat step 5 for item 2, the HexLines Tunnel Comp.

7 In Output Module for the Hexagon Tunnel Comp, select Custom to open the Output Module Settings dialog box, and set the following options:

• In Format, select QuickTime Movie.

• Select Import into Project When Done.

• Click Format Options.

8 In the Compression Settings dialog box, select Animation and Millions of Colors+. Make sure that the slider is set to Best, and then click OK.

9 In the Output Module Settings dialog box, review the settings: Channels is now set to RGB + Alpha, indicating that this item will be rendered with an alpha channel. Depth is set to Millions of Colors+, and Color is set as Premultiplied (Matted). When you are ready to continue, click OK to close the dialog box.

10 Repeat steps 7-9 for item 2, the HexLines Tunnel Comp.

11 Save the project one more time, and then click Render. After Effects renders the two compositions in order: first the Hexagon Tunnel Comp and then the HexLines Tunnel Comp.

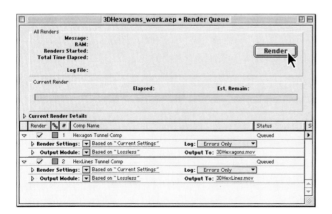

When the render is complete, close the Render Queue and double-click the 3DHexagons.mov item in the Project window to view the rendered movie. Do the same to view the 3DHexLines.mov.

If you need to make any changes, reopen the appropriate composition and make those adjustments. Remember to save your project and render the composition again, using the same render settings.

You have now completed Lesson 6. You have two more elements ready to add to the final piece.

Lesson 7

7 | Combining 2D Elements in a Composite

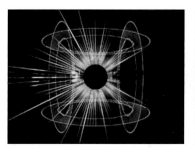 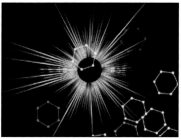 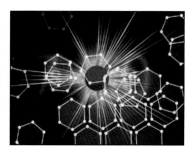

Up to this point, you've worked on individual elements—most of them abstract, geometric images. Now, you start bringing your work together. This lesson sets up the first "scene" of your final project, with the flat sheets of hexagons, stars, circles, and other two-dimensional elements working together to create an upbeat, integrated sequence.

In this lesson you'll learn to do the following:

• Import movies that you rendered earlier and use them as layers of a composition

• Change opacity by dragging points in the Opacity Values graph

• Rearrange layers in the stack

• Apply Color Dodge and Soft Light transfer modes

• Trim layer In points and Out points

• Apply the Tint effect to colorize layers

• Copy and paste effects from layer to layer

• Apply the Channel Blur effect

• Apply the Gaussian Blur effect

• Rearrange the order in which effects are processed

You'll begin combining your previously rendered elements in a two-dimensional environment. You'll set the proper timings for the elements and add effects to refine them so that they are ready for placement in the final project.

This lesson takes about an hour to complete, not including the time required to render the elements.

Getting started

Make sure that the following files are in the AE_CIB job folder on your hard drive, or copy them from the *After Effects Classroom in a Book* CD now.

• In the Sample_Movies folder: 2DComposite_final.mov and RingMix_final.mov from the Sample_Movies/Lesson07 folder on the CD

• In the Finished_Projects folder: 2DComposite07_finished.aep

Open and play the sample movies 2DComposite_final.mov and RingMix_final.mov to see the work you'll create in Lesson 7. When you finish, quit the QuickTime player. You can delete the sample movies now to save storage space, if necessary.

The only source files you need are QuickTime movies that you've rendered in previous lessons and saved in the _mov folder inside your AE_CIB job folder. These movies are not available on the Classroom in a Book CD; you must create them yourself in Lessons 1-6. Make sure that the following eight files are in your _mov folder:

• DotCircles.mov, Hexagons.mov, HexOutlines.mov, LightRays.mov, LineCircles.mov, Numbers.mov, Rings.mov, and Starburst.mov

Note: You will not render the final composition in this lesson. Instead, you'll import this project into your final project in a later lesson. This gives you the flexibility to make last-minute changes to these layers within the final project before the final render.

Creating the project

You'll do all the work for this lesson within a single project. Your first task is to create that project.

1 Start After Effects 5.0, if it is not already running.

2 Choose File > New > New Project.

3 Choose File > Save As.

4 In the Save Project As dialog box, find and open the _aep folder in the AE_CIB job folder you created earlier.

5 Type **2DComposite07_work.aep** to name the project, and then click Save.

Importing and organizing the source files

This project requires a number of source files. You'll now import these; most of the elements are movies you rendered in previous lessons.

1 Choose File > Import > Multiple Files.

2 Open the _mov folder inside your AE_CIB job folder. Then select the following files, one at a time, and click Open (Windows) or Import (Mac OS) each time:

• DotCircles.mov

• Hexagons.mov

• HexOutlines.mov

• LightRays.mov

• LineCircles.mov

• Numbers.mov

• Rings.mov

• Starburst.mov

3 Open the audio folder inside your AE_CIB job folder, select the Soundtrack.aif file, and click Open (Windows) or Import (Mac OS). Make sure that all nine files appear in the Project window, and then click Done to close the Import File dialog box.

4 Choose File > New > New Folder.

5 In the Project window, type **audio files** to name the new folder.

6 Select the Soundtrack.aif file, drag it into the audio files folder, and expand the folder so that you can see the Soundtrack.aif file inside it.

7 Create a second folder and name it **mov files**.

8 Select all the other imported files (the eight movies) and drag them into the mov files folder. Expand the folder so that you can see the eight .mov files inside it.

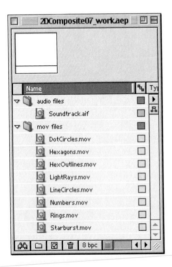

Note: Each of these files (except Soundtrack.aif, which is an audio file) contains a labeled alpha channel. Labeled alpha channels already contain the interpretation information After Effects needs, so the Interpret Footage dialog box does not appear during the import process.

Now all the files you'll need for this project are imported and you have a well-organized Project window for your work.

Creating a new composition

Before you begin building the final 2D composite, you need to create a composite of the three circle elements. You'll combine these elements in one composition so that you can treat it as a single layer in the final composite.

1 Choose Composition > New Composition.

2 In the Composition Settings dialog box, type **Ring Mix Comp** in Composition Name.

3 Enter the following options:

• In Width, type **800**.

• Deselect the Lock Aspect Ratio option.

• In Height, type **800**.

• In Pixel Aspect Ratio, select Square Pixels.

• In Frame Rate, type **29.97**.

• In Duration, type **500**, to specify five seconds.

• (Optional) In Resolution, select Half or lower, as needed for your system.

4 Make sure that you have entered all these options correctly, and then click OK.

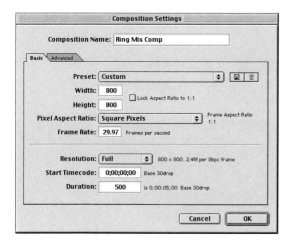

Combining the circles layers and applying transfer modes

Next you'll add the three circle elements to the composition and apply transfer modes to blend the layers.

1 If the background color of the composition is not set to black, choose Composition > Background Color, and select black.

2 Make sure that the current-time marker is at 0:00.

3 In the mov files folder in the Project window, select the Rings.mov, the LineCircles.mov, and the DotCircles.mov and drag them directly to the Timeline window to automatically center them in the Composition window.

Note: To select all three files and drag them together, hold down Ctrl (Windows) or Command (Mac OS) as you click. In the Timeline window, the file layers will stack in the order in which you select them, with the file you click first as Layer 1, and so on.

4 If necessary, select the files in the layer stack and drag them so that they are in the following order:

• Layer 1: LineCircles.mov

• Layer 2: Rings.mov

• Layer 3: DotCircles.mov

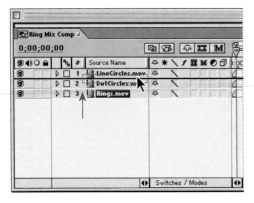

5 Move the current-time marker to 3:00 so that you can see more images in the Composition window.

6 In the Timeline window, click the Switches/Modes bar to open the Modes panel (if it is not already open). Or, choose Panels > Modes from the Timeline window menu.

7 In the Mode pop-up menus for Layer 1 and Layer 2, select Screen. Leave Layer 3 in Normal transfer mode.

Note: You can also select a layer and choose Layer > Transfer Mode > Screen to set the transfer mode.

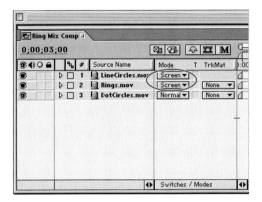

The Screen transfer mode creates a blended appearance among the three layers, visually uniting them.

Animating the rings opacity

In this procedure, you'll set a simple dissolve-in for one of the layers.

1 In the Timeline window, select the DotCircles.mov (Layer 3) and press T to open its Opacity property.

2 With the current-time marker at 0:00, type or scrub **0%** for the Opacity value and then click the stopwatch to set a keyframe.

3 Move the current-time marker to 1:00, and scrub or type **100%** for the Opacity value to create a second keyframe.

4 Press T to hide the Opacity property.

5 Preview the animation and then save the project.

The DotCircles.mov layer now dissolves-in during the first second of the composition.

Setting opacity to create randomly flashing layers

Next, you'll experiment with the opacity of the other two layers. Rather than entering specific values, you'll randomly change Opacity values and add keyframes so that the layers appear to flash in and out of view at irregular intervals. Exactly when and how large those changes are is up to you.

1 In the Timeline window, select Rings.mov (Layer 2) and press T to reveal its Opacity property.

2 Move the current-time marker to 0:00, and then click the stopwatch for Layer 2 to set a keyframe at 100% opacity.

3 Move the current-time marker forward approximately 10 to 30 frames (the exact position is not important) and press Alt + Shift + T (Windows) or Option + T (Mac OS) to set a keyframe. Or, you can set the keyframe by clicking the keyframe check box in the A/V Features panel.

4 Continue to set Layer 2 Opacity keyframes about every 10-30 frames (all at 100%) until you reach the end of the composition. Precise timing is not important because you want the results to appear to be random, not regular.

5 Click the arrow to expand the Opacity property so that you can see the Value and Velocity graphs. Then drag one of the square dots on the Value graph downward to lower the Opacity value. The Info palette shows the changing numerical value as you drag.

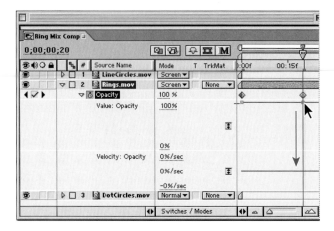

Note: The Opacity value in the Timeline window changes only if the current-time marker is lined up with the keyframe you drag.

6 Continue to drag other keyframe values on the Value graph so that some are at 100%, some at 0%, and a few are other values. The final result should be random flashing in and out, so big changes in adjacent keyframes create dramatic results.

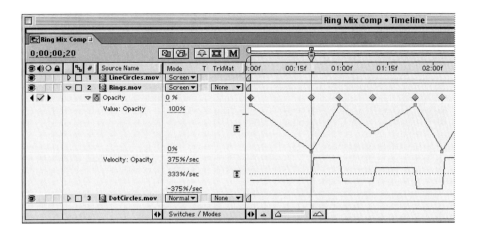

7 When you finish adjusting the graph, preview the animation. If you are not satisfied with the results, change the values as needed and preview again. Then collapse the Opacity property and save the project.

8 Repeat this entire process (steps 1 through 7) for LineCircles.mov to create a different set of randomly flashing Opacity keyframes on Layer 1.

Now both the Rings.mov and LineCircles.mov elements flash as the animation plays.

Rendering the Ring Mix Comp

You have completed uniting the ring and circles elements in the Ring Mix Comp so now you'll render the composition. This composition renders in just a few minutes on an average system.

1 Close the Composition and Timeline windows for the Ring Mix Comp.

2 In the Project window, select the Ring Mix Comp, and then choose Composition > Make Movie.

3 In the Output Movie To dialog box, type **RingMix.mov** as the name and specify the _mov folder in the AE_CIB job folder. Then click Save.

4 In the Render Queue, click the underlined words *Current Settings* to open the Render Settings dialog box, and then set the following options:

- In Quality, select Best.

- In Resolution, select Full.

- In Time Span, select Length of Comp.

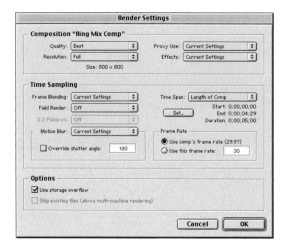

5 Click OK to return to the Render Queue.

6 In the Output Module pop-up menu, choose Custom to open the Output Module Settings dialog box, and then set the following options:

- In Format, select QuickTime Movie.

- Select Import into Project When Done.

- Click Format Options.

7 In the Compression Settings dialog box, select Animation and Millions of Colors+. Make sure that the slider is set to Best, and then click OK.

8 In the Output Module Settings dialog box, review the settings: Channels is now set to RGB + Alpha, indicating that this item will be rendered with an alpha channel. Depth is set to Millions of Colors+, and Color is set as Premultiplied (Matted). When you are ready to continue, click OK.

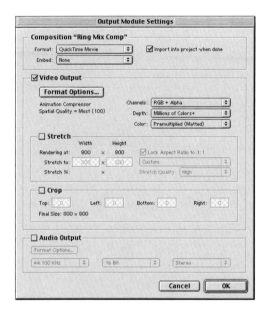

9 Save the project one more time, and then click Render.

10 When the render is complete, close the Render Queue and double-click RingMix.mov in the Project window to view the rendered movie. Or, press Alt + double-click (Windows) or Option + double-click (Mac OS) to open it in the After Effects Player so that you can change the magnification and window size. When you are ready to continue, close the player.

Note: The playback may appear jerky or have slight pauses. This is not a problem with your work or with the rendering process. Rather, this indicates that the system is not able to play back such a high-data-rate movie in real time. The rendered movie is OK.

11 In the Project window, drag the RingMix.mov into the mov folder.

If you need to make any changes, reopen the Ring Mix Comp and make those adjustments. Remember to save those changes and render the composition again, using the same render settings.

Creating a second composition

In the previous section, you combined the three circle elements into one movie. You'll use the rendered movie as a layer in the final 2D composite, which you start building now. In this composition, you'll combine all your 2D elements to create the composite required for the final piece. You'll also set up the timing, effects, and interactions between these elements in 2D space.

Your first task is to create the composition.

1 In the Project window, click the New Composition icon (▣) at the bottom of the window to create a new composition.

2 In the Composition Settings dialog box, type **2D Composite Comp** for the name.

3 In Preset, select NTSC D1 Square Pix, 720 x 540 to automatically set the Width, Height, Pixel Aspect Ratio, and Frame Rate to the appropriate selections.

4 In Resolution, select Full. Or, if required by your system, select Half or lower.

5 In Duration, type **900** to specify nine seconds, and then click OK.

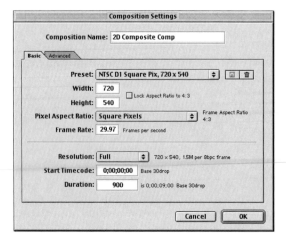

Placing the elements in the composition layer stack

Now you'll place the imported elements into this composition. You'll adjust the stacking order, duplicate one of the layers, and set layer In Points.

1 Move the current-time marker to 0:00.

2 In the mov files folder in the Project window, select all the movies *except* the DotCircles.mov, LineCircles.mov, and Rings.mov, and drag them directly into the Timeline window. You should have six movie layers. Each layer is automatically centered in the Composition window.

3 In the audio files folder in the Project window, select the Soundtrack.aif and drag it to the Timeline window.

4 In the Timeline window, drag individual layers up or down in the layer stack to arrange them in the following stacking order:

- Layer 1: Numbers.mov

- Layer 2: HexOutlines.mov

- Layer 3: Hexagons.mov

- Layer 4: RingMix.mov

- Layer 5: Starburst.mov

- Layer 6: LightRays.mov

- Layer 7: Soundtrack.aif

5 Select the RingMix.mov and choose Edit > Duplicate. You now see two RingMix.mov layers (Layers 4 and 5) in the layer stack.

Changing the layer In points

Next, you'll set each of the layer In points to establish the order in which the layers appear in the composition.

1 If the In/Out panel is not open in the Timeline window, click the double-arrow (◆▶) button to open those panels.

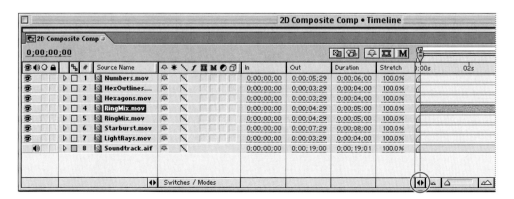

2 For RingMix.mov (Layers 4 and 5), set the In point at 0:17 by doing one of the following:

• Select both layers, move the current-time marker to 0:17, and press [(left bracket). The layer duration bar shifts on the timeline to start at frame 17.

• For Layer 4, click the underlined In value in the In/Out panel to open the Layer In Time dialog box, type **17**, and click OK. Repeat this step for the Layer 5 In value.

• Click the solid area (not the ends) of each layer duration bar and drag until the Info palette displays 0:17 as the In point.

3 Using any method described in step 2, set the LightRays.mov (Layer 7) In point at 1:06.

4 Set the HexOutlines.mov (Layer 2) and Hexagons.mov (Layer 3) In points at 4:02.

5 Leaving the Numbers.mov (Layer 1), Starburst.mov (Layer 6), and Soundtrack.aif (Layer 8) In points at 0:00, preview the composite. Then close the In/Out panel and save the project.

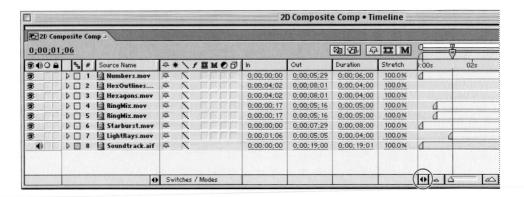

All the layers are set to enter the composition at the correct times.

Adjusting opacity and trimming a layer

You'll set keyframes for the Hexagons.mov layer so that it fades in and out, interacting with the HexOutlines.mov layer above it. You'll trim the layer to hide all frames beyond the 8-second mark because the Opacity value is 0 (zero) then and no longer changes.

1 In the Timeline window, select the Hexagons.mov layer (Layer 3) and press T to reveal its Opacity property.

2 Press I to move the current-time marker to the layer In point (4:02).

3 Scrub or type **0%** as the Layer 3 Opacity value. Click the stopwatch to set a keyframe.

4 Set three more Opacity keyframes for Layer 3 at the following times and values:

- At 5:17, set 19%.

- At 6:16, set 100%.

- At 7:21, set 0%.

5 With the current-time marker still at 7:21, press Alt +] (right bracket) (Windows) or Option +] (right bracket) (Mac OS) to set the Layer 3 Out point. Then press T to close the Opacity property.

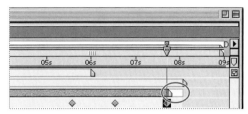

Area of suppressed (trimmed) footage

6 Move the current-time marker to 4:00 and press B to begin the work area at 4 seconds.

7 Move the current-time marker to 8:00 and press N to end the work area at 8 seconds.

8 Preview the animation and save the project.

The Hexagons.mov layer now gradually dissolves in over two-and-a-half seconds and then fades as the hexagons move out of the frame. Because you trimmed Layer 3 at 7:21 (when the layer opacity is zero), the duration bar more accurately represents the time at which this layer appears in the composition.

Trimming and moving duration bars

There are two types of keyboard shortcuts that use the bracket keys. Both types change the In and Out points of the selected layer. However, the difference between the two types is significant.

If you press only a bracket key ([ ) or ( ]), you move the layer—and its keyframes—in time. The duration bar of the selected layer shifts so that the In or Out point aligns with the position of the current-time marker. The length of the duration bar does not change. You can also drag a duration bar by the shaded area (not the end) to manually change the In and Out points.

In contrast, if you also press Alt (Windows) or Option (Mac OS) and a bracket key, you trim the layer. The duration bar doesn't move but it becomes shorter or longer in length. All the keyframes also remain in their original time positions. Trimming hides the portion of the layer that is either before or after the current-time marker position so you don't see that part of the layer when you view the composition. You can also drag either end of the duration bar to manually trim the layer. Because trimmed footage is only hidden, not removed, you can restore it later, even after you save and close the project. For more information, see "Understanding trimming" and related topics in After Effects online Help.

Applying the Tint effect

Currently, all the movie layers are white shapes over the black background color. You'll now add color to each of these layers by applying the Tint effect. You'll apply the effect to one layer and then copy and paste that effect into other layers that use the same effect settings.

1 Move the current-time marker to about 2:00 so that you can see the results of the effects as they are applied.

2 In the Timeline window, select the Numbers.mov layer (Layer 1).

3 Choose Effect > Image Control > Tint. The Effect Controls window appears.

4 In the Effect Controls window, click the Map White To option color swatch and use the color picker to select an orange-yellow color. The color value used in the sample movie has values of: R=207 (81%), G=153 (60%), and B=0 (0%).

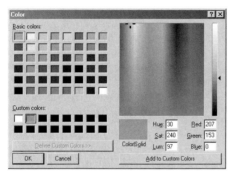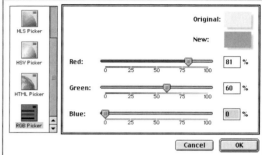

Windows color picker (left) and Mac OS color picker for RGB (right)

5 In the Effect Controls window, in Amount to Tint, scrub or type **60%**. The Numbers.mov layer appears in the selected color.

Copying and pasting an effect, with variations

Now you'll copy and paste this effect and its settings onto a few other layers, and then switch the color for some of them.

1 In the Effect Controls window, click the word *Tint* to select the effect, and then press Ctrl + C (Windows) or Command + C (Mac OS) to copy it.

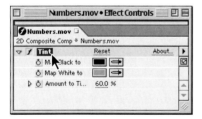

2 Select the top RingMix.mov layer (Layer 4) and press Ctrl + V (Windows) or Command + V (Mac OS) to paste the effect onto this layer. A RingMix.mov tab appears in the Effect Controls window and the RingMix.mov layer changes color.

3 In the Timeline window, select the following layers one at a time and choose Edit > Paste to apply the Tint effect to each one: RingMix.mov (Layer 5), Starburst.mov (Layer 6), and LightRays.mov (Layer 7).

4 Save the project and preview the animation. If necessary, reset the work area to preview only the frames where the applied Tint effect appears—that is, from about 0:00 to 5:00.

5 Move the current-time marker to 6:00.

6 Select the HexOutlines.mov and paste the Tint effect. A HexOutlines.mov tab appears in the Effect Controls window.

7 Click the Map White To color swatch, and then choose a bright green color in the color picker. The color value used in the sample movie had RGB values of: R=117 (46%), G=184 (72%), and B=10 (4%). Leave the Amount to Tint value at 60%. The HexOutlines.mov changes to green.

8 In the Effect Controls window, click the word *Tint* to select the effect and choose Edit > Copy.

9 Select the Hexagons.mov and choose Edit > Paste. The solid hexagons become green.

10 With the Hexagons.mov layer still selected, press F3 to open the Tint controls (if they are not already open). In Map White To, change the color to a darker green, using R=61 (24%), G=72 (28%), and B=10 (4%). Then in Amount to Tint, scrub or type **100%**.

11 Preview the animation and save the project.

Building your elements in black and white gives you more flexibility at later stages of the workflow. You can use the Tint effect to apply any color, even sampling colors from other layers in the composition with the eyedropper. This makes colorizing black and white elements incredibly simple.

Applying blur effects

Next you'll apply blur effects to two of the layers. You'll use the Channel Blur effect to blur the edges of the hexagons (Hexagons.mov), and the Gaussian Blur effect to give just a hint of softness to Layer 4 (the first of the two RingMix.mov layers). It is important that the Tint effect comes after the Channel Blur to achieve the desired effect. You can change the order of effects just as you would arrange layers in the layer stack.

1 Move the current-time marker to about 6:00, select Hexagons.mov (Layer 3) in the Timeline window, and choose Effect > Blur & Sharpen > Channel Blur. The Effect Controls window lists the Channel Blur effect below the Tint effect.

2 Scrub or type to set the Alpha Blurriness at **24** and leave all other options at their default settings. The edges of the hexagons soften as the blur is applied to the alpha channel of this layer.

3 In the Effect Controls window, select Channel Blur (click the effect name) and drag it above the Tint effect. You can now see the results of the Channel Blur in the Composition window.

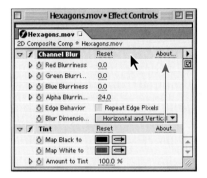

4 Move the current-time marker to about 4:00 so that you can see the results as you work.

5 Select the upper RingMix.mov layer (Layer 4), and choose Effect > Blur & Sharpen > Gaussian Blur.

6 In the Effect Controls window under Gaussian Blur, set Blurriness to 3.2. Leave the Blur Dimensions set to Horizontal and Vertical. This effect is subtle, but adds a slight softness to the layer.

7 Close the Effect Controls window, and save the project.

If you cannot see the Gaussian Blur effect, try setting your layer Quality switches to Best and toggle the effect off and on with the Show Effect (*f*) switch in the Effect Controls window. When you are ready to continue, be sure to reset the Quality switches to Draft and leave the Show Effect switch on.

For more information about blur effects, see After Effects online Help. See also the effects PDF files on your After Effects 5.0 application CD and on the Adobe Web site in the In Depth pages about After Effects 5.0.

Setting layer transfer modes

With all the necessary effects applied to your layers, you'll add a finishing touch: applying transfer modes to four of the layers in the composite. The layers then interact and affect one another, based upon the lightness and color values of each. As the layers move and change, so do the effects of the transfer modes.

1 Set the current time to about 2:00 so that you can see the results as you work, and make sure that the Modes panel in the Timeline window is open. Then apply transfer modes to individual layers as follows:

• For Numbers.mov (Layer 1), select Color Dodge. A warm glow appears where the Numbers.mov and the RingMix.mov layers overlap.

• For the upper RingMix.mov (Layer 4), select Soft Light.

• For the lower RingMix.mov (Layer 5), select Screen. The warm gold color from the Numbers.mov and the Starburst.mov elements leaks through to the RingMix.mov layers.

2 Move the current-time marker to about 5:15, after the hexagons start appearing in the composition.

3 For HexOutlines.mov (Layer 2), select Screen mode. The gold color of the Numbers.mov and the Starburst.mov show through the hexagons where the layers overlap.

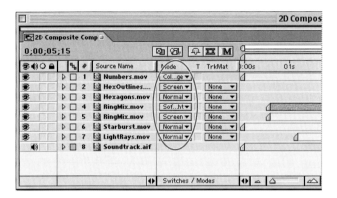

4 Preview the composition, noticing the way that the layers now interact. Then save the project.

Note: *If the amount of available RAM makes previewing difficult, you can preview this composition in sections. To do this, set a work area for the first half of the composition; then build and watch that preview. Then set a work area for the second half of the composition and preview.*

For more information about individual transfer modes, see "Specifying a layer mode" in After Effects online Help.

You won't render this composition now. Instead you'll import this project into the final project in a later lesson. For now, check your final preview against the sample movie you watched at the beginning of this lesson. Make any necessary adjustments, and save the project again.

You have now completed lesson 7.

Lesson 8

8 | Beginning the 3D Composite

Sophisticated camera work with advanced technical capabilities requires sophisticated software when you work with the captured footage. Adobe After Effects can do the job—and so can you, with a little careful planning and many skills you've already mastered as you've worked through this book.

In this lesson you'll learn to do the following:

- Import and use camera footage and data

- Use various 3D views

- Animate a still image (hexagon) in 3D space

- Add and use composition-time markers

- Apply Fast Blur and Echo effects

- Use the Hue/Saturation effect to color-correct a layer

- Use the Linear Wipe effect to reveal a layer

In this chapter, you'll work primarily with live-action footage of an actress, captured by a motion-control camera. You'll add a virtual camera layer to the composition and apply settings to match those of the actual camera used to film the footage. By re-creating the physical camera movement in the camera layer, you can place the actress in a virtual world so that later you can surround her with graphics. Fasten your seat belts…here you go.

This lesson takes about one hour to complete.

Getting started

Make sure that the following files are in the AE_CIB job folder on your hard drive, or copy them from the *After Effects Classroom in a Book* CD now.

- In the _mov folder: Girl_Alpha.mov

- In the _psd folder: Hexagon01.psd

- In the _txt folder: CameraData.txt

- In the Sample_Movies folder: 3DComp08_final.mov from the Sample_Movies/Lesson08 folder on the CD

- In the Finished_Projects folder: 3DComposite08_finished.aep

Refer to "Note: (Windows only) If you do not see the Prefs file, be sure that the Show all files option is selected for Hidden files on the View tab of the Folder Options dialog box." on page 4 for the procedure, if necessary.

Open and play the sample movie 3DComp08_final.mov, to see the work you'll create in Lesson 8. When you finish, quit the QuickTime player. You can delete the sample movie now to save storage space, if necessary.

You'll do all the work for both Lesson 8 and Lesson 9 within a single project. Your first task is to create that project.

1 Start After Effects 5.0, if it is not already running.

2 Choose File > New > New Project.

3 Choose File > Save As.

4 In the Save Project As dialog box, find and open the _aep folder in your AE_CIB job folder.

5 Type **3DComposite08_work.aep** to name the project, and then click Save.

You'll build several compositions within this project, adding the elements necessary for the 3D-compositing portion of the final animation.

Importing and organizing the source files

You need to import two footage files for this lesson.

1 Choose File > Import > Multiple Files.

2 Open the _mov folder inside your AE_CIB job folder, select the Girl_Alpha.mov, and click Open (Windows) or Import (Mac OS).

3 Open the _psd folder inside your AE_CIB job folder, select the Hexagon01.psd file, and click Open (Windows) or Import (Mac OS).

4 In the Interpret Footage dialog box, make sure that Straight – Unmatted is selected, and click OK.

5 In the Import Multiple Files dialog box, click Done.

6 Choose File > New > New Folder to create a new folder in the Project window.

7 Type **mov files** to name the folder, and then drag the Girl_Alpha.mov file into the mov files folder.

8 Create another new folder and type **psd files** as the name. Then drag the Hexagon01.psd file into this folder.

9 Click the arrows to expand both folders so that you can see the files inside.

Creating a composition

To begin building the final 3D composite, you create a new composition for the 3D composite.

1 Choose Composition > New Composition.

2 In the Composition Settings dialog box, type **3D Composite Comp** in Composition Name.

3 In Preset, select NTSC D1 Square Pix, 720 x 540 to automatically enter the settings for Width, Height, Pixel Aspect Ratio, and Frame Rate.

4 (Optional) In Resolution, select Half or lower, as needed for your system.

5 In Duration, type **1100**, to specify 11 seconds, and then click OK.

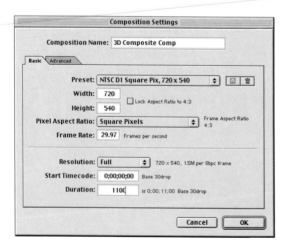

Adding the Girl_Alpha.mov

Now you'll add the Girl_Alpha.mov to the composition and look at the footage.

1 If necessary, choose Composition > Background Color, select black, and click OK.

2 Move the current-time marker to 0:00, if it is not already there.

3 In the Project window, select the Girl_Alpha.mov and drag it into the Timeline window to automatically center it in the Composition window.

4 At the bottom of the Composition window, click the alpha channel button to see the alpha matte for this layer.

Image in composition frame (left) with alpha channel button selected (right) in Composition window

5 In the Time Controls palette, use the Jog or Shuttle controls to scrub through the composition. The matte matches the footage throughout the composition.

6 In the Composition window, deselect the alpha channel button.

7 Press 0 on the numeric keypad to create a RAM preview of this layer. If necessary, lower the resolution so that you can preview all the frames. When you are ready to continue, stop the preview.

In this movie, the alpha channel designates the area of transparency around the actress. The alpha channel was created using keying effects and masking tools to remove the green screen placed behind her during filming.

Notice the camera movement in this footage, which was recorded using a motion-control camera. This camera physically swoops down and moves closer to the actress as it films. In your project, the goal is to re-create this camera movement with an After Effects camera, using data taken from the motion-control camera. By matching the camera move, you can re-create the shot, building a 3D environment around the actress. It is essential that you precisely match the original camera move so that the perspective in the final composite looks believable.

Keying the Girl_Alpha.mov

Many keying effects and matte tools are available in the Production Bundle version of After Effects and in plug-in packages for After Effects available through other developers. If you want to experiment with those tools and try keying an element yourself, you use a slightly different procedure when you import the file that ignores the existing alpha.

To ignore existing alpha:

1. In the Project window, select the footage item you want to key (such as the Girl_Alpha.mov).

2. Choose File > Interpret Footage > Main.

3. At the top of the Interpret Footage dialog box, under Alpha, select Ignore, and click OK.

When you place the Girl_Alpha.mov in a composition, you see the green screen behind the actress in the Composition window. The floor, stands, and other objects that were in the stage area have already been masked out for you. You can then use your keying effects and matte tools to key the file yourself. For information about using these features, see "Using keying effects," "Keying effects," "Matte Tools effects," and related subtopics in After Effects online Help.

Creating the background layer

You'll add a solid layer to act as the composition background. Later, you'll apply effects to this layer.

1 Make sure that the current-time marker is at 0:00.

2 Choose Layer > New > Solid.

3 For the Name, type **Background Solid,** and set the remaining settings as follows:

• In Width, type **720.**

• In Height, type **540.**

- Under Color, select white.

4 Click OK. The white solid fills the Composition frame and a Background Solid layer appears in the Timeline window.

Applying effects to the background

The solid layer is uniformly white at this point. You'll change that by adding a radial gradient with a small amount of random scatter.

1 Select the Background Solid layer and choose Effect > Render > Ramp. The Effect Controls window opens with the Ramp effect selected.

Note: If you don't see the gradient in the composition, make sure that you deselected the alpha channel button at the bottom of the Composition window.

2 For Start of Ramp, click the cross hairs (+) and drag to the center of the Composition window. Or, type **360, 270** as the coordinates so that the Start Color begins at the center of the solid.

3 For Start Color, click the swatch and use the color picker to select a dark green color. The color values used in the sample are: R=94 (37%), G=120 (47%), and B=28 (11%).

4 For End of Ramp, type **360, 670** as the outer edge of the gradient End Color. This sets the gradient ends outside the composition frame.

5 For End Color, use the color picker to select black.

6 In Ramp Shape, select Radial Ramp.

7 In Ramp Scatter, type or scrub **8** to add a little noise to the gradient.

8 Leave the setting for Blend with Original at the default value, 0.

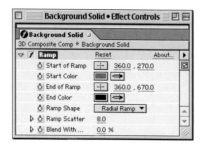 

Effect Controls settings for Ramp effect (left) and results in Composition window (right)

9 With the Background Solid layer still selected, choose Effect > Stylize > Noise.

10 In the Effect Controls window, in Amount of Noise, scrub or type **2%**. Leave the Clip Result Values and Use Clip Noise options selected.

Reducing the opacity of the solid

Next, you'll increase the transparency of the solid layer.

1 In the Timeline window, select the Background Solid layer and press T to reveal the Opacity property.

2 Scrub or type **60%** as the Opacity value.

3 Press T again to hide the Opacity property.

4 In the Timeline window layer stack, drag the Background Solid layer below the Girl_Alpha.mov, and then save the project.

You have completed your work with the Background Solid layer. It will remain in the background throughout this composition.

Working with cameras

In this section, you'll create the camera within the same composition as the previous section. In these procedures, you'll adjust settings and create relationships in a virtual three-dimensional world.

Your first task is to add a camera layer to that composition.

1 With the current-time marker at 0:00, choose Layer > New > Camera to create a new camera layer.

2 In the Camera Settings dialog box, in Preset, select 35mm. Leave Camera 1 as the camera name, and click OK.

Note: An error message may appear, telling you that there are no 3D layers in your composition. Click OK to ignore this message because you'll make some three-dimensional layers later in this lesson. The Camera 1 layer now appears in the Timeline window.

3 Choose View > Switch 3D View > Active Camera to select the camera view for the Composition window, if it's not already selected.

You used a camera earlier, in Lesson 6, when you created the tunnel-like rings of spinning hexagons. In that case, the camera shows the view as if the viewer is traveling straight through the center of the hexagon tunnel. In this lesson, the view is more complex because you'll make the camera swoop in along an arc-like path through three-dimensional space, mimicking the movement of the actual camera that filmed the footage of the actress. This automatically makes the elements you lay out in 3D space appear to change size and orientation as the camera layer moves. As a result, the various layers appear exactly as they would if they were actual objects captured on film by the real camera.

Adding a null object and a parent-layer relationship

Next, you'll link the camera to a null object, which will help translate some of the original motion-control data that you'll import in a later procedure.

1 With the current-time marker still at 0:00, choose Layer > New > Null Object to add a null object to the composition.

2 In the Timeline window, open the Switches panel, and on the Null 1 layer select the 3D Layer switch (⬚).

3 With the Null 1 layer selected, press P to reveal the Position property for the null object.

4 Scrub or type the following Position coordinates: **149.1, 44.0, 83.7.**

Note: These coordinates control the position of the camera and, therefore, the appearance of the rendered composition. It is important to be precise when entering these values.

5 Press S to reveal the Scale property for the null object.

6 Scrub or type **474%** as the Scale value, and then press S to close the Scale property.

7 In the A/V Features panel for the Null 1 layer, click the Video switch (⊛) to turn off its video.

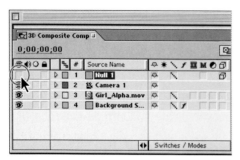

Turning off the Video switch in the A/V Features panel

8 In the Parent panel, drag the pick whip (◎) for the Camera 1 layer to the Null 1 layer so that a dark rectangle appears around the layer name. Then save the project.

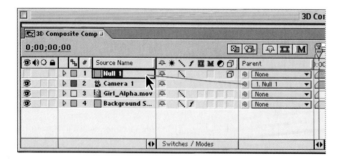

Note: If the Parent panel is hidden, right-click (Windows) or Option + click (Mac OS) any panel heading in the Timeline window to open the contextual menu and choose Panels > Parent. Or, click the arrow above the vertical scroll bar and use the Timeline window menu.

The pop-up menu in the Camera 1 layer Parent panel lists Null 1 as the parent layer, reflecting the new relationship between these layers. The null object now acts as a parent to the camera so that the camera will take on any changes you apply to the null object. For more information about parenting, see "Understanding parent layers" and related topics in After Effects online Help.

Note: Because of this parent-child relationship between the layers, the Scale value of the null object increases the scale of the camera. In this context, scale refers to all the attributes of the After Effects camera: the camera move, the pan, the tilt—the entire world of the camera.

Importing the camera data

Now it's time to import the data from the motion-control camera and apply it to the camera layer in the composition. This data includes information regarding all aspects of the camera and its movement. The information has been saved in a text file, which you copied from the CD at the beginning of this lesson. You'll now open that file and copy the data into the current composition.

1 On your desktop Explorer (Windows) or Finder (Mac OS), open your AE_CIB job folder and double-click the CameraData.txt file. The file opens in your default text-editing application, such as Notepad or WordPad (Windows) or SimpleText (Mac OS).

2 Select all the text in the file, being careful to include everything.

3 Press Ctrl + C (Windows) or Command + C (Mac OS) to copy all the text.

4 In After Effects, make sure that the current-time marker is set to 0:00, select the Camera 1 layer, and press Ctrl + V (Windows) or Command + V (Mac OS) to paste all the data into the layer. As you paste, keyframes are added to the Camera 1 layer.

5 In the After Effects Timeline window, select the Camera 1 layer and press U to reveal all its keyframed properties. You now see the keyframes that control the animation of the Point of Interest, Position, and Z Rotation for this camera. All of this information was taken from the actual motion-control camera data and stored in the text file.

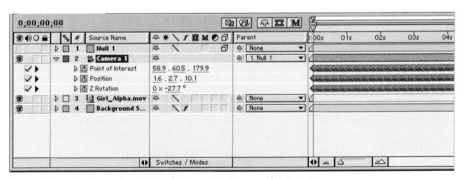

Camera layer keyframes for Points of Interest, Position, and Z Rotation

6 Press U again to hide all keyframed properties.

7 In your text-editing application, close the text file and quit the application.

Note: *Importing motion-control camera data is one of the more sophisticated After Effects features. It requires a great deal of research and experimentation with each camera used.*

Importing Motion-Control Camera Data—An Advanced Topic

After Effects can import data from motion-control camera equipment. Doing so requires research and experimentation with your particular motion-control camera system. Although this feature can be incredibly useful to those who work regularly with motion-control cameras, it should not be attempted by the inexperienced. It is much more difficult than importing camera data from a 3D software application.

The difficulty is not importing the data into After Effects. The tricky part is preparing the raw camera data. Motion-control systems usually generate camera-movement data as text files with columns of data. You can use spreadsheet software to manipulate the data before copying the motion data to the After Effects camera.

If your production requires the use of a motion-control camera and you plan to import the camera data into After Effects, consider the following issues both before and during production.

Recording camera stats: You need these statistics in order to match the After Effects camera to the motion-control camera. These include (but are not limited to): Film size, Depth of Field, Angle of View, Lens Focal Length, Focal Distance, Aperture, F-stop, Point of Interest, Position, and Rotation.

Measuring the scene: Take accurate measurements of the relationship between camera and objects recorded, noting the zero coordinates. Shoot a registration pass using an object of exactly known size and position. This gives you a reference object that you can use to help align the After Effects camera.

Accounting for lens distortion: This is particularly important if the subject being filmed approaches the edges of the frame when you shoot. Lens distortion can cause misalignment with the CGI footage, which then requires correction. You can use the After Effects Optics Compensation filter to add or remove lens distortion from your footage.

It's best to use only a prime lens. Zoom lenses are not recommended because it is more difficult to measure and match the focal length and distortion of a zoom lens.

Transferring film footage to video: Use 100% speed and full frame when you transfer film footage to video. Changes to the footage (such as cropping, scaling, and aspect ratio) often occur when footage is transferred from film to video. Again, for this reason it is important to perform tests that help you make these adjustments and which take into account these inconsistencies.

Giving yourself lots of time for testing: Even those who are most experienced in this area shoot multiple tests and make multiple attempts at matching the data before the final shoot. You can safely assume that this type of experimentation is required in order to get it right because every system, camera, and lens is different.

Viewing the results of the imported camera data

Next, you'll inspect the results of importing the data by examining the composition from different three-dimensional points of view.

As you look at the views, it's important to know that the word *frame* in this context refers to the field of vision for the camera—comparable to what you see when you look through the viewfinder of a physical camera. The camera focuses on the *point of interest;* by default, the point of interest is the center of the frame area.

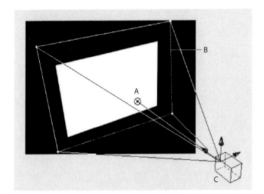

A. Point of Interest B. Frame C. Camera

Note: *Choose View > Switch 3D View, and make sure that the shortcut for Front is F10, for Top is F11, and for Active Camera is F12. If not, reset the shortcuts now. Refer to the procedure in "Setting and using 3D-views shortcuts" on page 218, if necessary.*

1 In the Composition window, select Front (or press F10) in the view pop-up menu. If the current-time marker is still set to 0:00 and the Camera 1 layer is still selected, the wireframe box representing the camera appears in the upper left area of the composition frame.

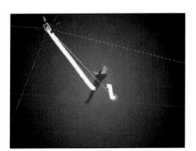

2 In the Composition window, select Top view (or press F11) and select 25% (or lower) magnification. The wireframe display represents the view of the camera, including its frame and point of interest, and the camera itself. A row of *X*'s (so close together they look like a thick black line) illustrates the position keyframes on the pasteboard.

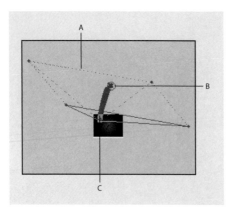

*A. Point of Interest **B**. Frame **C**. Camera*

3 On the Time Controls palette, drag the Jog or Shuttle (⟨▭ ▭▶⟩) control to scrub along the timeline, and watch the camera travel along this path.

4 In the Composition window view pop-up menu, select Right view, and then continue scrubbing along the timeline. You can see the camera moving toward the Girl_Alpha.mov layer as it zooms in to the point of interest: the woman's hands.

5 Select Active Camera view (or press F12) and drag the Jog or Shuttle controls in the Time Controls palette to preview the movement. The view appears to move closer and closer to the actress's hands.

By applying the motion-control camera data to the camera layer in this composition, you have re-created the same movement for the After Effects camera in this composition. As a result, you are now able to construct a 3D environment around the actress with accurate perspective.

Viewing 3D layers

In the world of 3D After Effects, what you see in the composition frame is not necessarily how your composition will look. Only Active Camera view accurately displays the image as it will be rendered. The other orthogonal (right-angle) views show you the relative positions of layers in 3D space, as if you were looking at the set of a theatrical production from different points of view: overhead, off in the stage wings, and so forth. What's important in the end is what appears in the camera field of vision—what the audience sees. The other views are available simply to help you visualize the relationships among the various layers, especially the relationship to the camera.

As the camera-path views in the previous steps show, the layers are positioned on the pasteboard, far from the composition frame. The position of the layers in relation to the composition frame is somewhat irrelevant. It is possible to reposition your 3D layers within a view so that they fall within the composition frame. You do this by deselecting all layers, setting the view to any except the Active Camera view, and using the track X,Y or the track Z camera tools. The layers appear within the composition frame from the selected point of view. Some layers are represented in full color and others as gray lines, depending on their positions in 3D space.

Adding the hexagon layer

Next you add the hexagon element, rotating and positioning it in 3D space so that it resembles a platform on which the actress stands.

1 Move the current-time marker to 0:00 and set the Composition window magnification to a convenient level for your monitor size.

2 In the Project window, select the Hexagon01.psd file and drag it to the Timeline window so that it is Layer 1 in the layer stack.

3 In the Switches panel, click the 3D layer switch (⬚) to make the hexagons a 3D layer. The layer disappears in the Composition window.

4 In the Composition window, select Top view (or press F11), and notice where the Hexagon01.psd layer is in relation to the camera. To see this, click the Camera 1 layer to see its path (the condensed line of *X*'s), and then click the Hexagon01.psd layer to see its layer handles. Layer 1 is behind the camera, so it does not appear in Active Camera view.

5 Move the pointer over the blue Z-axis arrow of the Hexagon01.psd layer so that the pointer appears with a small Z. Drag the layer toward the top of the Composition window so that it is positioned in front of (above) the camera. If necessary, reduce the magnification even further (choose View > Zoom Out) to see the pasteboard as you do this.

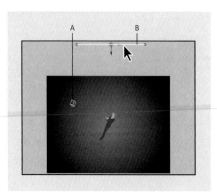

*A. Camera **B**. Hexagon01.psd layer*

6 Select Active Camera view (press F12). The Hexagon01.psd layer now appears in the Active Camera view because it is in front of the camera in 3D space.

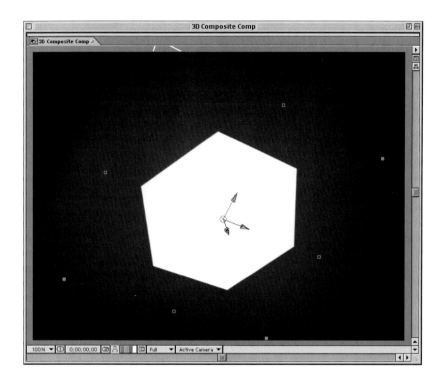

💡 *To confirm which layer is which, select layers in the Timeline window and look for the layer handles in the Composition window. Sometimes you may need to significantly reduce the magnification to find a selected layer on the pasteboard.*

Adding a composition-time marker

Next you'll add a marker to the timeline so that you can easily reference a specific frame in the composition. Then—just for practice—you'll use the shortcut to jump to that frame.

1 In the Timeline window, drag a composition-time marker from the Composition marker bin (▽) to the right of the timeline. Using the Info palette display to see the exact composition-time marker position on the timeline, drag the marker to 2:03.

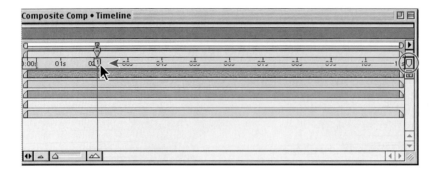

2 Move the current-time marker (▽)—*not* the composition-time marker (◉)—to any point on the timeline except 2:03, if necesssary.

3 Press 1 on the main keyboard (not the numeric keypad). The current-time marker jumps to 2:03, aligned with the composition-time marker.

This 2:03 frame is an important time in this composition because several different animation events take place here. You can use the composition-time marker to jump easily to that frame. You'll have opportunities for more practice with markers in the next lessons. For more information about composition-time markers, see "Using markers" and related topics in After Effects online Help.

Animating the hexagon

Now that the hexagon layer is properly positioned in the camera view, you'll animate the layer so that it tumbles into the composition frame. Then you'll add an effect and a transfer mode to adjust its color.

1 With the current-time marker set to 0:00, select the Hexagon01.psd layer in the Timeline window.

2 Press P to reveal the Position property, and then press Shift + R, Shift + S, and Shift + T to open all the Orientation and Rotation, Scale, and Opacity properties.

3 In Position, scrub or type **184, 91, 170** and click the stopwatch to set a keyframe.

4 In Scale, scrub or type **37%**. (Do not set a Scale keyframe.)

5 With the X Rotation value at 0°, click the X Rotation stopwatch to set a keyframe.

6 In Opacity, scrub or type **30%** to set the value. (Do not set an Opacity keyframe.)

7 Press 1 to jump to the composition-time marker at 2:03, and change the Position coordinates to **414, 461, 911** to set a second Position keyframe.

8 Still at 2:03, change the X Rotation value to **–270°**, being careful to include the minus sign.

9 Press accent grave (`) to close the layer properties.

Because Active Camera view is selected, you see the composition as it will appear after you render it. The Hexagon01.psd layer now animates from its original position, filling the frame and tumbling into place at the actress's feet. At this point, the hexagon does not match the actress's feet exactly. However, you'll trim the girl footage layer later in this lesson, and then the hexagon position will be perfect.

Applying effects and modes to the hexagon

In this short procedure, you'll add an effect and transfer mode to adjust the color of the Hexagon01.psd layer.

1 With the Hexagon01.psd layer still selected, choose Effect > Channel > Invert. The hexagon now appears as black instead of white. Leave the settings at the default values and close the Effect Controls window.

2 Open the Modes panel in the Timeline window, and select Overlay transfer mode for the Hexagon01.psd layer, to blend this layer with the background and with other elements that you'll place behind it in the next lesson.

3 Preview the animation and save the project.

The hexagon now blends a little better with the overall color of the scene.

Adjusting the live-action footage

In this section, you'll work with the Girl_Alpha.mov layer. You'll duplicate the layer and precompose it with the duplicates to help organize your work. Then you'll use various techniques to add a kind of aura to the image of the actress. Finally, you'll adjust the In point (which lines up the actress's feet with the Hexagon01.psd image) and add a transition effect (so that the girl appears to materialize over time, beginning at her feet, as if a fog around her is lifting).

Duplicating and precomposing the Girl_Alpha.mov

You'll duplicate the layer, precompose to group the layers together, and apply effects to add color correction and blurs to the individual layers.

1 In the Timeline window, drag the Girl_Alpha.mov layer to the top of the layer stack.

2 Choose Edit > Duplicate twice to create two more copies of the layer.

3 Select all three Girl_Alpha.mov layers and choose Layer > Pre-compose. The Pre-compose dialog box opens.

4 In New Composition Name, type **Girl Pre-comp**. Leave the second option (Move All Attributes into the New Composition) selected.

5 Select the Open New Composition option (if it's not already selected) so that the tab for this composition opens in the Composition and Timeline windows, and click OK.

6 In the Composition or Timeline window, click the Girl Pre-comp tab to bring it to the front of both windows.

In the Timeline window, the three Girl_Alpha.mov layers are now stacked in the Girl Pre-comp.

Creating a hazy background shape

Your next task is to add effects to the individual Girl_Alpha.mov layers in the Girl Pre-comp. After you apply these effects, After Effects automatically updates in the Girl Pre-comp layer in the 3D Composite Comp to reflect this change.

1 In the Timeline window for the Girl Pre-comp, select the first Girl_Alpha.mov layer (Layer 1).

2 Choose Effect > Blur & Sharpen > Fast Blur.

3 In the Effect Controls window under Fast Blur, scrub or type **50** for Blurriness. This layer now appears quite blurred. Leave the other settings at their default values.

To better see the results of the effects as they are applied, use the Solo switch (○) in the A/V Features panel. When the Solo switch is on, the Composition window temporarily displays only that layer, so that all the other layer Video switches (☻) are dimmed. When you finish viewing the single layer, click the Solo switch again to turn it off.

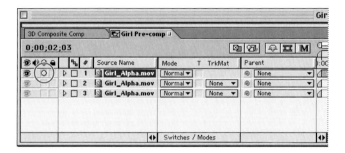

4 In the Timeline window Modes panel, select the Overlay transfer mode for Layer 1.

5 Press T to open the Opacity property and scrub or type **80%**.

6 Press T again to hide the Opacity property, and then save the project.

The blurred layer blends with the two layers behind it, creating a slight haze around the actress.

Correcting color with the Hue/Saturation effect

Small changes in the color can help you coordinate elements in your compositions. You'll apply the Hue/Saturation effect now, which helps you control these refinements.

1 In the Timeline window, select Layer 2.

2 Choose Effect > Adjust > Hue/Saturation.

3 In the Effect Controls window under Hue/Saturation, scrub or type to set the following values:

• In Master Hue, set **10°**.

• In Master Saturation, set **–20**, being careful to make the number negative.

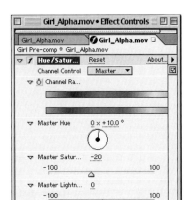

This effect applies a subtle color correction to Layer 2, reducing the red values.

💡 *You can see the change by clicking the Hue/Saturation effect switch (ƒ)in the Effect Controls window to toggle the effect off and on. As you toggle, watch the Composition window to see how the effect changes the image colors.*

Applying the Echo effect

In After Effects, you can add motion blur only to animated layers in a composition; you cannot add it to movement within video footage. However, you can simulate motion blur in video footage by applying the Echo effect to a layer. This effect can display several previous frames from the footage along with the current frame. Because those frames can be progressively muted, the results resemble a motion blur.

Note: *The order in which effects appear is important in achieving the desire result here—the Echo must come before the Fast Blur effect in the Effect Controls window.*

1 In the Timeline window, select Layer 3.

2 Choose Effect > Time > Echo.

3 In the Effect Controls window, make the following changes:

• In Echo Time (seconds), scrub or type **–0.25**, to specify the amount of time between echoes.

• In Number of Echoes, scrub or type **10**, so that 10 frames combine to produce the echo effect.

• Leave the Starting Intensity at 1.00 to display the starting frame in the echo sequence at full intensity.

• In Decay, scrub or type **0.70** to set the intensity of the echoes.

• In Echo Operator, select Composite In Back, so that the echoed frames appear behind the original layer.

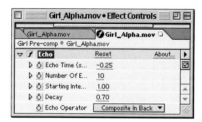

💡 *Try clicking the Solo switch (○) in the A/V Features panel on and off to see the results of this effect more clearly.*

4 With Layer 3 still selected, choose Effect > Blur & Sharpen > Fast Blur.

5 In the Effect Controls window under Fast Blur, scrub or type **10** as the Blurriness value. A slight blur is added to this layer, smoothing the results of the Echo effect.

6 Press T to open the Opacity properties for Layer 3, and scrub or type **50%**. Then press T again.

7 Make sure that the Video switches for all layers are turned on and that all Solo switches are turned off.

8 Click the close box on the Girl Pre-comp tab in either the Composition or Timeline window to close the Girl Pre-comp in those windows. The 3D Composite Comp now reappears in the Composition and Timeline windows. Then save the project.

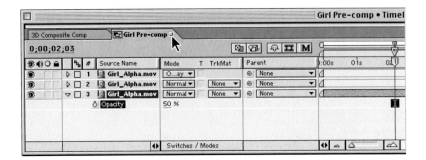

You have now combined the three Girl_Alpha.mov layers and the settings for these layers into one layer in the 3D Composite Comp. The color correction, blur, and echo effects all appear in the Girl Pre-comp layer.

For more information on the Echo effect, see After Effects online Help and the Effects documentation on the *After Effects Classroom in a Book* CD.

Setting the duration, In point, and opacity of a layer

Your next job is to trim, move, and animate the Opacity of the Girl Pre-comp layer.

1 In the Timeline window for the 3D Composite Comp, move the current-time marker to 1:18.

2 Select the Girl Pre-comp layer, and press Alt + [(left bracket) (Windows) or Option + [(Mac OS) to trim the layer In point.

3 Press Home to return the current-time marker to 0:00 and press [(left bracket) to move the layer In point to 0:00. The actress will appear to stand on the hexagon when it falls into place.

4 Move the current-time marker to 2:07, and press T to reveal the Opacity property for the Girl Pre-comp layer.

5 Scrub or type **0%** as the Opacity value and click the stopwatch to set a keyframe.

6 Move the current-time marker to 2:28 and change the Opacity value to 100%. You have now created a 20-frame dissolve for this layer.

Revealing a layer with a transition effect

Finally, you'll apply a transition effect to reveal the Girl Pre-comp layer in the 3D Composite Comp.

1 With the Girl Pre-comp still selected, choose Effect > Transition > Linear Wipe.

2 In the Timeline window, use the Opacity keyframe navigation arrows under the A/V Features panel to move the current-time marker to 2:07. Or press J.

3 In the Effect Controls window under the Linear Wipe effect, set the following:

• In Transition Completion, scrub or type **73%** and click the stopwatch to set a keyframe.

• In Wipe Angle, scrub or type **–160°**, being careful to make the number negative.

• In Feather, scrub or type **50** to add a softness to the edge of the wipe.

Note: At this point, you do not see the footage of the girl because the layer opacity is zero and also because of the 73% Transition Completion value you just set.

4 In the Timeline window, move the current-time marker to 3:17.

5 In the Effect Controls window, in Transition Completion, scrub or type **0%** to set another keyframe and complete the wipe that reveals the Girl Pre-comp layer. Close the Effect Controls window.

6 With the Girls Pre-comp layer selected, press U to see all the keyframes. When you are ready to continue, press U again to hide them, and then deselect all layers.

7 Move the current-time marker to 9:00 and press N to set the end of the work area. Move the current-time marker to 0:00, preview the animation, and then save the project.

The actress is revealed by both a dissolve-in and a linear wipe.

You have now completed Lesson 8, which does not include rendering the 3D Composite Comp. You'll continue working with this composition in Lesson 9 before you render it for use in the final composite.

Lesson 9

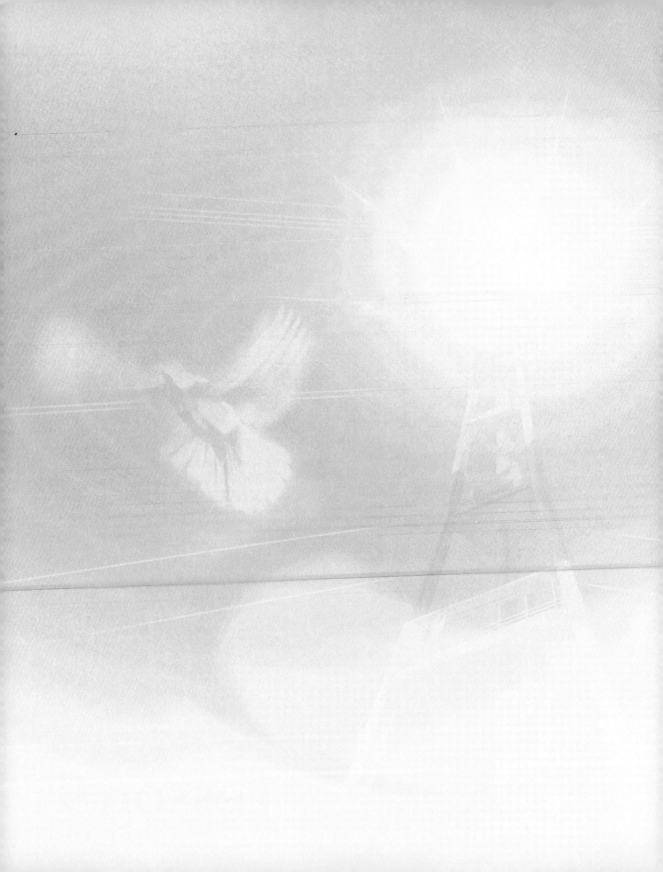

9 | Finishing the 3D Composite

Now things are getting really interesting as you continue to combine elements. You can use 2D elements—such as text and numbers—as 3D layers in this composition. That means you can arrange them any way you like around the camera to create a compelling virtual world around the 2D movie of the actress.

In this lesson you'll learn to do the following:

• Precompose and collapse 3D layers

• Apply the Tint effect

• Position and duplicate layers in 3D space

This lesson picks up the work you began in Lesson 8, using the same project as its basis. In that lesson, you worked with cameras, null objects, and imported camera data. In this lesson, you bring that work together with other 3D elements into a complete 3D composite that you render at the end of this lesson.

You'll work with two new 3D elements that have been prepared for you: a rings element, much like the ring image that you used to create circles in Lesson 3, and a starburst element, similar to the one you created in Lesson 4. You'll also work with four more elements that you built in Lessons 2 and 5.

This lesson takes about one hour to complete.

Getting started

At this phase of the work, the memory load is large enough that you may notice some sluggishness as After Effects processes your work. It's a good idea to take advantage of the various configurations that minimize the RAM requirements so that you can see the changes to your work as quickly as possible. See "Allocating RAM to After Effects" on page 2.

Make sure that the following files are in the AE_CIB job folder on your hard drive, or copy them from the *After Effects Classroom in a Book* CD now:

• In the _mov folder: 3DRings.mov and 3DStarburst.mov

• In the Sample_Movies folder: 3DComp09_final.mov from the Sample_Movies/Lesson09 folder on the CD

• In the Finished_Projects folder: 3DComposite09_finished.aep

Besides the two prepared movies provided on the CD, you'll use movies that you created and rendered in earlier lessons. Make sure that these files are in your _mov folder:

• BoxLightsLine.mov, Squares01.mov, TextCircle.mov, TextLine.mov.

Open and play the sample movie 3DComp09_final.mov to see the work you'll create in Lesson 9. When you finish, quit the QuickTime player. You can delete the sample movie now to save storage space, if necessary.

Importing and organizing the source files

Before you import the source files required for this lesson, you'll reopen and then rename the project you worked on in Lesson 8. By saving it under a new name, you give yourself the option of going back to the original project file and reexamining your work there.

1 Start After Effects and open the 3DComposite08_work.aep project, which is in the _aep folder inside your AE_CIB job folder.

2 Choose File > Save As, and type **3DComposite09_work.aep**.

3 Choose File > Import > Multiple Files.

4 Open the _mov folder in your AE_CIB job folder. Then select the following files one at a time, and click Open (Windows) or Import (Mac OS) each time:

• 3DRings.mov

• 3DStarburst.mov

• BoxLightsLine.mov

• TextCircle.mov

• TextLine.mov

5 Click Done to close the Import Multiple Files dialog box.

6 In the Project window, drag all the .mov files into the mov files folder, and expand the folder, if necessary, so that you can see the files inside it.

Now all the files you'll need for this project are imported and you have a well-organized Project window for your work.

Adding prepared 3D footage

Two of the imported movies are prepared files that you copied from the After Effects 5.0 Classroom in a Book CD. In this section, you'll incorporate these files into your composition.

The first prepared element, the 3DRings.mov, uses the same rings.psd image that you worked with in Lesson 3. This image was duplicated and animated in 3D space. The rendered movie uses the same camera move as the current 3D Composite Comp.

The second prepared element, the 3DStarburst.mov, is based on a starburst element like the one you created in an earlier lesson. This involved duplicating the Starburst.mov, positioning it in 3D space, and then rendering it, using the same camera move as the current 3D Composite Comp.

Adding and tinting the rings

Your first task in bringing the 3D elements together is to add the 3DRings.mov element to the 3D Composite Comp. You'll also adjust its color after you place it in the composite by applying the Tint effect and adding a transfer mode.

1 Open the 3D Composite Comp and move the current-time marker to 0:00.

2 In the Project window, select the 3DRings.mov and drag it into the Timeline window below the Girl Pre-comp in the layer stack, so that the 3DRings.mov is Layer 2.

3 Set the current-time marker to about 1:15 so that you can see the layers as you work.

4 In the Modes panel, select Screen as the Layer 2 transfer mode. The rings begin to blend with the background.

5 With the layer still selected, choose Effect > Image Control > Tint.

6 In the Effect Controls window, in Map White to, select the same orange-yellow color you used in Lesson 7. The color used in the sample has the RGB values of R=207 (81%), G=153 (60%), B=0 (0%), but if you used different values, be sure to enter those numbers.

7 In Amount to Tint, scrub or type **60%.** The rings now take on the yellow hue.

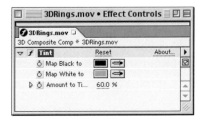

8 Press T to open the Opacity property in the Timeline window, and scrub or type **80%.**

9 Preview the animation. Press T to hide the Opacity property, and then save the project.

The timing of the 3DRings.mov layer works with the Girl Pre-comp layer dissolve to create the impression that the rings wipe her onto the screen.

Adding the glowing-ball element

Next you'll add the prepared 3DStarburst.mov to the 3D Composite Comp. In this task, you'll position the layer in the 3D Composite, set the proper timing, and then apply a transfer mode to blend this layer with the layers behind it.

1 Move the current-time marker to 3:27 and drag a composition-time marker from Composition marker bin at the right side of the Timeline window, pressing Shift as you drag to snap the new marker to the current time.

2 In the Project window, select the 3DStarburst.mov and drag it into the Timeline window above the Girl Pre-comp layer in the layer stack, so that the 3DStarburst.mov is now Layer 1 and its In point is at 3:27.

3 Move the current-time marker to 8:00 so that you can see the results as you continue working.

4 With Layer 1 selected, choose Effect > Image Control > Tint.

5 In the Effect Controls window, in Map White to, select the same orange-yellow color you used for the rings. The color used in the sample has the RGB values of R=207 (81%), G=153 (60%), B=0 (0%), but if you used different values, be sure to enter those numbers.

6 In Amount to Tint, scrub or type **30**.

7 In the Modes panel, select Hard Light as the Layer 1 transfer mode.

8 Press 2 (on the main keyboard, not the keypad) to move the current-time marker to the marker at 3:27, and then press B to define the beginning of the work area.

9 Move the current-time marker to 9:00 and press N to define the end of the work area.

10 Preview the animation, and save the project.

Hard Light transfer mode creates the look of a harsh spotlight shining on the layer images, adding highlights and deepening the shadows. This contrast makes the glowing ball more brilliant and dramatic because Hard Light makes the starburst take on more color from the layers behind it.

If your redraw speed is becoming sluggish, you can temporarily turn off the layer Video switches (☻) for the 3DStarburst.mov and the 3DRings.mov layers. This will increase the redraw speed as you continue working. You must turn on these Video switches before rendering. If the Video switches are left turned off, these layers are not rendered.

Adding the TextCircle element

In this task, you add the circular text element that you built in an earlier lesson. After you duplicate the layer twice, you have all the TextCircle 3D layers you need.

1 Set the current-time marker at 3:13.

2 In the Project window, select the TextCircle.mov and drag it into the Timeline window, placing it into the Layer 1 position in the layer stack.

3 Choose Edit > Duplicate twice to create two copies of the layer. You now have a total of three TextCircle.mov layers: Layer 1, Layer 2, and Layer 3.

4 Set the current-time marker to 5:10 and select Layer 2.

5 Press [(left bracket). The layer duration bar moves so that the Layer 2 In point is at 5:10.

6 Set the current-time marker to 6:11, select Layer 3, and press [(left bracket) to set the Layer 3 In point at 6:11.

7 In the Timeline window, open the Switches panel. Then select all three TextCircle.mov layers and click one of the 3D Layers switches to make them all 3D layers.

All the layers now temporarily disappear in the Composition window because they are not positioned in the camera view. You'll correct that in another procedure.

Setting transformation properties for the TextCircle layers

You'll configure the duplicates separately so that one layer circles around the actress, while the other two revolve around the glowing-ball element in her hands.

1 With all three TextCircle.mov layers still selected, press S, and then press Shift + P and Shift + R to open the Scale, Position, and Orientation and Rotation properties for each layer.

2 Deselect all layers and then move the current-time marker to about 5:00 so that you can see the results as you work.

3 Set the following transformation properties for Layer 1:

• In Position, scrub or type **406, 292, 928**.

• In Scale, scrub or type **36%**.

• In Orientation, scrub or type **270˚, 0˚, 145˚**. This orientation value hides the start point of the text animation behind the Girl Pre-comp layer.

4 Move the current-time marker to about 6:00 so that you can see the results as you work.

5 Set the following transformation properties for Layer 2:

- In Position, scrub or type **380, 292, 928**.

- In Scale, scrub or type **10%**, so that the layer passes around the glowing-ball element.

- In Orientation, leave the default settings unchanged: 0°, 0°, 0°.

6 Move the current-time marker to about 7:00.

7 Set the following transformation properties for Layer 3:

- In Position, scrub or type **380, 292, 928**.

- In Scale, scrub or type **8%**.

- In Orientation, scrub or type **90°, 0°, 180°**.

8 Select all three TextCircle.mov layers and press accent grave (`) to close the layer outlines. Keep the three layers selected.

9 Open the Modes panel, and select Screen transfer mode for one of the layers to set it for all three TextCircle.mov layers. Then deselect all layers.

10 Preview the animation, using the work area set from 3:27 to 9:00, and then save the project.

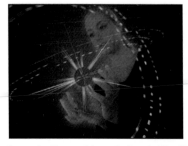

Image in Composition window (with all layer Video switches turned on)

Precomposing the TextCircle layers

Next, you'll combine the three TextCircle layers into one by precomposing. This keeps these element layers grouped together and makes your Timeline window less cluttered.

1 Select all three TextCircle.mov layers and choose Layer > Pre-compose. The Pre-compose dialog box appears with the second option already selected.

2 Type **TextCircle Pre-comp** for the name. Deselect the Open New Composition option, if it is selected, and then click OK.

3 In the Timeline window, click the Switches/Modes bar to open the Switches panel.

4 Click the Collapse Transformations switch (✱) for the TextCircle Pre-comp layer, and then save the project. Keep the TextCircle Pre-comp layer selected.

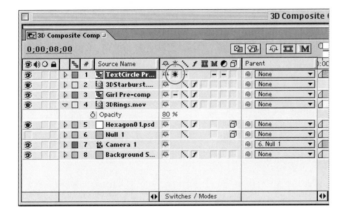

5 Move the current-time marker to 3:13, and press Alt + [(left bracket) (Windows) or Option + [(left bracket) (Mac OS) to trim the TextCircle Pre-comp layer In point.

The duration bar now represents the layer more accurately because this is when the TextCircle layers appear in the composition. Collapsing this layer is necessary to preserve the 3D state of the layers in the precomposition.

Adding the TextLine element and setting a position

You'll place several instances of the TextLine element so that they'll look like little cross-roads laid out on the platform on which the actress appears to stand. You start by adding the element to the composition and making it a 3D layer.

1 Press 1 on the main keyboard to move the current-time marker to composition-time marker 1 (at 2:03).

2 In the Project window, select the TextLine.mov and drag it into the Timeline window so that it is now Layer 1 in the layer stack. The Layer 1 In point is 2:03.

3 Move the current-time marker to about 3:00 so that you can see the layer in the Composition window as you work.

4 In the Switches panel, click the 3D Layer switch (⬚) to make the TextLine.mov a 3D layer. The layer temporarily disappears in the Composition window because it is not in the camera view.

5 In the Composition window, select Top view, or press F11, and then select 25% magnification.

6 Examine the positions of the layers by selecting these layers in the Timeline window so that you can see the layer handles:

• Select the Hexagon01.psd layer. If necessary, reduce the magnification again or resize the Composition window so that you can see the selection handles on the Composition window pasteboard.

• Select the TextLine.mov layer.

7 In the Composition window, drag the TextLine.mov layer by the blue Z axis to about the middle of the square that represents the Hexagon01.psd layer.

8 In the Composition window pop-up menu for orthogonal views, choose Camera 1. Then increase the magnification in the Composition window.

The TextLine element appears just as the hexagon layer tumbles into place.

Setting transformation properties for the TextLine elements

Your next task is to move the elements into position. You won't set keyframes here, so the position of the current-time marker doesn't matter.

1 In the Timeline window, select the TextLine.mov layer (if it's not already selected).

2 Press P and then press Shift + S and Shift + R to open the Position, Scale, Orientation, and Rotation properties for this layer, and enter the following values:

• In Position, scrub or type **412, 461, 920**.

• In Scale, scrub or type **55%**.

- In Orientation, scrub or type **270°, 0°, 0°**. The text line runs horizontally.

3 With the TextLine.mov layer still selected, choose Edit > Duplicate.

4 Select Layer 2, and enter these values (the properties you need are already open):

- In Position, scrub or type to change the third coordinate to **914**. Leave the first two values (412, 461) unchanged.

- Leave Scale set to 55%.

- In Orientation, scrub or type to change the third coordinate to **90°**. Leave the first two (270°, 0°) unchanged. The new text line is nearly vertical.

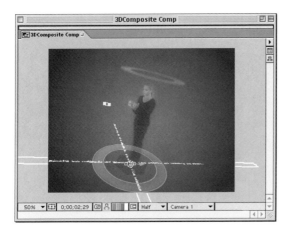

5 Close the layer properties for Layers 1 and 2, and then save the project.

In 3D space, Layer 2 now lies perpendicular to Layer 1: Layer 1 runs horizontally and Layer 2 is vertical, slanting slightly to the left.

Duplicating and moving TextLine layers

To form a simple grid, you'll duplicate and move each of the TextLine layers.

1 Move the current-time marker to 3:00, if necessary.

2 Select Layer 1 (the horizontal TextLine.mov layer), and choose Edit > Duplicate.

3 In the Composition window, drag Layer 1 by its green Y axis toward the top of the slanted vertical line of text.

Note: Increasing the magnification may help you see the green Y-axis line and arrow.

4 In the Timeline window, select Layer 3 (the vertical TextLine.mov layer) and choose Edit > Duplicate again.

5 In the Composition window, drag Layer 3 by its green Y axis to the right edge of the lower horizontal line of text.

Now, Layers 2 and 4 intersect at the actress's feet. Layers 1 and 3 appear to intersect behind her: above and to the right.

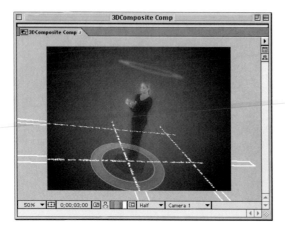

Setting In points and Y coordinates for TextLine layers

Next, you'll adjust some of the In points so that the layers start to appear at different times. Your final task with TextLines is to apply the Screen transfer mode to all the TextLine layers.

1 Make sure that the current-time marker is at 3:00.

2 Select Layer 1 and press [(left bracket) to set the Layer 1 In point at the current time (3:00).

3 Select Layer 3 (the slanted vertical TextLine.mov layer), and again press [(left bracket) to set its In point at 3:00.

4 Move the current-time marker to about 3:15 so you can see the results of the next steps.

5 Select all four TextLine.mov layers, and then open the Modes panel in the Timeline window.

6 Under Modes, select Screen for one of the layers to set this transfer mode for all four layers.

7 With Layers 1 through 4 still selected, press T to open the Opacity properties and type (don't scrub this time) **60%** to set the opacity value for all four layers. Then press T again.

8 Save the project and preview the animation. If necessary, change the work area so that you can see your work, and then change it back to its previous settings (4:00 to 9:00).

Precomposing the TextLine layers

To keep your Timeline window layer stack easier to manage, you'll precompose the four TextLine layers. After precomposing, you'll need to select the Collapse switch (∗) to preserve the quality of the images and the 3D character of the layer.

1 In the Timeline window, select all four TextLine layers.

2 Choose Layer > Pre-compose.

3 In the Pre-composition Settings dialog box, type **TextLine Pre-comp** as the name.

4 With the Open New Comp option deselected, click OK. The TextLine Pre-comp appears as Layer 1 in the Timeline window, replacing the four TextLine layers.

5 In the Switches panel, click the Collapse switch (∗) for Layer 1.

6 Drag the TextLine Pre-comp layer to the Layer 4 position in the layer stack, just below the Girl Pre-comp layer.

7 Press 1 to move the current-time marker to 2:03.

8 Press Alt + [(left bracket) (Windows) or Option + [(left bracket) (Mac OS) to trim the Layer 4 In point so that it accurately represents the time at which the layer appears in the composition. Then save the project.

That's all the work you need to do with the TextLines for now.

Adding BoxLightsLine elements

This element is ready for you to place in the 3D composite, where you'll position it in 3D space.

1 With the 3D Composite Comp open, move the current-time marker to 0:11.

2 Drag the BoxLightsLine.mov from the Project window to the Timeline window and position it as Layer 1. In the Composition window, the layer looks like a black bar.

3 Press 1 (on the main keyboard) to move the current-time marker to the composition-time marker at 2:03 so that you can see the results as you continue working.

4 In the Switches panel, click the 3D Layer switch (⊟) for Layer 1. The layer disappears. (You'll adjust it in the next step so that it is again visible.)

5 Press P, and then press Shift + R, Shift + S, and Shift + T to open the Position, Orientation, Rotation, Scale, and Opacity properties for Layer 1 and make the following changes:

- In Position, scrub or type **360, 384, 1240**.

- In Scale, scrub or type **50%**.

- Make sure that Orientation is 0, 0, 0.

- In Opacity, scrub or type **20%**.

6 In the Modes panel, select Screen.

Duplicating and shifting the BoxLightsLine elements

Next you'll duplicate this element and give the duplicates a variety of settings in three-dimensional space. As the result, you'll see different sets of box lights running at right angles to each other parallel to the floor of the image.

1 Choose Edit > Duplicate. Leave Layer 1 selected.

2 Move the current-time marker to 0:18 and press [(left bracket) to set the Layer 1 In point at this time.

3 Press P to open the Layer 1 Position property, and scrub or type **1222** to change the first position coordinate. Leave the other coordinates at 384 and 1240.

4 Choose Edit > Duplicate.

5 Move the current-time marker to 2:12 and press [(left bracket) to set the Layer 1 In point at this time.

6 Press P and then Shift + R to open the Position, Orientation, and Rotation properties.

7 In Position, scrub or type **720, 386, 1240**.

8 In Orientation, scrub or type **0, 90, 0**.

9 Choose Edit > Duplicate four more times, and then use the same techniques to change the In point and the third position coordinate for each of the first four layers as follows:

• Layer 1: In point = 2:06, third Position coordinate = **4680**. (Leave the first coordinates set to 720 and 386.)

• Layer 2: In point = 3:07, third Position coordinate = **3820**.

• Layer 3: In point = 1:17, third Position coordinate = **2960**.

• Layer 4: In point = 0:24, third Position coordinate = **2100**.

10 Select all layers and press accent grave (`) to hide all properties, and then deselect all layers. Save your project.

You now have seven BoxLightsLine.mov layers, all set to Screen transfer mode in the Modes panel.

Precomposing layers

Finally, you'll combine all the BoxLightsLine.mov layers into a single layer by precomposing. Grouping layers together in this way helps simplify the layer stack so that you can work more efficiently.

1 Press Shift + click to select all seven BoxLightsLine.mov layers.

2 Choose Layer > Pre-compose.

3 Type **BoxLights Pre-comp** as the name. Leave the second precompose option selected, leave Open New Composition deselected, and click OK.

4 In the Timeline window layer stack, move the BoxLights Pre-comp layer below the 3DRings.mov layer and above the Hexagon01.psd layer.

5 In the Switches panel, select the Collapse switch (✱) for the BoxLightLine Pre-comp layer to preserve the 3D qualities of the BoxLights layers.

6 Reset the work area to show the entire composition, and then preview your work. When you finish, save the project.

That's all the work needed on the BoxLights, which is the final element in the 3D Composite composition. You're almost finished with this lesson.

Rendering the 3D Composite composition

Now that you have finished building the 3D Composite, it is time to render the composition.

1 Turn on the video switches for any layers that are turned off (except the Null 1 layer).

2 Close the Composition, Timeline, and Effect Controls windows.

3 In the Project window, select the 3D Composite Comp and choose Composition > Make Movie.

4 In the Output Movie To dialog box, type **3DComposite.mov** in Name, and specify the _mov folder inside the AE_CIB job folder. Then click Save. The Render Queue opens with the 3D Composite Comp as the first item in the queue.

5 Click the words *Current Settings* to open the Render Settings dialog box, and then set the following options:

- In Quality, select Best.

- In Resolution, select Full.

- In Time Span, select Length of Comp, and then click OK to return to the Render Queue.

6 Click the word *Lossless* to open the Output Module Settings dialog box, and then set the following options:

- In Format, select QuickTime Movie.

- Select Import into Project When Done.

- Under Video Output, make sure that Animation Compressor and Spatial Quality = Most are listed. Also make sure that Channels is RGB, and Depth is set to Millions of Colors (not Millions of Colors+). There is no need to render an alpha channel for this composition because it contains a solid background. When you are ready to continue, click OK.

7 Save the project one more time and then click Render.

8 When the rendering finishes, close the Render Queue.

9 In the Project window, drag the 3DComposite.mov file into the mov files folder.

10 Open the 3DComposite.mov by double-clicking it in the Project window and click the Play button to view the movie.

Compare your final rendered movie to the sample movie you played at the beginning of this lesson. If necessary, make any changes, save the project, and render it again, using the steps listed above.

You have now completed Lesson 9. This QuickTime movie is ready for importing into the final composition. There, it will be combined with the 2D composite project, this project, and a few final elements to complete the piece.

Lesson 10

10 | Building the Final Animation

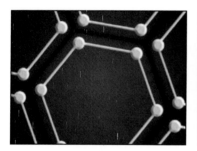 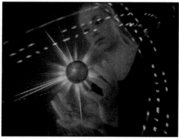 

At this point, you bring everything together in one overall project, and your careful organization really pays off. Finding the files you need is much easier because you've thought ahead and taken the time to keep your file structure logical and tidy—setting a good example for when you go on to create even larger and more complex After Effects projects of your own.

In this lesson, you'll learn to do the following:

- Import After Effects projects
- Organize the Project window with multiple imported projects
- Apply a track matte
- Work with the Spherize, Lens Flare, and Bevel Alpha effects
- Add a light to a composition and animate it
- Place items in compositions at specific points in time
- Rotoscope an image, using the mask tools
- Create a realistic reflection layer

You continue compositing both 2D and 3D layers in a final composition to complete the animation. You'll start by building a reflection that you'll position on the glowing ball and add a light burst to it. Then, after making a number of adjustments and creating a some new layers, you'll import, place, and set properties for the final image files, which come together as the final scene, showing the client's logo. Then you'll be completely finished building the visuals and ready to render your final animation—which you'll do in Lesson 11.

This lesson takes approximately an hour and a half to complete.

Getting started

Make sure that the following files are in the AE_CIB job folder on your hard drive, or copy them from the *After Effects Classroom in a Book* CD now.

- In the _psd folder: A.psd, R.psd, and Adobe.psd
- In the Sample_Movies folder: FinalComposite_final.mov from the Sample_Movies/Lesson10 folder on the CD
- In the Finished_Projects folder: FinalComposite10_finished.aep

This lesson also uses several files you created in earlier lessons. Make sure that the following files are also stored in the appropriate folders in your AE_CIB job folder:

- In the _aep folder: 2DComposite07_work.aep and 3DComposite09_work.aep
- In the _mov folder: 3DHexagons.mov, 3DHexLines.mov, LensFlare.mov, and Squares01.mov

Open and play the sample movie FinalComposite_final.mov, to see the work you'll complete in this lesson. When you finish, quit the QuickTime player. You can delete the sample movie now to save storage space, if necessary.

Begin by creating a new project.

1 Start After Effects 5.0, if it is not already open.

2 Choose File > New > New Project.

3 Choose File > Save As.

4 In the Save Project As dialog box, find and open the _aep folder in the AE_CIB job folder you created earlier.

5 In File Name, type **FinalComposite10_work.aep** and click Save.

Importing the source files

You start by importing all your source files, including two After Effects projects.

1 Choose File > Import > Multiple Files.

2 Locate the _mov folder inside your AE_CIB job folder and individually select and import the following movie files that you built in earlier lessons:

• 3DHexagons.mov

• 3DHexLines.mov

• LensFlare.mov

• Squares01.mov

3 Locate the _psd folder and import each of the following Photoshop files. Each time the Interpret Footage dialog box appears, be sure that the Straight – Unmatted option is selected, and then click OK.

• A.psd

• Adobe.psd

• R.psd

4 Locate the _aep folder and import each of the following After Effects project files:

• 2DComposite07_work.aep

• 3DComposite09_work.aep

5 Click Done to close the Import Multiple Files dialog box.

The two After Effects projects you imported appear as folders in the Project window. Inside, you'll find all the compositions and source files you used when you created these projects. You'll reuse some of these source files to create new images in the final composite.

Organizing the Project window

The number of items in your Project window is larger than any previous project in these lessons. Keeping the window logically and efficiently arranged makes your work faster and easier, so it's well worth the small effort required to do this.

1 Choose File > New > New Folder to create a new folder in the Project window, and then type **mov files** as the folder name, and press Enter or Return.

2 Drag the 3DHexagons.mov, 3DHexLines.mov, LensFlare.mov, and Squares01.mov files into the mov files folder. Click the arrow to the left of the folder to expand it so that these files inside are visible.

3 Create two more folders, and type **psd files** to name the first one and **aep files** to name the second one.

4 Drag the A.psd, R.psd, and Adobe.psd files into the psd files folder.

5 Drag the 3DComposite09_work.aep and 2DComposite07_work.aep folders into the aep files folder.

6 Click the arrows next to the folders to expand them so that you can see the folder contents.

7 In the aep files folder, expand each of the project folders. All the compositions and source files you used in these projects are stored within these folders. Leave them organized as they are.

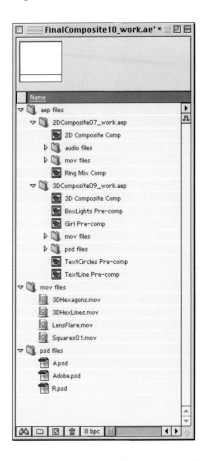

8 To save space in the Project window, close all the folders.

Now all the files you need for this project are imported and you have a well-organized Project window.

Note: *Leaving the original source files nested under the two imported projects helps you keep track of which files are associated with the different projects. The location of these file references in the Project window does not affect what happens in your compositions.*

Creating the glowing-ball reflection

In this section, you'll build a reflection element and apply it to the glowing ball that the actress appears to hold in her hands. This reflection of the composition image helps to convey a more believable impression of the ball shape, as if it were a three-dimensional sphere with a mirror finish. Then you'll add a light burst to the reflection, to give it another realistic touch.

Duplicating to create a new composition

You'll create the reflection image by making a few adjustments to a duplicate of the 3D Composite Comp that you built in Lessons 8 and 9.

1 In the Project window, expand the aep files folder and the 3DComposite09_work.aep folder, and then select the 3D Composite Comp.

2 Press Ctrl + D (Windows) or Command + D (Mac OS) to duplicate the composition.

3 Select the duplicate (named *3D Composite Comp**) and press Ctrl + K (Windows) or Command + K (Mac OS) to open the Composition Settings dialog box.

4 In Composition Name, type **Reflection Comp**. Leave all other settings as they are, and click OK.

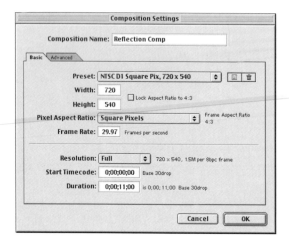

5 In the Project window, drag the Reflection Comp to the top level of the Project window hierarchy.

You duplicated the composition as an easy way of re-creating the camera layer and its movement, which is governed by the null object.

Adding and removing files from a composition

You can delete the layers you don't use from the duplicated composition and add other files that you need for the design. Then, you'll place another movie of the same scene, which will become a reflection in the surface of the glowing-ball element.

1 In the Project window, double-click the Reflection Comp to open it in the Composition and Timeline windows, and make sure that the current-time marker is at 0:00.

2 Select and delete all the layers in the composition except the Camera 1 layer and the Null 1 layer so that only these two layers remain in the composition.

3 In the Project window, expand the 3DComposite09_work.aep folder and its nested _mov folder to find the 3DComposite.mov. Drag this movie into the Timeline window so that it is Layer 1 in the layer stack.

4 Select the 3DComposite.mov layer and choose Edit > Duplicate.

5 Press Enter or Return and type **Reflection** to rename Layer 1. Then press Enter or Return again.

6 Move the current-time marker to 3:21, select Layer 1, and press [(left bracket) to set the In point at this frame.

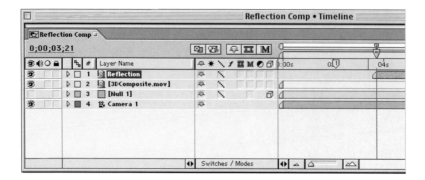

Drawing a mask

You now mask the reflection layer to create a circular shape for the image. Then, when you place the reflection above the glowing-ball image in the composite, the reflection matches the glowing ball and appears to be coming from the surface of the ball.

1 In the Tools palette, select the oval mask tool. Make sure that the Reflection layer is still selected in the Timeline window.

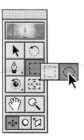

2 Move the tool to the center of the Composition window. Start to drag and then press Ctrl + Shift (Windows) or Command + Shift (Mac OS) to draw a circle from the center, making the circle slightly smaller than the height of the composition frame.

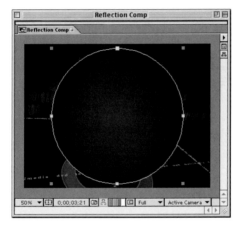

3 In the Tools palette, select the selection tool (⬉).

4 With the Reflection layer selected, press F to reveal the Mask Feather property in the Timeline window.

5 Scrub or type **20** to create a 20-pixel feather, softening the edge of the mask.

Setting transform properties for the Reflection layer

You placed the second (reflection) version of the 3DComposite.mov on top of the original layer so that it appears as a reflection on the glowing ball, and then you masked it to the appropriate shape. The reflection layer needs just a few more adjustments.

1 With the Reflection layer selected, click the 3D Layer switch (⬚) to make it a 3D layer, and make sure that the Active Camera view is selected. The yellow mask circle moves partly out of view in the upper left corner of the composition frame.

2 Press S to reveal the Reflection layer Scale property, and set the Scale value to **1.4%**.

3 Press P to reveal the Position property, and scrub or type **383.3, 291.9, 932.3** as the Position coordinates. The mask now moves back into view.

Note: *Precision is important here, so that the reflection element exactly matches the position of the glowing ball.*

4 Press R to reveal Rotation and Orientation properties. For the Orientation values, scrub or type **35°, 20°, 0°**. In the Composition window, small yellow handles show the layer position in the actress's hands. The second image of the girl is visible as a ghost image inside the glowing ball.

5 Move the current-time marker to 5:00, and press T to reveal the Opacity property for the Reflection layer. Scrub or type **0%** as the Opacity value, and set a keyframe.

6 Move the current-time marker to 6:00 and change the Opacity value to **60%** so that a second keyframe appears. Press T to hide the Opacity property, and save the project.

If you preview the composition, you'll see the reflection on the glowing ball. However, it looks as if it were reflected from a flat mirror rather than from a spherical surface, so it needs a little more work.

Applying effects to the Reflection layer

Now you add three effects and make a few final adjustments to this layer to give it a ball-shaped appearance.

1 Move the current-time marker to about 9:00 so that you can see the results as you work.

2 Select the Reflection layer and choose Effect > Distort > Spherize.

3 In the Effect Controls window, under Spherize, scrub or type **250** as the Radius value. Leave the Center of Sphere at its default position. The image appears warped, as if it were wrapped around a sphere.

4 Choose Effect > Render > PS+Lens Flare.

5 In the Lens Flare options dialog box, enter the following:

• In Brightness, drag the slider or type **116%**.

• In Lens type, select 35mm prime, and then click OK.

6 In the Effect Controls window, under PS+Lens Flare, make sure that Flare Center is at 288, 216 and that Blend with Original is at 0%. A lens flare appears on the Reflection layer.

7 Choose Effect > Perspective > Bevel Alpha.

8 In the Effect Controls window, scroll if necessary to see the Bevel Alpha controls, and enter the following:

- In Edge Thickness, scrub or type **20**.

- In Light Angle, scrub or type −**139°**.

- Select the Light Color eyedropper and click the edge of the starburst element in the Composition window to select a light brown color.

- In Light Intensity, scrub or type **0.50**.

9 Close the Effect Controls window, collapse the Reflection layer properties (if any are expanded), and save the project.

Note: To see the results of applying the Bevel Alpha effect more easily, deselect the Reflection layer now.

The Spherize effect warps images, as if wrapping them around a sphere. The Bevel Alpha effect helps to define the edges of an image—in this case, the reflective surface of the glowing ball. The PS+Lens Flare effect is familiar to you from your work in Lesson 2. It also helps create a believable image of a three-dimensional reflective surface.

You have now finished creating the reflection element.

Building the LightBurst element

To add some sparkle to the reflection, you now use the LightRays.mov and the LensFlare.mov that you created in earlier lessons to create a LightBurst element. To do this, you place these elements in a new composition and apply a track matte to blend them together. You will use this element in the final composite to create a glowing highlight that radiates from the reflection of the glowing ball. Begin by creating the composition.

1 Choose Composition > New Composition and enter the following in the Composition Settings dialog box:

- In Name, type **Light Burst Comp**.

- In Width, type **720**.

- In Height, type **540**.

- In Pixel Aspect Ratio, select Square Pixels.

- In Frame Rate, set **29.97.**

- (Optional) In Resolution, select Half (or lower), if needed for your system.

- In Duration, type **400,** to specify four seconds.

2 Click OK to close the Composition Settings. The composition automatically opens in the Composition and Timeline windows.

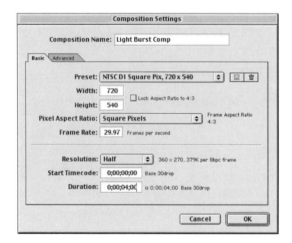

3 In the Project window, drag this composition to the top level of the window hierarchy.

Note: *If the composition background color is not black, change it now by choosing Composition > Background Color and selecting black.*

Adding layers and preparing your working view

You next add two layers to the Light Burst Comp and examine them. You also change the working view now so that you'll be able to see the differences in the alpha channel when you do the procedure following this one.

1 Make sure that the current-time marker is at 0:00.

2 In the Project window, expand the mov files folder and drag the LensFlare.mov into the Timeline window.

3 Also in the Project window, expand the 2DComposite07_work.aep folder and then expand the mov files folder inside it to find the LightRays.mov.

4 Drag the LightRays.mov into the Timeline window, positioning it as Layer 1, above the LensFlare.mov. The Composition window is now entirely black.

5 Move the current-time marker to about 2:15 so that you can see the results as you work.

6 In the A/V Features panel, click the Layer 1 Solo switch (○) so that only the LightRays.mov appears in the Composition window.

7 In the Composition window, click the alpha channel button. You now see the layer in black (representing the areas of transparency) and white (areas of 100% opacity, where the layer image is visible).

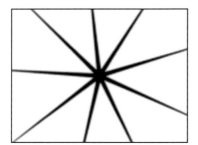

8 Deselect the alpha channel button. In the Timeline window A/V Features panel, deselect the Solo switch.

You'll use the LightRays layer as an alpha matte in the next procedure, so that the image behind it will appear only where the LightRays layer is transparent.

Applying a track matte and effect

You now create a special relationship between the LightRays and LensFlare layers so that the LightRays layer acts as an inverted *track matte*—a stencil through which the LensFlare layer appears. Although the beginning and final look of the image seem to be the same, the use of the track matte ensures that the alpha channel of the combined layers is correct when you place the LightBurst element into the Reflection composition.

1 In the Timeline window, open the Modes panel.

2 For the LensFlare.mov (Layer 2), under TrkMat, select the Alpha Inverted Matte "LightRays.mov" option from the track matte pop-up menu. The LensFlare.mov now appears only through the inverted alpha channel of the LightRays.mov layer. An icon (■) beside the layer name serves as a reminder that this layer now includes a track matte.

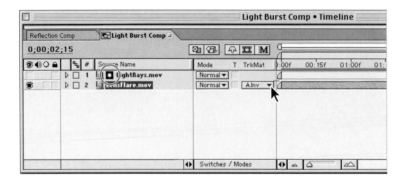

Note: The Video switch (⊛) for the LightRays layer is turned off. This happens automatically when you apply a track matte. The upper layer in the track-matte relationship is used only for its alpha or luma values; the layer itself is not displayed in the Composition window.

3 Select the LensFlare.mov and choose Effect > Blur & Sharpen > Fast Blur.

4 In the Effect Controls window, scrub or type **15** as the Blurriness value to soften the lens flare image.

5 Preview the animation. Then close the Composition, Timeline, and Effect Controls windows for the Light Burst Comp (click the small square on the composition tab), and save the project.

For more information about track mattes, see "Creating track mattes and traveling mattes" and related subtopics in After Effects online Help.

Combining the LightBurst and Reflection compositions

Next you add the Light Burst Comp to the Reflection Comp, creating an animated glowing light source radiating from the reflective glowing ball in the actress's hands. You'll then adjust the Opacity and Scale values of the Light Burst Comp layer.

1 Move the current-time marker to 5:00.

2 In the Project window, select the Light Burst Comp and drag it into the Timeline window so that it is Layer 1 in the layer stack.

Note: This element is not yet visible in the Composition window.

3 In the Switches panel, click the 3D Layer switch (⊕) to make the Light Burst Comp a 3D layer. Then, in the Composition window, make sure that the view is set to Active Camera.

4 Press T to reveal the Opacity property for the Light Burst Comp layer and scrub or type **40%** as the Opacity value.

5 Press S to reveal the Scale property, and scrub or type **10%**. Press S again to hide the Scale property.

6 Click the Switches/Modes bar at the bottom of the Timeline window to open the Modes panel.

7 For Layer 1, select Add transfer mode.

Adding expressions and setting the work area

You now use expressions to link the LightBurst position and orientation with those of the Reflection layer. Your goal in this procedure is to line up the LightBurst with the glowing ball. That move is already embedded in the Reflection layer because it contains the original null object and camera that you created in Lesson 8.

1 In the Timeline window, select both the Light Burst Comp layer and the Reflection layer, and press P to reveal the Position properties. Then deselect both layers.

2 Select the word *Position* under the Light Burst Comp layer, and choose Animation > Add Expression.

3 Drag the Expression: Position pick whip from the Light Burst Comp layer to the Position property of the Reflection layer to create an expression, being careful to drag to the word *Position*, not one of the Position coordinate values.

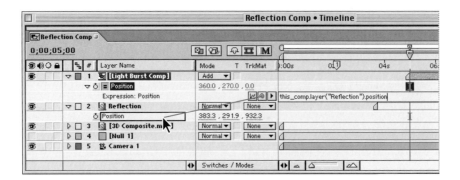

4 Select both the Light Burst Comp and the Reflection layers again, and press R to reveal the Orientation and Rotation properties. Then deselect both layers.

5 Select the word *Orientation* under the Light Burst Comp layer, and choose Animation > Add Expression.

6 Drag the Expression: Orientation pick whip to the Orientation property of the Reflection layer.

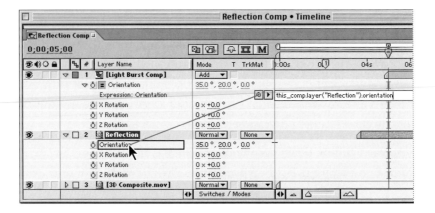

7 Click a white area of the Timeline window to deselect the expression. Select all the layers and press accent grave (`) to hide all the layer properties. Then deselect all the layers.

8 With the current-time marker at 5:00, press B to set the beginning of the work area.

9 Move the current-time marker to 9:00 and press N to set the end of the work area.

10 Preview the animation and save the project.

The first expression makes the LightBurst element take on the Position values of the Reflection layer, which helps it to line up perfectly with the reflection in the glowing ball. The second expression makes the light burst adopt the Orientation values of the Reflection layer.

Rendering the Reflection Comp

It's time to render this new 3D composite, which includes the Reflection elements you have just created. By adding a word to the movie name, the filename helps you recognize this rendering as the one with the reflective ball in it.

1 Close the Composition and Timeline windows for the Reflection Comp.

2 In the Project window, select the Reflection Comp and press Ctrl + M (Windows) or Command + M (Mac OS) to start making a movie.

3 In the Output Movie To dialog box, type **3DComposite_ball.mov**, specify the _mov folder inside the AE_CIB job folder, and click OK. The item appears in the Render Queue.

Note: You may see other items listed in Render Queue. These represent movies that you rendered in the 2DComposite07_work.aep and 3DComposite09_work.aep projects, before you imported them into the Reflection Comp.

4 In the Render Settings pop-up menu, select *Best Settings*, and then click the underlined words *Best Settings* to open the Render Settings dialog box.

5 In Time Span, select Length of Comp, and then click OK to close the dialog box.

6 In Output Module, select Custom to open the Output Module Settings dialog box, and do the following:

- In Format, select QuickTime Movie.

- Select the Import into Project when Done option.

- Under Video, click Format Options to open the Compression Settings dialog box.

7 In the dialog box, select Animation Compression and Millions of Colors, and then click OK.

8 In the Output Module Settings, make sure that Channels is set to RGB and Depth is set to Millions of Colors, and then click OK.

9 Save the project one more time, and click Render.

When the render is finished, close the Render Queue. Then select the 3DComposite_ball.mov, which appears at the top of the Project window, and drag it into the mov files folder.

You can double-click the movie to play it. When you are ready to continue, close the player.

Building the final composition

Now you can begin building the final composition. Using the composition that you built in Lesson 7 as a starting point, you add other elements to complete the animation. You'll also add a number of subtleties, creating a visual complexity and richness to the design.

1 In the Project window, select the 2DComposite Comp located inside the 2DComposite07_work.aep folder and choose Edit > Duplicate. A copy of this composition appears with an asterisk (*) at the end of its name.

2 Press Ctrl + K (Windows) or Command + K (Mac OS) to open the composition settings for the duplicate composition.

3 In Composition Name, type **Final Composite Comp**.

4 In Duration, type **18:00**.

5 Leaving all other composition settings unchanged, click OK to close the Composition
Settings dialog box.

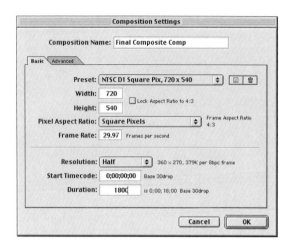

6 In the Project window, drag the Final Composite Comp out of the
2DComposite07_work.aep folder so that it sits at the top level of the project window
hierarchy, and double-click to open it in the Composition and Timeline windows.

Saving a still frame

Next you save a single frame of this composition as a still image (psd) file. This frame
looks rather empty: It's just a black field with a subtle radial green ramp. This background
serves as a transition element so that the scene changes more smoothly.

You create the still image by rendering a single frame. The process is similar to the
procedure you follow when you render a movie.

1 In the Project window, select the 3DComposite_ball.mov and drag it into the Layer 1
position in the Timeline window and continue dragging it to the right until the current-
time display reads 7:07. Then release the mouse.

Note: The current-time marker does not move when you use this technique.

2 Press I to move the current-time marker to the current In point (7:07).

3 Choose Composition > Save Frame As > File to save this frame as a still image.

4 In the Output Frame To dialog box, type **3DComp_still.psd** as the filename and save
it in the _psd folder inside the AE_CIB job folder. The item appears in the Render Queue.

5 In Render Settings, select Best Settings.

6 In Output Module, select Custom.

7 In the Output Module Settings dialog box, set the following:

• In Format, select Photoshop Sequence to save it as a single Photoshop file.

• Select the Import into Project When Done option, and then click OK to close the dialog box.

8 Save the project and click Render.

You'll be using the 7:07 time position several more times, so it may be convenient to have a composition-time marker at this point. To create one, drag a marker from the bin ( ), pressing Shift to snap the new marker into alignment with the current-time marker. Later, you can move the current-time marker back to this composition-time marker by pressing 1 on the keyboard (not on the numeric keypad). You can set up to 10 composition-time markers.

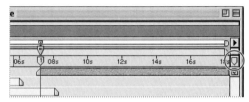

Composition-time marker bin

When rendering is complete, close the Render Queue. The still frame is rendered and imported, appearing in the Project window as 3DComp_still.psd. Drag this file into the psd files folder in the Project window. You can double-click the file to open and view it in the Footage window. When you are ready to continue, close the Footage window.

Adding more elements to the Final Composite Comp

Now it's time to add more elements to the Final Composite Comp. The still frame you just finished creating provides a transition image as the composition moves from the two- to the three-dimensional section of the animation.

1 Move the current-time marker to 5:05.

2 In the Project window, select 3DComp_still.psd and drag it into the Timeline window so that it is Layer 8, below the Starburst.mov in the layer stack. The In point is automatically set at the current-time marker (5:05).

3 Move the current-time marker to 7:07 and press Alt +] (right bracket) (Windows) or Option +] (right bracket) (Mac OS) to trim the 3DComp_still.psd layer Out point at the current time (7:07).

4 Select the Starburst.mov layer, press T to reveal the Opacity property, and set keyframes as follows:

• Move the current-time marker to 6:11, and click the stopwatch to set a keyframe at 100% opacity.

• Move the current-time marker to 6:22, and scrub or type **0%**. A second keyframe appears, creating an 11-frame dissolve of the Starburst.mov. Then press T to hide the Opacity property.

5 With the Starburst.mov still selected, press Alt +] (right bracket) (Windows) or Option +] (right bracket) (Mac OS) to trim the layer Out point.

6 Move the current-time marker to 6:00 and press B to set the beginning of the work area.

7 Move the current-time marker to 8:00 and press N to set the end of the work area.

8 Preview the animation and save the project.

The 3DComp_still.psd provides a transitional background image, appearing between the end of the Starburst.mov (at 6:22) and the beginning of the 3DComposite_ball.mov (at 7:07). Because the Starburst opacity is zero after 6:22, that image is not visible after that point, so it makes sense to trim the footage there. Trimming essentially empty frames from layers makes the timeline a better visual reference, giving you at-a-glance information about which layers are contributing at which times.

Adding edges to the HexOutlines.mov

Now you work with the HexLines element, which is already in the composition. You use one of the After Effects perspective effects to add texture to the HexOutlines.mov.

1 In the Timeline window, select HexOutlines.mov and drag it above 3DComposite_ball.mov in the layer stack. Leave the HexOutlines layer selected.

💡 *It may be helpful to widen the source-name panel in the Timeline window so that you can read more of the names that identify the layers. To do this, just drag the divider tab on the right side of the panel heading.*

2 Choose Effect > Perspective > Bevel Alpha.

3 In the Effect Controls window, the Bevel Alpha effect appears below the Tint effect you applied in an earlier lesson. Adjust the following Bevel Alpha settings:

• In Edge Thickness, scrub or type **10**.

• In Light Angle, scrub or type **60°**. Make sure that the value is positive this time.

• In Light Color, click the swatch and use the color picker to select a gray color. The sample uses the 128 (50%) for each of the R, G, and B values.

• In Intensity, scrub or type **1.00**.

4 Using the current work area (between 5:00 and 8:00), preview your work. When you are ready to continue, stop the preview and save the project.

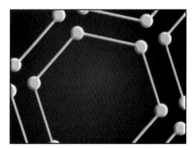

The HexOutlines.mov now has a raised appearance. The Bevel Alpha effect gives the hexagon outlines an embossed look, almost like 3D objects.

Dissolving the Hexagons.mov

One more adjustment is necessary for the solid Hexagons.mov element.

1 Press 1 (on the main keyboard) to move the current-time marker to 7:07 (or use some other method if you did not create a composition-time marker here).

2 Select the Hexagons.mov layer and press T to reveal the Opacity property. Several keyframes you created earlier appear in the timeline.

3 Select the fourth opacity keyframe (at 7:21) and drag it to the current-time marker (at 7:07), pressing Shift as you drag to snap the keyframe into alignment with the current-time marker.

4 Press T to hide the Opacity property.

5 Press Alt +] (right bracket) (Windows) or Option +] (right bracket) (Mac OS) to trim the layer Out point.

6 Drag the Hexagons.mov layer from the Layer 4 position to the Layer 3 position, just above Numbers.mov in the layer stack.

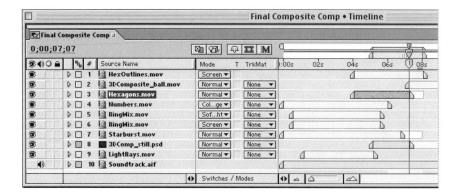

7 Using the current work area (between 5:00 and 8:00), build a RAM preview. When you are ready to continue, stop the preview and save the project.

This change creates a better transition between the hexagons and the 3DComposite_ball.mov layer.

Time-remapping the 3DComposite_ball.mov

Next you apply Time Remapping to the 3DComposite_ball.mov layer. In this case, Time Remapping is used to speed up the playback of the movie and to hold (freeze) the last frame. When you finish, the entire movie will play back in 6 seconds and 13 frames—twice as fast as the original 11 seconds.

1 In the Timeline window, move the current-time marker to 7:07, and select the 3DComposite_ball.mov layer.

2 Choose Layer > Enable Time Remapping.

3 In the Timeline window, expand the 3DComposite_ball.mov layer to see the Time Remap category. Two Time Remap keyframes are already in place, indicating the start and end frames of the 11-second movie: one at 7:07 with a timecode value of 0:00 (shown as underlined text in the Time Remapping properties); the other at 18:07 with a timecode value of 11:00.

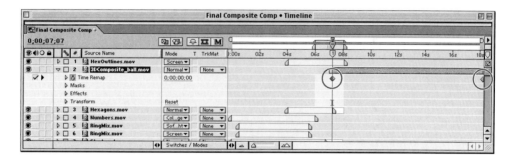

Note: The 18:07 Out point is actually beyond the defined duration for the composition.

4 Move the current-time marker to 13:20, click the underlined timecode value, and scrub or type **1100**. A new keyframe appears.

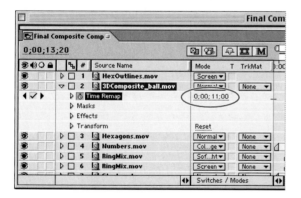

5 With the current-time marker still at 13:20, press N to set the end of the work area.

6 Move the current-time marker to 7:00 and press B to set the beginning of the work area.

7 Build a RAM preview. When you are ready to continue, stop the preview, select the layer and press accent grave (`) to collapse the layer outline, and save the project.

The Time Remap keyframes at 7:07 and 13:20 force the 11-second movie to play within the 6:13 time span between the two keyframes. Note that the layer duration bar extends beyond the keyframe at 13:20. This indicates that the last frame of the movie will hold (freeze) until the layer Out point. This is just what you want.

Adding another layer of numbers

You now add a second Numbers layer to the final compositions so that it appears just after the Hexagons leave the frame.

1 Set the current-time marker at 7:20.

2 In the Project window, select the Numbers.mov, (inside the 2DComposite07_work.aep folder, in the mov files folder) and drag it into the Timeline window, placing it as Layer 1 in the layer stack.

3 In the Timeline window, click the double-arrow button (◆▶) to open the In/Out/Stretch panel and click the Stretch value for the Numbers.mov layer.

4 In the Time Stretch dialog box, type **15%** for Stretch Factor, to shorten the layer duration bar and make the movie play back much faster. Then click OK.

5 In the Timeline window Modes panel for the Numbers.mov, select Color Dodge transfer mode to create a dark glow for the movie.

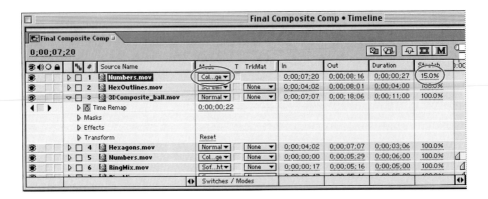

You'll use the In/Out/Stretch panel again soon, so leave it open for now.

Adding transformations to the second set of numbers

In this task, you'll use a different dialog box to set Scale values for the numbers, distorting their appearance.

1 With the current-time marker still set at 7:20 and the Numbers layer still selected, press T to reveal the Opacity property, set the value at **0%**, and create a keyframe.

2 Move the current-time marker to 8:16 and change the Opacity value to **100%**. The Numbers.mov now fades in over almost one second.

3 Press Shift + S to also reveal the Scale property. Then click the left keyframe navigation arrow next to Opacity to jump back to 7:20. Or, press J.

4 Press Ctrl + Shift + S (Windows) or Command + Shift + S (Mac OS) to open the Scale dialog box and enter the following options:

• In Preserve, select None. (Be careful to do this before you make the other changes.)

• In Width, type **100%**.

• In Height, type **800%**.

• In Units, make sure that the % of Source option is selected. Review your settings to make sure that they are correct, and then click OK.

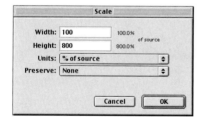

5 Set a keyframe for Scale.

6 Move the current-time marker to 8:16. The numbers now resemble streams of neon-green smoke rising up the composition frame.

7 Scrub or type the Scale values at **100%** for width and **30%** for height. A second keyframe is set.

8 Move the current-time marker to 7:00 and press B to set the beginning of the work area.

9 Move the current-time marker to 10:00 and press N to set the end of the work area.

10 Collapse the layer outline. Then preview the animation and save the project.

The Scale keyframes you set here cause the layer height to shrink as the layer fades up. In the composition, the numbers element provides a brief but flashy transition as the actress appears in her 3D world.

Adding the squares

Next you add the Squares01.mov that you built in Lesson 2. You then change the stretch and apply an effect so that the layer creates a subtle textural element.

1 Set the current-time marker to 1:14 and drag the Squares01.mov from the Project window into the Timeline window so that this movie is Layer 2 in the layer stack, below the Numbers.mov.

2 If the In/Out/Stretch panel is not still open, open it now.

3 In the Time Stretch value for the Squares01.mov layer, enter **50%** to play back the animation at twice the original speed.

4 Click the double-arrow button at the bottom of the Timeline window to hide the In/Out/Stretch panel.

5 In the Modes panel, select Overlay as the transfer mode for Layer 2.

6 With the Squares01.mov layer selected, choose Effect > Channel > Invert. Leave the effect default settings unchanged.

The Invert effect applies to the RGB channels, producing a dark glow where the Squares01.mov overlaps the starburst and rings layers.

Leave the Squares01.mov layer selected so that you're ready for the next procedure.

Setting transform properties and duplicating the squares

You now create a dissolve for the squares. With that accomplished, you then duplicate and reposition a squares layer so that they extend across the width of the composition frame.

1 Press S to open the Squares01.mov layer Scale property and scrub or type **13%**. The squares become very small behind the rings and starburst.

2 Press P to reveal the Position property, and scrub or type **180, 270** so that the layer moves to the left of the composition frame.

3 Press T to reveal the Opacity property. Scrub or type **0%**, and click the stopwatch to set an Opacity keyframe.

4 Move the current-time marker to 2:08 and change the Opacity value to **100%**.

5 Move the current-time marker to 2:29 and change the Opacity value to **0%**.

6 Press Ctrl + D (Windows) or Command + D (Mac OS) to duplicate the squares layer.

7 In the Composition window, drag the selected Squares01.mov layer (Layer 2) to the right to the 540, 270 coordinates, pressing Shift as you drag to constrain the movement. Use the Info palette to see the coordinate values updated as you drag.

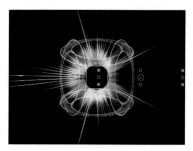

Layer 2 shown selected in Composition window

8 Move the current-time marker to 1:14 and press B to set the beginning of the work area.

9 Move the current-time marker to 3:00 and press N to set the end of the work area.

10 Select Layer 3 and press T to collapse the layer outline. Then preview the composition and save the project.

You have added another very subtle and brief transition element. The results may be especially difficult to see when you preview the composition at less than full size and full resolution. To work around that limitation, you can toggle the Video switch (👁) in the A/V Features panel for the Squares01.mov layer as you apply changes. Also, try increasing the magnification to 200% (with or without enlarging the Composition window). You should then be able to see the slight changes in the Composition window. In spite of its subtlety, this element adds a richness to the design, adding to the overall message the client wants you to convey.

Creating a blue solid

Next you create a blue solid layer which lends color to the ending frames of the animation, as the 3DHexagon layers appear.

1 Set the current-time marker to 11:21, and choose Layer > New > Solid.

2 In the Solid Settings dialog box, set the following:

• In Name, type **Blue Solid**.

• Click the Make Comp Size button to set the size at 720 x 540.

• Click the color swatch and use the color picker to specify a dark blue. The sample uses R=13 (5%), G=51 (20%), B=107 (42%).

3 Click OK to close the Solid Settings dialog box.

4 In the Timeline window, drag the Blue Solid layer below the 3DComposite_ball.mov layer so that the Blue Solid is Layer 6 in the layer stack.

5 Save the project.

Note: This layer does not appear in the Composition window until you add a mask. You'll do that in the following procedure.

Masking around the glowing ball

In this task, you use the Layer window because it offers a couple of advantages for the kind of work involved here. One advantage is that you see the layer you're working with by itself in the Layer window, but you can also still see the layer composited with the other layers in the Composition window. Another advantage is that it's often easier to see specific details—such as the edge of the reflecting ball in this case.

1 Set the current-time marker to 11:28 and double-click the 3DComposite_ball.mov layer in the Timeline window to open it in the Layer window. Drag the windows so that you can see both the Composition and Layer windows.

If your screen is getting crowded, you can move the Layer window over the Project window for now. You won't need to see that window while you work in the Layer window. It may be helpful to increase the magnification in the Layer window to 100% or higher, but you can leave the window itself at its current size because you don't need to see the entire image, just the area of the reflective ball.

2 In the Tools palette, select the oval mask tool and draw a mask around the reflective ball in the Layer window. You can press Ctrl + Shift (Windows) or Command + Shift (Mac OS) as you draw to drag a circle shape from its center. In the Composition window, the Blue Solid fills the area outside of the mask.

3 Press M to reveal the Mask Shape property for the 3DComposite_ball.mov layer, and click the stopwatch to set a keyframe (at 11:28).

4 In the Modes panel for Mask 1, select Subtract from the mask mode pop-up menu.

Your mask now reveals the blue solid within the glowing ball. Leave the Layer window open with the 3DComposite_ball.mov layer displayed.

Rather than displaying only the area inside of the mask shape (as with Add), Subtract removes what is inside the mask shape from the original image and displays the remaining image area.

Rotoscoping the reflection on the glowing ball

Rotoscoping refers to painting or altering an image frame-by-frame. This procedure follows in that tradition of hand-crafted image-creation. In this task, you advance a few frames at a time, setting keyframes for Mask Shape in the Timeline window and then adjusting the mask in the Layer window so that it continues to match the shape of the glowing ball as the frames advance. This meticulous work creates exactly the visual inter-actions that you want.

Currently, you have just one keyframe for the Mask Shape property, created in the previous procedure. Now you add more keyframes.

1 In the Timeline window, with the current-time marker at 11:28, select Mask 1 under the 3DComposite_ball.mov layer.

2 Make sure that Mask 1 is selected in the target menu in the Layer window.

3 Press Ctrl + A (Windows) or Command + A (Mac OS) to select all the mask points, and then press Ctrl + T (Windows) or Command + T (Mac OS) to display the transform handles for the Mask Shape. Adjust these handles in the Layer window to reshape the mask so that it matches the shape of the reflective ball.

4 Press the Page Down key twice to advance the current-time marker by two frames (to 12:00). Then adjust the mask again, using the instructions in step 2 (making sure that Mask 1 is selected) and step 3 (reshaping the mask to fit over the reflective ball).

5 Repeat step 4 at about every two frames until you reach 12:25, setting a total of over a dozen keyframes. You may need to reduce the magnification of the Layer window when the glowing ball no longer fits in the viewing area. At 12:25, the edges of the glowing ball and the Mask 1 shape should be completely outside the composition frame.

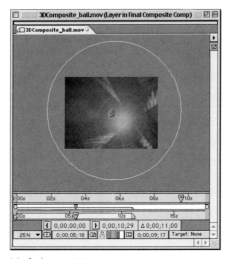

Mask size at 12:25

6 Close the Layer window. In the Timeline window, collapse the outline for this layer.

7 Set the work area to begin at 11:28 and end at about 14:00.

8 Preview the animation and save your work. Leave the Layer window open and the 3DComposite_ball.mov selected.

Now the glowing ball fills with the blue solid.

Animating the Mask Feather property

In this short procedure, you apply and animate a feather quality to the mask.

1 Move the current-time marker to 11:28.

2 With the 3DComposite_ball.mov layer selected, press F to reveal the Mask Feather property.

3 Set Mask Feather to **600**, and click the stopwatch to set a keyframe.

Note: Notice how much the edge of the masked layer softens. In this case, it softens so much that the image inside the mask is still visible. You now animate the Feather amount to help with this transition.

4 Move the current-time marker to 12:21, and scrub or type **24** as the Mask Feather value. The press F to hide the Mask Feather property.

5 Preview the animation and save the project.

Adding and time-remapping 3D hexagon elements

Now it's time to add the 3D hexagon elements you built in Lesson 6. These provide the transition between the two scenes: the zoom into the reflective glowing ball and the animation that resolves into the Adobe logo that completes the piece.

1 Move the current-time marker to 12:09.

2 In the Project window, drag the 3DHexagons.mov and the 3DHexLines.mov from the mov files folder into the Timeline window, placing them just below the 3DComposite_ball.mov. Make sure that the 3DHexagons becomes Layer 6 and the 3DHexLines is Layer 7.

3 Select only the 3DHexagons.mov layer and choose Layer > Enable Time Remapping.

4 Click the arrow to expand the layer properties. Two keyframes, indicating the start and end of the movie, are already in place: one at 12:09 (time) for 0:00 (timecode), and one at 15:09 (time) for 3:00 (timecode).

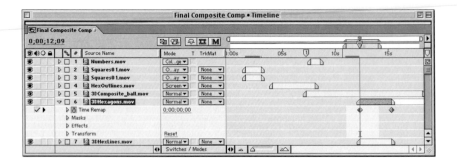

5 Click the right end of the layer duration bar, and drag the handle to 17:29, using the Info palette as your guide. This effectively holds the last frame of the 3DHexagons.mov until the end of the composition. The last frame remains on-screen until the Out point of the layer.

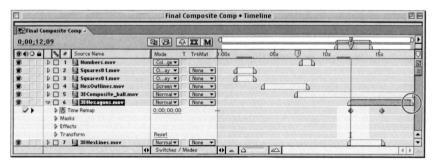

Layer duration bar extended to 17:29

6 Select the 3DHexLines.mov, and repeat steps 3 through 5 for that layer: to enable Time Remapping and change the length of the duration bar. Then collapse all layer properties.

Duplicating and adjusting the 3DHexagon.mov

You now create a blurry glow around the hexagons, using an effect and a transfer mode.

1 Select the 3DHexagons.mov layer and duplicate the layer.

2 With the top 3DHexagons.mov layer (Layer 6) selected, choose Effect > Blur & Sharpen > Fast Blur.

3 In the Effect Controls window, set **40** as the Blurriness value. Then close the Effects Controls window.

4 In the Modes panel, set both 3DHexagons.mov layers transfer modes to Overlay, to blend them with the layers below them in the layer stack.

Setting options and effects for the 3DHexLines.mov

Now that you've adjusted the solid hexagons, you apply effects and animate the opacity for the outline version of those images.

1 Drag the 3DHexLines.mov layer to the Layer 6 position, above the 3D Hexagons layers.

2 Choose Effect > Channel > Invert. Leave the effect controls at their default settings, and close the Effect Controls window.

3 In the Modes panel for Layer 8, select Hard Light transfer mode.

4 Press T to reveal the Opacity property for Layer 8, and set the following Opacity keyframes:

• With the current-time marker at 12:23, type or scrub **0%**. Click the Opacity stopwatch to set a keyframe.

• With the current time marker at 13:14, set **64%**.

• At 14:04, set **0%.** Then press T to hide the Opacity property.

5 Press Alt +] (right bracket) (Windows) or Option +] (right bracket) (Mac OS) to trim the layer Out point at the current time (14:04).

6 Use the current-time marker and the B and N keyboard shortcuts to set the work area from 12:09 to 16:00.

7 Preview the composition and save your project.

Positioning the 3DHexagons for transition

As the reflection layer dissolves, the 3DHexagons move into position, filling the frame. You'll set these Position keyframes now. They then shift with the glowing ball as they are revealed.

1 Set the current-time marker to 12:09.

2 In the Timeline window, select both 3DHexagon.mov layers and press P to reveal the Position properties.

3 Leaving both layers selected, type **288** and **234** to set the Position coordinates for both layers.

4 Press Alt + Shift + P (Windows) or Option + P (Mac OS) to set keyframes for both layers.

5 Move the current-time marker to 12:22 and set both layer positions at **360, 270** (at the center of the frame). Then press P to hide the Position properties for both layers.

6 Preview the animation and save the project.

Now, the 3DHexagons shift into position—from the center of the glowing ball to the center of the composition frame—as they are revealed through the mask shape. This is another subtle refinement that happens very quickly but it makes an important difference in maintaining a smooth transition between elements.

Adding another starburst element

Now you add another starburst element to the composition. This starburst creates an animated texture behind the 3DHexagons as the Adobe logo appears.

Ordinarily, it is not a good idea to scale an image larger than its original size. In this case, it's acceptable because of two special circumstances: First, the image you enlarge is merely part of the background and is revealed only through transfer modes, so it is not especially prominent. Second, you add a blur, which reduces the jagged edges that enlarging creates.

1 Set the current-time marker at 11:21.

2 In the Project window, expand the mov files folder in the 2DComposite07_work.aep folder, and then drag the Starburst.mov into the Timeline window between the 3DHexLines.mov and Blue Solid in the layer stack so that Starburst.mov is now Layer 9.

3 Move the current-time marker to 14:11. Then press S, and scrub or type **300%** for the Scale value. The edges of the starburst now appear jagged because of the increase in scale.

4 Press T, and set an Opacity keyframe (at 100%). Leave the Opacity property open.

5 In the Modes panel for the Starburst.mov, select Overlay transfer mode, to blend the starburst with the background layers.

6 Choose Effect > Blur & Sharpen > Fast Blur.

7 In the Effect Controls window, scrub or type **10** as the Blurriness. The blur eliminates the jagged edges of the image.

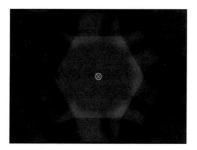

8 Press End to move to 17:29, and scrub or type **0%** as the Opacity value. Then press T to hide the Opacity property.

9 Using the current work area (12:09 to 16:00), preview the composition and save the project.

The starburst now twinkles behind the blue hexagons.

Putting together the final scene

In this section, you'll build the logo-resolve that completes the animation. This part of the composition combines the blue background and a hexagon tunnel with three Photoshop files that together represent the Adobe logo. You'll make these three files 3D layers so that they can interact with a spotlight that you'll create and move across them—your finishing touch to the project.

Creating the logo resolve: the A

You begin building the trademarked Adobe logo with the large letter A against a red background.

1 Set the current-time marker to 13:28.

2 In the Project window, select the A.psd (in the psd files folder) and drag it into the Timeline window to the top of the layer stack (Layer 1). The layer In point is automatically set at 13:28.

3 In the Switches panel, click the 3D Layer switch (⊞) to make A.psd a 3D layer.

4 Press P, and scrub or type **360, 234, 0** as the Position coordinates so that the image is slightly above the center of the frame.

5 Press S, and scrub or type **0%** as the Scale value. Then set a Scale keyframe.

6 Move the current-time marker to 14:09 and type **62%** for the Scale value. The logo now increases in size over 11 frames.

Creating the logo resolve: the R

The R.psd is a Photoshop image of the registered trademark symbol (®). Although this is a small element in the composition, it is often an essential part of a client's legal requirements. You'll satisfy that need without compromising the design by positioning, scaling, and dissolving the image so that it's visible without overwhelming the scene.

1 Set the current-time marker to 15:04, select the R.psd in the Project window, and drag it into the Timeline window to the top of the layer stack (Layer 1). The layer In point is automatically set at 15:04.

2 In the Switches panel, click the 3D Layer switch (⊞) to make R.psd a 3D layer.

3 Press P, and type **451, 165, 0** as the Position coordinates. This positions the R.psd at the upper right corner of the A.psd image.

4 Press S, and scrub or type **60%** as the Scale value.

5 Press T, and scrub or type **0%** as the Opacity value. Then click the stopwatch to set a keyframe.

6 Move the current-time marker to 16:04 and scrub or type **100%** as the Opacity value.

The R.psd now fades up over 1 second.

Creating the logo resolve: Adobe

The final part of the Adobe logo is the word *Adobe* in white type.

1 Move the current-time marker to 14:11, select the Adobe.psd in the Project window, and drag it into the Timeline window to the top of the layer stack (Layer 1). The layer In point is automatically set at 14:11.

2 In the Switches panel, click the 3D Layer switch (⬠) to make Adobe.psd a 3D layer.

3 Press S, and scrub or type **62%** as the Scale value.

4 Press P, and scrub or type **362, 355, 0** as the Position coordinates.

5 Press T, and scrub or type **0%** as the Opacity value. Then click the stopwatch to set a keyframe.

6 Move the current-time marker to 15:11 and scrub or type **100%** as the Opacity value.

💡 *To advance by exactly one second, click the current-time display in the Timeline window, to open the Go To Time dialog box. On the numeric keypad, press + (plus sign) and type **100** to jump ahead one second. If you wanted to go back one second, press + (plus sign), – (minus sign), and type **100**.*

7 Collapse the layer outlines for all three logo layers (A.psd, R.psd, and Adobe.psd).

8 Using the current-time marker and the B and N keyboard shortcuts, set the work area to begin at 12:00 and to end at 17:29.

9 Preview the animation and save the project.

The logo now appears to move toward the viewer (increasing in size) while the Adobe name and registration mark fade up. The timing used perfectly matches the sound track.

Adding the light sweep

The final touch is to add the sweeping light that shines over the logo. You create a simple spotlight in the composition and animate its Point of Interest. The Point of Interest indicates in which direction the light shines. You set the light to sweep across the composition frame, adding color to the Adobe logo as it falls into place.

1 With the current-time marker at 13:28, choose Layer > New > Light. The Light Settings dialog box appears.

2 Click OK to accept the following default settings (or, change them to these settings, if needed):

- Name: Light 1
- Light Type: Spot
- Intensity: 100%
- Cone Angle: 90°
- Cone Feather: 50%
- Color: white
- Casts Shadows: (not selected)

3 In the Timeline window, expand the Light 1 layer and then expand its Transform category.

4 In Light Position, scrub or type **156, 163, -334** (making sure that the last number is negative). The light moves to the upper left area of the composition frame.

Note: It is possible to simply select the Light 1 and drag it in the Composition window, but here we want the exact numbers shown above. Scrubbing or typing are the better techniques in this case. The same is true for the next step, in which you change the Point of Interest.

5 In Point of Interest, scrub or type **-37, 204, -50** (being careful to make the 37 and 50 negative numbers) and click the stopwatch to set a keyframe. The light now aims just outside of the upper left edge of the composition frame.

6 Move the current-time marker to 15:00, and change the Point of Interest coordinates to **357, 202, -58**, to aim the light directly over the Adobe logo. Then hide the properties for the Light 1 layer.

7 Using the current-time marker and the B and N keyboard shortcuts, set the work area to begin at 13:15 and to end at 16:00.

8 Create a RAM preview. When you are ready to continue, stop the preview and save the project.

The light now sweeps across the logo, illuminating its color as the light moves.

Congratulations! Now, all the elements are finally in place. To see your final results, you can preview the composition. However, this is a large and complex animation, so your system memory may not be able to handle a RAM preview of the entire composition. To work around this, try limiting the work area and viewing your work in small chunks, such as four-second segments.

By finishing Lesson 10, you have successfully completed the entire animation in this book—well done! In the final lesson, you will render this composition in several output formats.

Lesson 11

11 The Render Queue and Output Formats

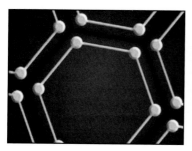 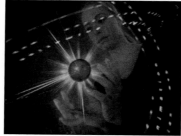 

The success of your project depends on your ability to deliver the job you promised in the formats your client needs. In this final lesson, you'll create time-saving templates and then render your final composition in a variety of formats and resolutions for broadcast or the Web.

In this lesson, you'll learn to do the following:

- Create render-settings templates
- Create output-module templates
- Render multiple output modules
- Select the appropriate compressor for your delivery format
- Use Pixel Aspect Correction
- Render the final animation for NTSC broadcast video output
- Render a test version of a composition
- Render a Web version of the final animation

In this lesson, you'll delve more deeply into rendering. In order to meet the client's request for several versions of this animation (as described in "How to use these lessons" on page 6), you'll explore options available within the Render Queue. After creating render-settings and output-module templates, you'll render both a broadcast version and a Web version of the final movie.

The total amount of time required to complete this lesson depends in part on the speed of your processor and the amount of RAM available for rendering. The amount of hands-on time required is less than one hour.

Getting started

You do not need to copy any new source files for this lesson because you finished building the final composition in Lesson 10. However, you should copy the following from the Sample_Movies/Lesson11 folder on the CD to the Sample_Movies folder on your hard disk and play them now:

- Final_Sorenson_final.mov
- Final_Cinepak_final.mov
- Final_NTSC_final.mov

This lesson continues from the point at which Lesson 10 ends: ready to render the Final Composite Comp. You begin by reopening your project from Lesson 10: FinalComposite10_work.aep.

1 Start After Effects 5.0, if it is not already open.

2 Choose File > Open Project.

3 Open the _aep folder inside the AE_CIB job folder, and select the FinalComposite10_work.aep.

4 Click Open.

♀ *If you finished Lesson 10 recently, you can choose File > Open Recent Project and then select FinalComposite10_work.aep from the list of projects on the submenu.*

The project opens with the windows and palettes displayed as when you last saved this project. If Composition, Timeline, or Effect Controls windows are open, close them now.

Creating templates for the rendering process

In previous lessons you selected individual render and output-module settings each time you rendered a composition. In this section, you'll create templates for both render settings and output-module settings. These templates are presets that you can use to streamline the setup process when you render items for the same type of delivery format. After you define these templates, they appear in the Render Queue window, on the appropriate pop-up menu (Render Settings or Output Module). Then, when you're ready to render a job, you can simply select the template that is appropriate for the delivery format your job requires, and the template applies all the settings.

Creating a Render Setting template for full resolution

The first template you create is for full-resolution the render settings.

1 Choose Edit > Templates > Render Settings to open the Render Settings Templates dialog box.

2 Under Settings, click New to open the Render Settings dialog box.

3 Under Render Settings, select Best for Quality and Full for Resolution.

4 Under Time Sampling, do the following:

• In Frame Blending, select On for Checked Layers.

• In Motion Blur, select On for Checked Layers.

• In Time Span, select Length of Comp.

• Under Frame Rate, make sure that the Use Comp's Frame Rate option is selected.

5 Click OK to return to the Render Settings Templates dialog box. All the settings you selected appear in the lower half of the dialog box. If you need to make any changes, click the Edit button and then adjust your settings.

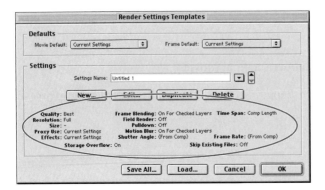

6 In Settings Name, type **Final Render_fullres** (for full resolution).

7 At the top of the dialog box, under Defaults, select Final Render_fullres as the Movie Default. Then click OK to close the dialog box.

Final Render_fullres is now the default Render Settings option and appears (instead of Current Settings) each time you open the Render Queue to make a movie.

If you want to save a render-settings template for use on another system, you can click the Save All button in the Render Settings Templates dialog box before you close it in step 7 (or, reopen the dialog box later by choosing Edit > Templates > Render Settings). Save the file in an appropriate location on your hard drive, such as in the After Effects application folder. All the currently loaded render settings are saved in a file with the .ars extension. Then copy this file to the drive of the other system. When you start After Effects on that system, choose Edit > Templates > Render Settings, click the Load button, and select the new .ars file to load the settings you saved.

Creating a render-settings template for test renderings

Next, you create a second render-settings template, selecting settings appropriate for rendering a test version of your final movie. A test version is smaller—and therefore renders faster—than a full-resolution movie. When you work with complex compositions that take relatively long times to render, it is a good practice to render a small test version first. This helps you find any final tweaks or blunders that you want to adjust before you take the time to render the final movie.

1 Choose Edit > Templates > Render Settings. The Render Settings Templates dialog box appears.

2 Under Settings, click New to open the Render Settings dialog box.

3 Select the following settings:

• In Quality, select Best.

• In Resolution, select Third, to render the movie at one-third the composition size.

4 Under Time Sampling, do the following:

• For Frame Blending, select Current Settings.

• For Motion Blur, select Current Settings.

• In Time Span, select Length of Comp.

5 Under Frame Rate, select Use This Frame Rate, and type **12** (fps). Then click OK to return to the Render Settings Templates dialog box.

6 In Settings Name, type **Test_lowres** (for *low resolution*).

7 Examine your settings, which now appear in the lower half of the dialog box. If you need to make any changes, click the Edit button to adjust the settings. Then click OK.

The Test_lowres option now appears in the Render Settings menu in the Render Queue.

You have now created two render-settings templates. One is for a full resolution final version, and one for a low resolution test version of your final composite.

Creating templates for output modules

Using similar processes to the previous section, you'll now create templates to use for output-module settings. Each will include unique combinations of settings that are appropriate for a specific type of output.

Creating an output-module template for broadcast renderings

The first template you create for output-module settings is appropriate for an NTSC broadcast-resolution version of your final movie.

1 Choose Edit > Templates > Output Module.

2 Under Settings, click New to open the Output Module Settings dialog box.

3 In the Output Module Settings dialog box, under Output Module, do the following:

• In Format, select QuickTime Movie.

• Select the Import into Project When Done option.

• Under Video, click Format Options to open the Compression Settings dialog box.

4 Under Compressor, in the two pop-up menus, select Animation and Millions of Colors. Click OK to close this dialog box, and then review the settings in the Output Module Settings dialog box to make sure that the Channels selection is RGB and Depth is Millions of Colors.

5 Select the Audio Output option, and then for Sample Rate, select the 44.100 kHz, 16 Bit, and Stereo options.

6 Then click OK to return to the Output Module Templates dialog box. Review the settings in the lower half of the dialog box and click the Edit button if you need to adjust your settings.

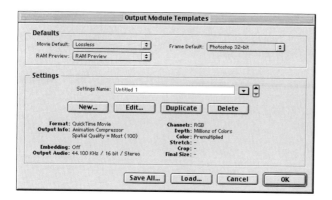

7 In Settings Name, type **Final Render_QT_audio** (to remind you that this template for QuickTime includes audio settings).

8 Under Defaults, in the Movie Default pop-up menu, select Final Render_QT_audio. Then click OK.

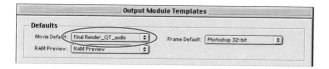

The Final Render_ QT_audio template is now the default selection in the Output Module menu, and appears (instead of Lossless) each time you queue a composition item to be rendered as a movie.

As with the render-settings templates, you can save output-module templates for use on other systems. Click the Save All button in the Output Module Templates dialog box. Name the file and save it to an appropriate location on your hard drive, such as in the After Effects application folder. All loaded output-modules are saved in a file with the .aom extension. Transfer this file to the drive of another system and launch After Effects. Choose Edit > Templates > Output Module, click the Load button, and select the .aom file to load the settings.

Creating a low-resolution output-module template

Next, you create a second output-module template with settings appropriate for rendering a low-resolution test version of the movie. In this case, the settings that you select are also appropriate for the World Wide Web version of the movie requested by the client in the scenario.

1 Choose Edit > Templates > Output Module to open the Output Module Templates dialog box.

2 Under Settings, click New to create a new template and to open the Output Module Settings dialog box.

3 In Format, select QuickTime Movie.

4 Select Import into Project When Done.

5 Click Format Options (under Video Output) and select the following settings in the Compression Setting dialog box:

• In the upper pop-up menu, select Sorenson Video. This compressor automatically determines the Color setting.

• Set the Quality slider to High.

• Under Motion, select the Key Frame Every option, and then type **30**.

• Select Limit Data Rate to, and type **150**.

6 Click OK to close the Compression Settings dialog box and return to the Output Module Settings dialog box.

7 Under Audio Output, click the Format Options button to open the Sound Settings dialog box and select the following:

• In Compressor, select IMA 4:1.

• In Rate, select 22.050.

• In Size, select 16 bit.

• In Use, select Stereo, and then click OK to close the Sound Settings dialog box. Your sound settings now appear under Audio Output in the Output Module Settings dialog box. Click OK to close the Output Module Settings dialog box.

8 In the lower half of the Output Module Templates dialog box, examine your settings, and click Edit if you need to make any changes.

9 In Settings Name, type **Test_Sorenson**, and then click OK.

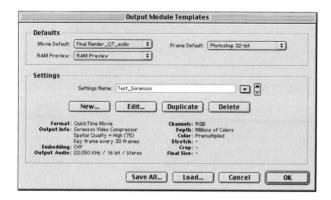

Note: The Sorenson Video compressor is available with QuickTime 4.0 or later. QuickTime is included on your After Effects application CD and is also available for download from the Apple Web site. The IMA 4:1 compressor is commonly used when compressing audio for Web or desktop playback.

As you might expect, greater compression and lower audio sample rates create smaller file sizes, but they also reduce the quality of the output. However, this low-resolution quality template is fine for creating test movies or movies for the Web.

For more information regarding specific compression settings, see "Setting QuickTime compression options" and "Setting Video for Windows compression options" in After Effects online Help.

Rendering to different output media

Now that you have created templates for your render settings and output modules, you can use them to render the movies the client in the scenario requested.

Preparing to render a test movie

First you render the test version, selecting the Test_lowres render settings and the Test_Sorenson output-module templates that you created.

1 In the Project window, double-click the Final Composite Comp to open it in the Composition and Timeline windows.

2 Review the switches in the A/V Features panel to make sure that the Video switch (👁) is on for all visual layers and that the audio switch (◀)) is on for that layer. Then close the Composition and Timeline windows.

3 In the Project window, select the Final Composite Comp, and then choose Composition > Make Movie.

4 In the Output Movie To dialog box, locate the AE_CIB job folder and click the New Folder button (▢).

5 Type **Final_Renders** to name the new folder, and then open the folder, if necessary.

6 In Name, type **Final_Sorenson.mov**, and then click Open (Windows) or Save (Mac OS). The Render Queue opens with this item queued to render.

7 In the Render Settings pop-up menu, select Test_lowres.

8 In the Output Module pop-up menu, select Test_Sorenson.

9 Save the project.

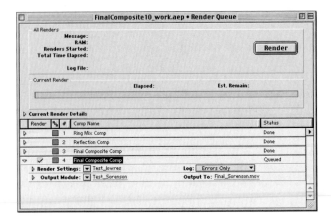

You'll do a few more things before you render the movie. Leave the Render Queue open as you go on to the next task.

Understanding compression

Compression is often necessary to reduce the size of movie files, which can be quite large. It is often essential for playing movies on a desktop computer. Animations intended for playback on the desktop, from a CD, or from a Web site must be compressed in order to ensure effective playback speeds. This is due to limited throughput: the amount of data a drive can process per second. A standard internal hard drive or CD ROM drive cannot process data fast enough to play a full-resolution movie back at real time. The same is true when playing movies from a Web site.

Compression is always a trade-off between quality and size. As you reduce the size of the file (increasing its ability to play back efficiently), you sacrifice image quality.

The compressor that you use determines how information is removed to compress the file; how information is removed determines the specific effect on the image. Different compressors affect your images in different ways. Some compressors are more suitable than others for a particular animation, based on the types of images and colors used. Some support alpha channels and some do not. It is important to select a compressor that gives you the maximum image quality at the minimum file size. This may require some experimentation on your part—rendering the movie using several different compressors at different compression settings— until you find the right combination for your purposes.

For Web or Desktop playback: *Both the Sorenson Video and Cinepak are standard compressors for items intended to be played back on the desktop, from a CD, or posted on a Web site. Both do a reasonably good job decreasing the size of the file so that it can be played back efficiently, without reducing image quality too severely. Reducing the frame rate (as you did in the Test_lowres Render Settings template) and the resolution (the size of the movie) also help you generate a movie that plays back at low data rates.*

For Video resolution playback or output: *If you have a video-capture or playback card (or both) installed in your system, you'll want to render your animation using the compressor or codec for that card. Most manufacturers' video-capture and playback cards are based upon one of the following compression algorithms: DV compression, Motion JPG, MPEG 2, or Uncompressed Serial Digital output. By rendering with the appropriate compressor or codec (and using the frame size that correlates to your compressor), you can take advantage of the hardware installed—playing the animation back at real time and at video resolution on an external NTSC or PAL monitor. Then, if your system is hooked up to a deck, you can also use this hardware to lay off the animation to video tape.*

Working with multiple output modules

Next you add another output module to this render queue so that you can compare the appearance of two compressors. You set this one for Cinepak compression.

1 With the Final Composite Comp still selected in the Render Queue, choose Composition > Add Output Module. A second set of Output Module and Output To options appears directly beneath the first.

2 In the lower Output Module pop-up menu, select Test_Sorenson.

3 Click the underlined words *Test_Sorenson* to open the Output Module Settings dialog box, and then click the Format Options button under Video Output.

4 In the Compression Settings dialog box, do the following:

• In the upper pop-up menu, select Cinepak.

• In the lower pop-up menu, select Millions of Colors.

• Make sure that the following settings are selected: Quality slider at High, Frames per second at 12, Key Frame Every at 30 frames, and Limit Data Rate at 150K/second. Then click OK to close the dialog box.

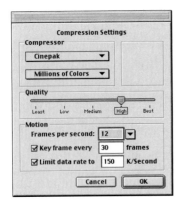

5 Click OK again to close the Output Module Settings dialog box.

6 Next to Output To, click the words *Not Yet Specified* to open the Output Movie To dialog box.

7 In Name, type **Final_Cinepak.mov** and save it in the Final_Renders folder inside the AE_CIB folder.

8 In the Render Queue, save the project and click Render. After Effects renders both of these formats simultaneously.

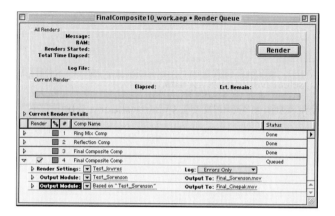

When the render is complete, close the Render Queue. Both the Final_Sorenson.mov and Final_Cinepak.mov appear in the Project window. You can double-click each to preview the movies in the Footage window and compare their appearances. You can now select the movie that looks better to you and rename it **Final_Web.mov** (on the desktop; you do not rename it within After Effects). This version is ready for handoff to your client.

Note: When the render is complete, you may find it helpful to further reduce the size of the movie before posting it to a Web site. You may want to create streaming video, or simply reduce the size based on the majority of the audience's available bandwidth. You can do this with a media-compression or media-cleaner application specifically designed for this purpose.

If you need to make any final changes to the animation, reopen the appropriate composition and make those adjustments now. Remember to save your work when you finish and then render the test movie again, using the appropriate settings. After examining the test render and making any necessary changes, you'll proceed with your final render.

Exporting to SWF

You can use After Effects to export compositions as MacroMedia Flash (.swf) files, for playback within a Web-browser application. However, certain types of artwork are more suitable than others for export to SWF. Rasterized images and some effects cannot be represented by vectors, and therefore are not efficiently saved to SWF format. It is possible to export them, but the files will be larger in size.

Also, it is helpful when exporting items to SWF to place all your layers within a single composition rather than using precompositions or nested compositions. Using a single composition also tends to reduce the size of the exported file.

In this project, you have used many rasterized images, so this movie is best rendered in some other format. For more information, see "Exporting to MacroMedia Flash (SWF) format" in After Effects online Help.

Preparing the composition for full-resolution rendering

Next, you prepare to render the Final Composite Comp. This animation is intended primarily for NTSC video output, as specified by the client in this scenario. You begin by placing the Final Composite Comp in a new composition that you create at the appropriate size for your final delivery format.

1 If the Composition, Timeline, and Effect Controls windows are open, close them now.

2 Choose Composition > New Composition, and choose the following Composition Settings:

• In Name, type **Final Comp NTSC.**

• In Preset, select: NTSC D1, 720 x 486 to automatically enter the correct dimensions (720 x 486), Pixel Aspect Ratio (D1/DV NTSC), and Frame Rate (29.97).

• In Resolution, select Full (or lower if necessary for your system).

• Make sure that Start Timecode is 0:00.

• In Duration, type **18:00**, to specify 18 seconds, and then click OK. The composition opens in the Composition and Timeline windows.

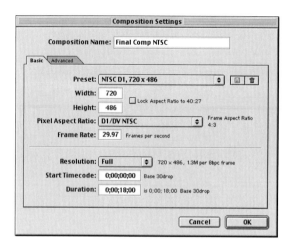

3 In the Project window, select the Final Composite Comp and place it in the new composition by dragging it to the Final Comp NTSC icon. When the Final Comp NTSC icon becomes highlighted, release the mouse.

Using Pixel Aspect Correction

As you scrub through or preview the animation, you may notice that the items in the Composition window now appear a bit wider than before. This D1 NTSC composition has a non-square pixel aspect ratio. However, your computer monitor displays images using square pixels. Therefore, the images that you see in the Composition window appear stretched unless you enable a feature called Pixel Aspect Correction. Pixel Aspect Correction squeezes the Composition window slightly to display the image as it will appear on a video monitor. By default, this feature is turned off. Follow the steps below to turn it on.

1 Place the current-time marker at 6:00 where the hexagons fill the composition frame, and look carefully at the shape of the image in the Composition window.

2 In the Composition window menu, select Pixel Aspect Correction (if it is not already checked).

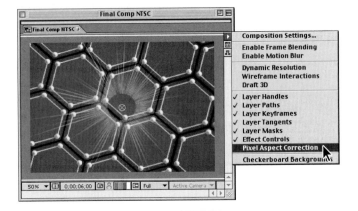

3 A Warning appears stating that this adjusted view is for preview purposes only. Decide whether you want this Warning to appear once each time you run After Effects or never again, and then select that option from the Show Warning pop-up menu. Then click OK.

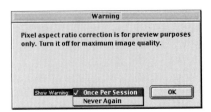

The image in the Composition window is squeezed, appearing (at a modified pixel aspect ratio) as it will once this item is rendered, laid off to tape, and viewed on a video monitor. The layers in the Composition window may appear a bit jagged while you have this view turned on. You'll want to turn it off to see your images with full anti-aliasing. This view does not effect rendering.

Note: If Pixel Aspect Correction is already enabled on your system, that means that it was enabled in the last open composition. Select it in the Composition window menu now to disable it. Note the difference in the shape of the hexagon layer. Select it again in the menu to turn it back on.

Using Pixel Aspect Correction, you can work in a Composition with a non-square pixel aspect ratio but still view your images as they would appear on a video monitor. This is a very useful feature because most broadcast formats require that you build your final compositions at a non-square pixel aspect ratio (720 x 486).

You build your full-frame compositions at the equivalent square pixel aspect ratio (720 x 540) in these lessons for two reasons: First, you were working with elements of many different sizes. Second, it means that you can view your work at the proper aspect ratio (unstretched) and full resolution with full anti-aliasing.

Rendering the final movie for broadcast

Now you render the NTSC broadcast version of your final animation. This may take half an hour or more, depending on your system.

1 Close the Composition and Timeline windows.

2 In the Project window, select the Final Comp NTSC and press Ctrl + M (Windows) or Command + M (Mac OS) to open the Output Movie To dialog box.

3 In File Name, type **Final_NTSC** (indicating that this item will be rendered at NTSC D1 resolution) and specify the Final_Renders folder inside the AE_CIB job folder, and click Save. The item appears in the Render Queue.

4 The Final Render_fullres Render Setting already appears selected in the Render Settings pop-up menu because you set this as the default movie settings when you created the template.

5 The Final Render_QT_audio setting appears selected in the Output Module menu, again because you set this as the default earlier in this lesson. This item is now ready to render.

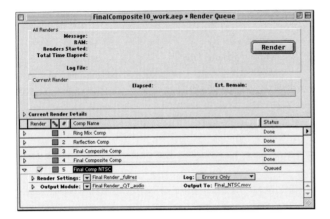

6 Save the project one more time, and click Render.

7 When the render is finished, close the Render Queue.

8 In the Project window, double-click the Final_NTSC.mov to open it in the Footage window.

As you play the movie, compare your final render to the sample movie you watched at the beginning of this lesson. If necessary, reopen the appropriate composition and make any necessary changes. Then save the project and render the movie again, using the steps listed above.

Note: *Because this movie is so large, it does not play back at real time in the QuickTime Player. If you have a video playback card installed on your system, render the movie choosing the appropriate compressor and frame size for that card in the Compression Settings. Import the movie into your editing software and play it back using your hardware for real-time playback.*

You now have both a Web version and a broadcast version of the final animation ready for delivery to your client.

Congratulations! You have now completed the Adobe *After Effects Classroom in a Book*. To learn more about After Effects 5.0, go to the Adobe Web site and search the Technical Support and Knowledgebase pages.

Index

Credits

Design and Production

Belief

Steve Kazanjian - Managing Director

Mike Goedecke - Executive Creative Director

Shari Trout - Executive Producer

Rick Gledhill - Lead Designer

Marc Sylvan - Music/Sound Design

GOMOCO

George Hladky - Motion control rig shoot

Lesson Development

Beth Roy

Technical Writer/Editor

Patricia Solon

Print Production

Command Z

Jan Martí